American Choral Music Since 1920

Other books by David DeVenney
in this series

AMERICAN CHORAL MUSIC
An Annotated Guide

EARLY AMERICAN CHORAL MUSIC
An Annotated Guide

AMERICAN MASSES AND REQUIEMS
A Descriptive Guide

American Choral Music
Since 1920

An Annotated Guide

David P. DeVenney

Fallen Leaf Press

Berkeley, California

Published by Fallen Leaf Press
P.O. Box 10034
Berkeley, CA 94709 USA

Library of Congress Cataloging–in–Publication Data

De Venney, David P., 1958-
    American choral music since 1920: an annotated guide / David P.
DeVenney.
        p.   cm. — (Fallen Leaf reference books in music, ISSN 8775-
268X; no. 27)
    Includes bibliographical references and indexes.
    ISBN 0-914913-28-X (cloth: alk. paper)
    1. Choral music--United States--20th century--Bibliography.
I. Title. II. Series.
ML128.C48D45 1993
016.7825'0973--dc20   93-21428
                                                                CIP
                                                                MN

The paper used in this book meets the minimum requirements of the
American National Standard for Information Services—Permanence of
Paper for Printed Library Materials, ANSI Z39.48-1984.

iv

To RWC and CWM

Table of Contents

List of Composers

Introduction

Anyone searching for a single word or phrase to capsulize twentieth-century American choral music would be hard pressed to find one that would suffice. The seventy-six composers included in this volume have written a cornucopia of music in widely varying styles, penned from the years immediately following the first World War until the present day. The music ranges from the lush Romanticism of Charles Wakefield Cadman to the stark, dissonant harmonies of Morton Feldman, from the easily singable style of Gail Kubik to the more vocally demanding works of Richard Felciano or Charles Wuorinen. While little holds this music together as a whole, these works can be divided into chronological or stylistic subgroups for closer examination. I have done so below, with a listing of about one hundred noteworthy pieces.

The Romantic Tradition

Nineteenth-century Romanticism did not fade away immediately following World War I or with the advent of new compositional techniques. Many composers whose styles were formed before the war continued to write in a Romantic manner after others had departed from it. One can find reminders and echoes of an earlier age in the works of Cadman, Frederick Converse, Arthur Farwell, Philip James, Arthur Shepherd, Charles Skilton, and the naturalized American, Percy Grainger, as well as in the works of later composers like Randall Thompson and Emma Lou Diemer.

Both Cadman and Farwell wrote many works that were influenced by Native American music, sometimes utilizing authentic melodies or other musical material. Cadman frequently drew upon the writings of poet Nelle Richmond Eberhart for his text sources: their best collaborations include not only *The Father of Waters* (223) and *Naranoka* (242), but also shorter works like "From the Land of Sky-blue Waters" (226), and "The Rainbow Waters Whisper" (250). Farwell wasn't as prolific as Cadman in this genre, but his "Four Indian Songs" (589) fit easily into this same style.

Other composers drew upon common Romantic themes like nature or history for their texts. Frederick Converse left several lengthy works that bear closer study, most notably *The Peace Pipe* (299). The prolific Percy Grainger wrote numerous folk song arrangements that are complemented by his settings of texts by Rudyard Kipling. His choral works on texts from *The Jungle Book* are interesting, including

"Morning Song in the Jungle" (767), "Mowgli's Song against the People" (768), and "Night-song in the Jungle" (771).

Philip James and his contemporary Leo Sowerby each left many choral works, the best of which are their religious music. Typical works by these stylistically conservative men include James's anthem "By the Waters of Babylon" (998) and Sowerby's "The Armor of God" (1660). I also recommend several of Sowerby's more lengthy cantatas, including *The Canticle of the Sun* (1674) and his masterwork *Forsaken of Man* (1701).

The little-known but accomplished composer Charles Skilton wrote secular music almost exclusively. His longest piece, *From Forest and Stream* (1637), is thoroughly Romantic in style, and uses nature as its subject; individual movements have titles like "Hollow Oak," "The Night Hawk," and "Pussy Willow."

Perhaps the most familiar name among the Romantic composers is Arthur Shepherd, who may also have been the best of this group. He left fewer than twenty choral works, but several are among the finest listed in this book. They include the cantata *The City in the Sea* (1618), as well as the shorter, delightful "A Ballad of Trees and the Master" (1615), and "Psalm XLII" (1626), one of his best-known choral works.

I mentioned Randall Thompson and Emma Lou Diemer as two composers whose musical style depends much on Romanticism. Thompson's choral works are among the best-known body of American choral literature. His "Alleluia" (1874) is frequently performed and much-loved, and his oratorio *The Peaceable Kingdom* (1902) is certainly one of the finest twentieth-century works in this genre, though receiving fewer performances than it should. Thompson's other lengthy works include the *Mass of the Holy Spirit* (1894), *The Nativity of St. Luke* (1896), *The Passion According to St. Luke* (1901), and the eloquent, haunting double-choir *Requiem* (1907).

While Diemer has written prolifically in a wide variety of idioms and styles, most of her music is highly singable and extremely melodic, with lush, colorful harmonies and imaginative orchestrations. Many of the shorter works are particularly delightful, such as "Come Hither, You that Love" (486) and "The Shepherd to His Love" (540), both for women's voices. Among her longer choral works meriting further investigation is the recent *There is a Morn Unseen* (548) for chorus, soprano, and large orchestra.

Another clue to understanding the continuing influence of Romanticism on twentieth-century American choral music is the choice of texts composers have set. A quick glance at the Index to Authors and Sources of Texts shows that the favorite poet for these composers is Walt Whitman, followed closely by other

Romantics like Emerson, Thoreau, Millay, and Longfellow. Only liturgical or biblical texts are set more frequently by contemporary composers than these nineteenth-century writers.

The "American" Composers

A second group of composers might be characterized as those who sought and used "American" influences for their music. Among these men, Ernst Bacon, Aaron Copland, Roy Harris, Gail Kubik, and Halsey Stevens became prominent in the 1920s and '30s. Bacon was a prolific composer. While he felt more comfortable with shorter compositions, he also wrote several cantata-length pieces worth noting, particularly *The Ecclesiastes* (32) and *The Last Invocation* (42). Copland's choral works continue to be performed frequently and need little introduction to most conductors and singers. Among his most popular choral music are the settings of *Old American Songs* (311), the two choruses from *The Tender Land* (312 and 314), and the challenging motet "In the Beginning" (308).

Roy Harris arranged many folk songs besides writing a number of choral works in a folk-like manner. His two longest works, the *Folk Fantasy for Festivals* (837) and the *Folk-song Symphony* (838), are both written in this style. Harris remained a champion of choral singing throughout his life, and the reader will find some of his ideas quoted in the article by Nick Strimple cited in the Bibliography of Writings (B210). Gail Kubik not only arranged many folk songs for chorus, but also composed a number of longer works in a more serious style, including *A Mirror for the Sky* (1122) and *A Record of Our Time* (1132). Halsey Stevens's music is more contemporary sounding than the others in this group, perhaps because he is slightly younger. His best work is the cantata *A Testament of Life* (1842).

The Composers of Mid-century

The group of composers who reached their creative maturity in the 1940s and '50s include some of the most important and influential American musicians in this century. Samuel Barber, Norman Dello Joio, Howard Hanson, Douglas Moore, Vincent Persichetti, Walter Piston, William Schuman, Roger Sessions, and Virgil Thomson wielded an enormous influence on the history of music in this country through their composition, teaching, and positions as music administrators. All wrote important works that have become part of the standard choral music canon.

Among Barber's best works are the well-known "Reincarnations" (74) and the oratorio *The Prayers of Kierkegaard* (73). Dello Joio, one of the more conservative members of this group, is well represented by the short "A Jubilant Song" (390), and the longer *The Mystic Trumpeter* (397) and *Song of Affirmation* (411). Hanson's interesting "Cherubic Hymn" (803) and *Lament for Beowulf* (807) continue to receive occasional performances, as do some of the choral works of William Schuman, especially the eloquent *Carols of Death* (1585).

Roger Sessions left only a few choral works, but among them is the masterpiece composed to Whitman's *When Lilacs Last in the Dooryard Bloom'd* (1611). Readers familiar with Hindemith's more frequently performed setting of this work will also want to explore Sessions's piece, which is equally moving, though musically more dissonant. Virgil Thomson, long considered the dean of American composers, left a large and noteworthy catalog of choral music, represented well by both the *Missa pro defunctis* (1934) for men's and women's choruses and orchestra, and the *Seven Choruses from Medea* (1944) for women's voices and percussion.

More Recent Composers

Four of the most prolific American choral composers included in this Catalog were born in the early 1920s, including Daniel Pinkham and Ned Rorem, both born in 1923. These men write in a relatively conservative style, more progressive harmonically than melodically, and both favor shorter over longer pieces. Pinkham experimented for a while with electronic tape as choral accompaniment and wrote some interesting music in this medium, notably "In the Beginning of Creation" (1426). Rorem's melodic style is more disjunct than Pinkham's, although his music is almost always highly singable. His choral masterwork, *An American Oratorio* (1524), like much of his choral music, so perfectly reflects the poetry he chooses for texts.

Kirke Mechem and Alice Parker, two years younger than Pinkham and Rorem, are also frequently performed. Mechem has written a number of choral cycles, defined as works of several constituent parts forming a whole, although each part may stand alone in performance. *Five Centuries of Spring* (1169) and *Seven Joys of Christmas* (1186) both belong in this genre. Parker is at her best writing shorter works, exemplified by the four "Mountain Hymns" (1302). Her commitment to spirited hymn and congregational singing is also reflected in her choral output.

Finally, there are many younger composers included here whose works reflect a variety of musical styles, especially Paul Chihara, Libby Larsen, Thomas Pasatieri, and Stephen Paulus. Chihara's unmetered Magnificat (285) for six-part women's chorus is unusual and evocative, in a highly singable, melodic idiom. The other three composers have made their mark predominantly in the world of opera, and their choral music often reflects a love of drama that makes their music rewarding to perform. Larsen's "Dance Set" (1142) is delightful, and Paulus's charming, clever "Christmas Tidings" (1330) and amusing "Personals" (1338) are both representative of his work. Pasatieri's Mass (1327) is both beautiful and moving.

Conclusions

Space prevents me from mentioning many of the composers included in this Catalog, some of whose works are very well known, and some whose music is rarely performed. Leonard Bernstein's choral oeuvre needs little introduction to any modern conductor or listener, although one cannot say the same about a number of other fine composers whose names, if not their music, are widely known. Composers like Leslie Bassett, William Bergsma, Elliott Carter, David Diamond, Jacob Druckman, Lukas Foss, Peter Mennin, and Douglas Moore have exerted a lasting influence on musical and choral life in this country, and the reader is encouraged to browse through the listings of their works to appreciate the choral legacy these composers have given us.

This Catalog annotates nearly 2,000 choral works; when individual, separately performable movements are counted, the number reaches over 3,000 pieces. No one can doubt that there is a wealth of contemporary American music with which to enliven, enlarge, and broaden the current choral repertory. Only recently has this country begun to re-discover its long musical and artistic heritage. There is no better place to continue the search than with this rich body of choral literature, culled from the recent past.

Acknowledgements

I extend my appreciation to Ralph Pearson, former Vice President for Academic Affairs and to the Humanities Advisory Committee at Otterbein College for their financial support of this project. Mary Ellen Armentrout, research librarian of the Courtright Memorial Library at Otterbein, was, as always, cheerful and efficient in dealing with my many requests for interlibrary loan and computer searches. Eero Richmond, of the American Music Center in New York City, where I first located many of these scores, was generous with his time and assistance. I would also like to thank the staffs at the following locations for allowing me to use their facilities and collections: Music and Dance Library, The Ohio State University; Eda Loeb Kuhn Music Library at Harvard University; Music Collection, Boston Public Library; Americana Collection, Music Division, New York Public Library; Music Division, The Library of Congress; and the many libraries that sent works on interlibrary loan, as well as the composers who graciously answered my queries for information. Finally, I extend my appreciation to Craig Johnson, my colleague at Otterbein, for his encouragement and interest in this book; and to the publisher of Fallen Leaf Press, Ann Basart, who always has good suggestions, and whose many editorial changes are not only useful but welcome.

Guide to Use

The Catalog of Works

Scope

The Catalog of Works lists original choral music written by composers active in the United States from roughly 1920 until the present. It includes works intended to be sung by a choral ensemble rather than by an ensemble of solo voices. It excludes arrangements, except those made by composers of their own works (for example, a song later arranged by its composer for chorus). For the most part, it also excludes hymns, arrangements of other composers' works, and arrangements of folk songs and spirituals. (A notable exception to the latter is the set of Aaron Copland's *Old American Songs*, arranged for chorus with the composer's permission.)

The Catalog also excludes works written specifically for the stage, individual choruses excerpted from stage works (with a few exceptions, such as the two choruses from Copland's opera *The Tender Land* and similar pieces, which in my view have entered the standard choral repertory), and choruses published separately from larger works.

Arrangement

The Catalog is arranged alphabetically by composer. Under each composer's name, entries appear alphabetically by title (given in the original language). Each entry is distinguished by a reference number. These numbers run consecutively through the Catalog and are also used in all of the indexes to the Catalog to refer the reader to a specific work.

Each Catalog citation gives, when applicable and available, the opus number, date of composition (or copyright date), author or source of the text, duration, publisher, and location of the composer's manuscript. Timings of each work, although based on careful examination of the scores, should be taken merely as a guide. Occasionally, some works have been published by little-known firms; in these cases, I have provided a library location to assist the user in obtaining a score.

An entry may refer the user to writings concerning that composition included in the Bibliography, by citing a number preceded by the identifying letter "B." An entry may also list performance reviews of a given work. If I have been unable to examine a given score, but have obtained a citation from an authoritative listing by another author, I have included the source of my information. Finally, a note at the end of the annotation may give other pertinent information about a work, such as arrangements for different voicings, and so forth.

Indexes

The choral works cited in the Catalog are indexed by genre, performing forces, title, and author or source of the text. Numbers in these indexes refer to the sequential numbers of the entries in the Catalog.

The Bibliography

Scope

The annotated Bibliography of Selected Writings cites works on the history and circumstances surrounding the composition of this music; on theoretical and analytical studies related to them; and on their performance practice and interpretation. It is intended primarily as a research tool for the choral conductor who wishes to have a list of important writings on twentieth-century American choral music, as well as the conductor who would like to explore this literature in more depth.

The Bibliography includes European and American doctoral dissertations and masters' theses, as well as articles in Festschriften and other collections, articles in scholarly journals, and books. I have also included memoirs, letters, and collected recollections of these composers when appropriate. Performance reviews of individual works are cited only under individual annotations in the Catalog of Works.

Excluded from the Bibliography are program notes, reviews of recordings, publishers' catalogs, thematic catalogs, and iconographies, except where these are contained in another source. Although I have excluded articles in dictionaries and encyclopedias, whenever possible I have consulted the bibliographies of these volumes for additional sources. When I have found a reference to a source that looked promising, but was unable to locate the source, I have included the reference with no annotation.

Arrangement

Citations in the Bibliography are arranged alphabetically by author. Each citation is given a reference number preceded by the letter "B." These numbers, independent of those in the Catalog of Works, are used in the index to the Bibliography to refer the reader to a specific writing, and in the Catalog as a cross-reference between a composition and a book, article, etc., that directly pertains to that work.

Index

The writings included in the Bibliography are given a comprehensive index of their own, using the "B" reference numbers, independent of the indexes for the Catalog of Works.

Guide to Annotations in Catalog of Works

0000   Composer, Name

Title of work, opus number, date of composition or copyright

Med: performing forces required for performance

Txt: author or source of text

Dur: duration

Pub: publisher

Mss: location of composer's manuscript

Src: source of annotation, if incomplete or if the work was not viewed during the compiling of this guide

Rev: performance reviews

Bib: references to works in the Bibliography of Selected Writings

Listing of individual movements or component pieces of longer works

N.B.   other relevant information about the work

Abbreviations

A	alto	kybd	keyboard
ACA	American Composers Alliance, New York City	LC	Music Division, Library of Congress, Washington, D.C.
adapt.	adapted	LU	Liber usualis
AMC	American Music Center, New York City	M	mezzo-soprano
		nar	narrator
AMP	Associated Music Publishers	n.d.	no date
anon.	anonymous	NYPL	Music Division, New York Public Library
arr.	arranged, arrangement		
B	bass	ob	oboe
Bar	baritone	opt	optional
bass	contrabass (string bass)	orch	orchestra
BH	Boosey & Hawkes Music Publishers	org	organ
		perc	percussion
BMI	Broadcast Music, Inc.	Ph.D.	Doctor of Philosophy
BPL	Music Division, Boston Public Library	pno	piano
		Ps.	Psalm
bsn	bassoon	rev.	revised
ch. orch	chamber orchestra	S	soprano
clar	clarinet	S.M.D.	Doctor of Sacred Music
cong	congregation	str	string(s)
DA	Dissertation Abstracts	T	tenor
D.A.	Doctor of Arts	tamb	tambourine
dbl	double	tape	pre-recorded electronic tape
div	divisi	tbn	trombone
D.M.A.	Doctor of Musical Arts	timp	timpani
D.S.M.	Doctor of Sacred Music	tpt	trumpet
Eng. hn	English horn	trad.	traditional (referring to origin of text)
fl	flute		
gtr	guitar	trans.	translated, translation
Harvard	Eda Loeb Kuhn Music Library, Harvard University	vla	viola
		vln	violin
hn	horn	vv	voices, voicing
hp	harp	WLSM	World Library of Sacred Music
hpschd	harpsichord		
inst.	instruments		

Bibliographic Guide to Source Listings

(Source listings with a "B" number refer the reader to works in the Bibliography of Writings)

Balough, Teresa. *A Complete Catalogue of the Works of Percy Grainger.* Melbourne, Australia: University of Western Australia, 1975.

Block, Adrienne Fried and Carol Neul-Bates. *Women in American music: a Bibliography of Music and Literature.* Westport, Conn.: Greenwood Press, 1979.

Farwell, Price, ed. *A Guide to the Music of Arthur Farwell and to the Microfilm Collection of His Work.* Briarcliff Manor, New York: for the composer's estate, 1972.

James, Helga. *A Catalog of the Musical Works of Philip James, 1890-1975.* New York: Judith Finell Music Services, 1980.

Locke, Arthur Ware and Charles K. Fassett. *Selected List of Choruses for Women's Voices.* Northampton, Mass.: Smith College, 1964.

McDonald, Arlys L. *Ned Rorem: a Bio-bibliography.* Westport, Conn.: Greenwood Press, 1989.

Paulin, Carolyn. "The Choral Music of Gordon Binkerd." *Research Memorandum Series* of the American Choral Foundation, 161 (July, 1992).

Roberts, Kenneth. *A Checklist of Twentieth-century Choral Music for Male Voices.* Detroit: Information Coordinators, Inc., 1970.

Sadie, Stanley, ed. *The New Grove Dictionary of American Music.* New York: Norton, 1986.

Catalog of Works

A

1 Albright, William
An alleluia super round (1973)
Med: 8 or more singers, any voicing,
     opt. unspecified inst.
Txt: "Alleluia"
Dur: indeterminate
Pub: Elkan-Vogel

2 Albright, William
Chichester Mass (1974, rev. 1979)
Med: SATB
Txt: LU
Dur: 11'
Pub: CF Peters
Rev: *Music* (AGO) 9 (Nov, 1975) p25

3 Albright, William
David's songs (c.1985)
Med: SATB, org
Txt: Ps. 149:1-3; 116:1-6; 137:1-2;
     150
Dur: 9'30"
Pub: CF Peters

4 Albright, William
Mass in D (1974)
Med: SATB, cong, org, perc
Txt: LU
Src: Grove

5 Albright, William
Pax in terra (1981)
Med: SATB div, ST soli
Txt: LU
Dur: 8'
Pub: CF Peters
Rev: *Notes* 43/4 (1987) p925-6

6 Albright, William
A song to David (1983)
Med: antiphonal choruses, soli, nar,
     orch
Txt: Christopher Smart
Dur: 60'
Pub: CF Peters
Rev: *American Organist* 18 (Feb, 1984)
     p30

7 Argento, Dominick
Easter day (c.1990)
Med: SATB
Txt: Richard Crashaw
Dur: 3'
Pub: BH

8 Argento, Dominick
Everyone sang (1991)
Med: SATB dbl choir
Txt: Siegfried Sassoon
Dur: 4'30"
Pub: BH

9 Argento, Dominick
I hate and I love (1981)
Med: SATB, perc
Txt: Catullus, trans. composer
Dur: 15'
Pub: BH
Bib: B29

10 Argento, Dominick
Jonah and the whale (1976)
Med: SATB, TB soli, nar, 3 tbn, perc,
     timp, pno, org
Txt: anon. medieval verses; Jonah 2:2-
     9; Ps. 130; folksongs
Dur: 60'

Pub: BH
Rev: *Music Educators Journal* 61 (Jan, 1975) p84
    The lesson
    The charge to Jonah
    His flight
    The storm at sea
    In the belly of the whale
    His prayer
    In Nineveh
    Jonah's despair
    The booth
    God's rebuke
    The lesson restated

11 Argento, Dominick
Let all the world in every corner sing (1980)
Med: SATB, brass quartet, timp, org
Txt: George Herbert
Dur: 3'
Pub: BH

12 Argento, Dominick
A nation of cowslips (1968)
Med: SATB
Txt: John Keats
Dur: 20'
Pub: BH
    The Devon maid
    On visiting Oxford
    Sharing Eve's apple
    There was a naughty boy
    A party of lovers at tea
    Two or three posies
    In praise of Apollo

13 Argento, Dominick
Peter Quince at the clavier (c.1980)
Med: SATB, pno
Txt: Wallace Stevens
Dur: 20'
Pub: BH

14 (not used)

15 Argento, Dominick
The revelation of St. John the Divine (1966)
Med: TTBB, T solo, brass, perc
Txt: Book of Revelations
Dur: 35'
Pub: BH
    Prologue and adoration
    The seven seals and seven trumpets
    Jubilation and epilogue

16 Argento, Dominick
Te Deum (1987)
Med: SATB, orch
Txt: LU and anon. Middle English lyrics
Dur: 40'
Pub: BH
Bib: B113

17 Argento, Dominick
A thanksgiving to God in his house (1979)
Med: SATB
Txt: Robert Herrick
Dur: 4'
Pub: BH
Rev: *American Organist* 22 (June, 1988) p44; *Musical America* 108/4 (1988) p37; *Das Orchester* 36 (Mar, 1988) p301; *Symphony Magazine* 38/5 (1987) p32; *Tempo* 163 (Dec, 1987) p53

18 Argento, Dominick
Tria carmina paschalia (1970)
Med: SSA, hp, gtr or hpschd
Txt: anon. Latin Easter lyrics
Dur: 15'
Pub: BH
Rev: *Pan Pipes* 64/3 (1972) p36-7

B

19   Bacon, Ernst
The animals' Christmas oratorio
    (1964)
Med: boys', junior, or women's cho-
    rus, nar, pno
Txt: medieval French, adapt. Manuel
    Komroff
Dur: 23'
Pub: Presser
Mss: copy in NYPL

20   Bacon, Ernst
Apothegms (n.d.)
Med: SATB, kybd
Txt: not indicated
Dur: 12'
Pub: unpubl.?
Mss: copy in NYPL

21   Bacon, Ernst
Babe of Bethlehem (c.1971)
Med: SATB, incidental soli, pno
Txt: trad.
Dur: 4'
Pub: Belwin-Mills

22   Bacon, Ernst
Bird talk (n.d.)
Med: SSA
Txt: not indicated
Dur: 3'
Pub: Summy Birchard

23   Bacon, Ernst
The birds (c.1955)
Med: SA, pno
Txt: not indicated
Dur: 1'
Pub: Rongwen Music

24   Bacon, Ernst
Buttermilk Hill song (Song of 1776)
    (n.d.)
Med: SA, vln, fl, bells, drum or tamb,
    pno or org
Txt: not indicated
Dur: 4'
Pub: BH

25   Bacon, Ernst
By blue Ontario (1958)
Med: SATB, ABar soli, orch
Txt: Walt Whitman
Dur: 45'
Pub: unpubl.
Mss: copy in NYPL

26   Bacon, Ernst
Canons (n.d.)
Med: 2, 3 or 4 vv, perc
Txt: composer?
Dur: various short works
Pub: unpubl.
Mss: copy in NYPL
    Evergreen
    Grieve not too long
    Love and the law
    Wisdom's modesty
    Definition
    The arts
    Politics
    Legality
    Flee or follow
    Two courages
    Surfeit
    Anomaly
    Speculation
    Money
    Grief
    Our friends
    Sierra high trip
    Rest in the mountains
    On belay
    Mountain meadow

The buyer beware
Sad thought
Foreign
Old Paint
Hair cut
The Colorado trail
Epitaph

27 Bacon, Ernst
A carol (c.1957)
Med: SSA, kybd
Txt: trad.
Dur: 2'
Pub: Galaxy

28 Bacon, Ernst
A Christmas carol (1956)
Med: SATB, pno
Txt: Robert Herrick
Dur: 2'30"
Pub: Peer Intl.

29 Bacon, Ernst
The Colorado trail (c.1954)
Med: SATB, pno
Txt: trad., arr. by composer
Dur: 10'
Pub: Lawson-Gould

30 Bacon, Ernst
Devilish Mary (1953)
Med: SATB, pno four hands
Txt: trad.
Dur: 4'
Pub: Shawnee Press

31 Bacon, Ernst
Down yonder (c.1955)
Med: SATB, pno
Txt: trad.
Dur: 4'
Pub: Rongwen Music

32 Bacon, Ernst
The Ecclesiastes (1936)
Med: TTBB, SB soli, orch
Txt: not indicated
Dur: 40'
Pub: unpubl.
Mss: Syracuse University; copy in NYPL
Src: Dox

33 Bacon, Ernst
Five hymns (c.1952)
Med: SATB, kybd
Txt: see below
Dur: 7'
Pub: CC Birchard
    The eternal goodness (John Greenleaf Whittier)
    Morn and night (Wm. Blake)
    The soule (Robert Herrick)
    Freedom (James Russell Lowell)
    Child's evening hymn (S. Baring-Gould)

34 Bacon, Ernst
Four innocent airs (c.1958)
Med: SA, pno
Txt: see below
Dur: 7'
Pub: Lawson-Gould
    Return of spring (A. Wynne)
    Where go the boats (Robert Louis Stevenson)
    The schoolboy (Wm. Blake)
    A cradle song (Wm. Blake)

35 Bacon, Ernst
From Emily's diary (1947)
Med: SSAA, SA soli, ch. orch
Txt: Emily Dickinson
Dur: 25'
Pub: G. Schirmer
    Preface
    My river runs to thee
    I dwell in possibility

A drop fell on the apple tree
The daisy follows soft the sun
What soft, cherubic creatures
When roses cease to bloom, dear
It's coming
"Unto me?"
Not what we did shall be the test
Afterthought

36 Bacon, Ernst
Give me Jesus (c.1958)
Med: SA, pno
Txt: trad.
Dur: 2'
Pub: Galaxy Music

37 Bacon, Ernst
Golden rules (c.1956)
Med: SATB, pno or org
Txt: *Talmud*
Dur: 2'
Pub: Peer Intl.

38 Bacon, Ernst
The houn' dawg (c.1952)
Med: TTBB, pno
Txt: trad.
Dur: 3'
Pub: Mercury Music

39 Bacon, Ernst
How many? (1951)
Med: SATB, pno
Txt: trad.
Dur: 4'30"
Pub: EB Marks

40 Bacon, Ernst
John Hardy (1954)
Med: SATB, pno
Txt: trad.
Dur: 4'
Pub: Lawson-Gould

41 Bacon, Ernst
Jonah (c.1956)
Med: SATB, kybd
Txt: Herman Melville
Dur: 3'
Pub: Peer Intl.

42 Bacon, Ernst
The last invocation (1971)
Med: SATB, SB soli, orch
Txt: Emily Dickinson, Walt Whitman
Dur: 50'
Pub: unpubl.
Mss: San Jose Symphony; copy in NYPL
Rev: *Symphony Magazine* 34/5 (1983) p30

43 Bacon, Ernst
The last train (c.1954)
Med: SATB, pno four hands
Txt: Paul Horgan
Dur: 6'
Pub: Shawnee Press
N.B. From his opera *A tree on the plains*.

44 Bacon, Ernst
The long farewell (c.1951)
Med: SATB, pno
Txt: trad.
Dur: 2'30"
Pub: EB Marks

45 Bacon, Ernst
The Lord star (c.1949)
Med: SATB, Bar solo, kybd
Txt: Walt Whitman
Dur: 12'
Pub: Music Press

46 Bacon, Ernst
Love somebody (c.1957)
Med: SATB, pno
Txt: trad.

Dur: 5'
Pub: Presser

47 Bacon, Ernst
Mid-winter's snow (c.1976)
Med: SA, pno
Txt: Spanish folk song
Dur: 4'
Pub: Lawson–Gould

48 Bacon, Ernst
Nature (c.1971)
Med: women's voices, pno
Txt: Emily Dickinson
Dur: 20'
Pub: EC Schirmer
   The mountain
   The gentlest mother
   A spider
   The arctic flower
   With the first Arbutus
   There came a day
   A wind like a bugle
   Winter afternoons
   The cricket song
   The sea

49 Bacon, Ernst
Ode (c.1951)
Med: SATB
Txt: Ralph W. Emerson
Dur: 4'
Pub: Mercury Music

50 Bacon, Ernst
Of music (c.1958)
Med: SA, kybd
Txt: not indicated
Dur: 2'30"
Pub: Galaxy Music

51 Bacon, Ernst
The precepts of Angelus Silesius (n.d.)
Med: SSA div
Txt: Johann Scheffer, trans. Paul Carus

Dur: 9'
Pub: Bennington College New Music
   Series
Src: Locke
   Prologue—Two eyes our souls possess
   Chorale—Thou needest not cry to
   God
   Sermon—God never did exist
   Ground—Dost think, poor man
   Air—The rose is without why
   Drone—Rain rains not for itself
   Chorale—All creatures are the voice
   Song—The nightingale will not
   Response—"Where is my residence?"
   Conclusion—Friend, it is now enough

52 Bacon, Ernst
The robe (c.1953)
Med: SATB, pno
Txt: trad.
Dur: 4'
Pub: Shawnee Press

53 Bacon, Ernst
Seven canons (c.1948)
Med: 2-4 voices, pno
Txt: see below
Dur: 17'
Pub: NY Music Press
Rev: *Music Review* 10 (Feb, 1949) p75
   God (Angelus Silesius)
   Sinai
   Schools and rules (William Blake)
   The pelican
   The little children
   Chop, cherry (Robert Herrick)
   Money

54 Bacon, Ernst
Shouting pilgrim (c.1954)
Med: SATB, pno
Txt: trad.
Dur: 3'30"
Pub: Lawson–Gould

55 Bacon, Ernst
Sleep song (c.1955)
Med: SATB
Txt: trad.
Dur: 2'
Pub: Rongwen Music

56 Bacon, Ernst
Sweet morning (c.1960)
Med: SA, pno
Txt: trad.
Dur: 2'
Pub: HW Gray

57 Bacon, Ernst
Usania (1972)
Med: SATB, SB soli, orch
Txt: Walt Whitman, et al.
Dur: 40'
Pub: unpubl.
Mss: Free Library of Philadelphia
Src: Dox

58 Bacon, Ernst
Waiting (c.1956)
Med: SATB, opt. kybd
Txt: John Burroughs
Dur: 2'
Pub: Peer Intl.

59 Bacon, Ernst
Water (c.1959)
Med: SA, kybd
Txt: Ralph W. Emerson
Dur: 2'
Pub: Galaxy Music

60 Barber, Samuel
Ad bibinem cum me rogaret ad cenam
     (1943?)
Med: SATB
Txt: Venantius Fortunatus
Dur: 2'

Pub: G Schirmer
Mss: holograph in LC

61 Barber, Samuel
Agnus Dei (1967)
Med: SATB
Txt: LU
Dur: 7'30"
Pub: G Schirmer
N.B. Transcribed from String Quartet,
     Op. 11, second movement; in-
     strumental version known as the
     Adagio for Strings.

62 Barber, Samuel
Christmas Eve (c.1924)
Med: SAA, 2 soli, org
Pub: unpubl.
Src: Grove

63 Barber, Samuel
Easter chorale, Op. 40 (1964)
Med: SATB, 3 tpt, 3 tbn, 2 hn, tuba,
     timp, opt. org
Txt: Pack Browning
Dur: 3'
Pub: G Schirmer

64 Barber, Samuel
God's grandeur (1938)
Med: SATB dbl choir
Txt: Gerard Manley Hopkins
Pub: unpubl.
Src: Grove

65 Barber, Samuel
Let down the bars, O death, Op. 8,
     No. 2 (1939)
Med: SATB
Txt: Emily Dickinson
Dur: 2'
Pub: G Schirmer
Mss: LC
Rev: *Musical Times* 91 (Jan, 1950) p31

66 Barber, Samuel
Long live Louise and Sidney Homer
(1944)
Med: canon
Pub: unpubl.
Src: Grove

67 Barber, Samuel
The lovers, Op. 43 (1971)
Med: SATB, Bar solo, orch
Txt: Pablo Neruda
Dur: 31'
Pub: G Schirmer
Rev: *ASCAP* 5/3 (1972) p30; *Hi-Fidelity/Musical America* 22 (Jan, 1972) pMA23; *International Musician* 70 (Dec, 1971) p11; *Music Educators Journal* 58 (Nov, 1971) p16; *Music Journal* 30 (Jan, 1972) p75; *Pan Pipes* 64/2 (1972) p28; *Saturday Review* 54 (Oct 10, 1971), p14-15; *Symphony News* 22/6 (1971) p24.
Body of a woman
Lithe girl, brown girl
In the hot depth of this summer
Close your eyes
The fortunate isles
Sometimes
We have lost even this twilight
Tonight I can write
Cemetery of kisses

68 Barber, Samuel
Mary Ruane (c.1936)
Med: SATB
Txt: James Stephens
Pub: unpubl.
Src: Grove

69 Barber, Samuel
The monk and his cat, Op. 29
(c.1945)
Med: SATB

Txt: trans. W.H. Auden
Dur: 4'
Pub: G Schirmer
N.B. Originally for solo voice.

70 Barber, Samuel
Motetto (1930)
Med: SATB div
Txt: Book of Job
Pub: unpubl.
Src: Grove

71 Barber, Samuel
A nun takes the veil (Heaven-haven),
Op. 13, No. 1 (c.1951)
Med: SATB
Txt: Gerard Manley Hopkins
Dur: 2'30"
Pub: G Schirmer
N.B. Also for SSAA, TTBB.

72 Barber, Samuel
Peggy Mitchell (c.1936)
Med: SATB
Txt: James Stephens
Pub: unpubl.
Src: Grove

73 Barber, Samuel
The prayers of Kierkegaard, Op. 30
(1954)
Med: SATB div, S solo (AT soli ad lib.), orch
Txt: Søren Kierkegaard
Dur: 20'
Pub: G Schirmer
Mss: LC
Rev: *American Choral Review* 24/4 (1982) p15-16; *American Music Digest* 1 (Oct, 1969) p7; *Christian Science Monitor*, Dec 4, 1954; *Music Journal* 34 (June, 1976) p70-1 and 35 (Dec, 1977) p36-7; *Musical Opinion* 79 (Dec, 1955) p157;

Music Review 19 (Aug, 1958)
p247ff

74   Barber, Samuel
Reincarnations, Op. 16 (1932–40)
Med: SATB
Txt: James Stephens
Dur: 10'
Pub: G Schirmer
Mss: LC
Bib: B96
    Mary Hynes
    Anthony O'Daly
    The coolin

75   Barber, Samuel
A stopwatch and an ordnance map,
    Op. 15 (1940)
Med: TTBB, timp
Txt: Stephen Spender
Dur: 7'
Pub: G Schirmer
Mss: LC
Rev: *Musical Opinion* 78 (Feb, 1955)
    p285ff; *Music Review* 16 (Nov,
    1955) p341–2

76   Barber, Samuel
Sure on this shining night (c.1961)
Med: SATB
Txt: James Agee
Dur: 3'30"
Pub: G Schirmer
N.B. Originally for solo voice.

77   Barber, Samuel
To be sung on the water, Op. 42,
    No. 2 (1969)
Med: SATB
Txt: Louise Bogan
Dur: 3'
Pub: G Schirmer
Mss: LC

78   Barber, Samuel
Twelfth night, Op. 42, No. 1 (1969)
Med: SATB
Txt: Laurie Lee
Dur: 4'30"
Pub: G Schirmer
Mss: LC

79   Barber, Samuel
The virgin martyrs, Op. 8, No. 1
    (c.1939)
Med: SSAA
Txt: Helen Waddell, after Siegebert
    of Gemboux
Dur: 3'30"
Pub: G Schirmer
Mss: LC

80   Bassett, Leslie
Cantata for the city, nation, world
    (c.1959)
Med: SATB, cong, 4 tbn, org
Txt: John White Chadwick
Dur: 11'
Pub: ACA
    Hymn: External ruler of the ceaseless
      round
    We are of thee
    Earth, hear thy maker's voice
    We would be one
    Lord, in the strength of grace
    Enough to know

81   Bassett, Leslie
Celebration in praise of earth (1970)
Pub: CF Peters
Src: B119

82   Bassett, Leslie
Collect (1969)
Med: SATB, tape
Txt: anon
Dur: 4'
Pub: WLSM
Bib: B129

83   Bassett, Leslie
Eclogue, encomium and evocation
    (1962)
Med: SSA, 4 inst
Pub: ACA
Src: Grove

84   Bassett, Leslie
Follow now that bright star (1977)
Med: SATB
Txt: Anne Sanders
Dur: 2'
Pub: ACA

85   Bassett, Leslie
Hear my prayer, O Lord (1965)
Med: SA, org
Txt: Ps. 44
Pub: CF Peters
Src: Grove

86   Bassett, Leslie
The lamb (1952)
Med: SATB, pno
Txt: William Blake
Dur: 3'
Pub: ACA

87   Bassett, Leslie
Lord, who has formed me (c.1987)
Med: SATB, kybd
Txt: George Herbert
Dur: 3'
Pub: CF Peters

88   Bassett, Leslie
Moon canticle (1969)
Med: SATB, nar, opt. cello
Txt: not indicated
Dur: 17'
Pub: CF Peters
    Introduction and hymn
    Query
    Incantation

    Forecast
    Conclusion

89   Bassett, Leslie
Moonrise (1960)
Med: SATB
Pub: ACA
Src: B119

90   Bassett, Leslie
Notes in the silence (1966)
Med: SATB, pno
Txt: Dag Hammarskjöld
Dur: 9'
Pub: CF Peters

91   Bassett, Leslie
Of wind and earth (1973)
Med: SATB, pno
Txt: Percy B. Shelley, William Jen-
    nings Bryant, and St. Francis
Dur: 9'
Pub: CF Peters

92   Bassett, Leslie
Out of the depths (1957)
Med: SATB, org
Txt: Ps. 130
Dur: 4'
Pub: ACA

93   Bassett, Leslie
Prayers for divine service (1965)
Med: TTBB, org
Txt: LU
Dur: 9'
Pub: ACA
Mss: composer
Src: Roberts
    Munda cor meum
    Domine Jesu Christe
    Agnus Dei

94   Bassett, Leslie
Remembrance (1960)
Med: SATB, org
Txt: Rupert
Dur: 4'
Pub: CF Peters

95   Bassett, Leslie
A ring of emeralds (1979)
Med: SATB, pno
Txt: see below
Dur: 10'
Pub: CF Peters
   Invitation (anon.)
   Madrigal 1 (Gerald Griffin)
   Riddle (Jonathan Swift)
   The blackbird's song (anon.)
   Madrigal 2 (John Boyle O'Reilly)

96   Bassett, Leslie
Sing to the Lord (c.1987)
Med: SATB, kybd
Txt: Ps. 95
Dur: 3'
Pub: CF Peters

97   Bassett, Leslie
Whoe'er she be (1987)
Med: SSA, pno
Txt: Richard Crashaw
Dur: 3'30"
Pub: CF Peters

98   Bauer, Marion
At the new year, Op. 42 (1947)
Med: SATB, pno
Txt: Kenneth Patchen
Dur: 3'
Pub: AMP

99   Bauer, Marion
China, Op. 38 (1943)
Med: SATB, pno
Txt: Boris Todrin

Dur: 6'
Pub: J Fischer
Mss: LC

100   Bauer, Marion
Death spreads his gentle wings (c.1952)
Med: SATB
Txt: Eunice Prosser Crain
Dur: 2'
Pub: AMP

101   Bauer, Marion
Fair daffodils (c.1914)
Med: SSA, pno
Txt: Robert Herrick
Dur: 3'
Pub: AP Schmidt
Mss: LC

102   Bauer, Marion
A foreigner comes to earth on Boston Common (c.1953)
Med: SATB, ST soli
Txt: Horace Gregory
Dur: 6'
Pub: NY: Composers' Facsimile Edition
Mss: LC

103   Bauer, Marion
A garden is a lovesome thing (c.1938)
Med: SSATBB
Txt: Thomas Edward Brown
Dur: 4'
Pub: G Schirmer

104   Bauer, Marion
Here at high morning, Op. 27 (1931)
Med: TTBB
Txt: May Lewis
Dur: 2'
Pub: HW Gray

105 Bauer, Marion
The lay of the four winds, Op. 8
(c.1915)
Med: TTBB, pno
Txt: Cale Young Rice
Dur: 6'
Pub: AP Schmidt
Mss: LC

106 Bauer, Marion
Lobster quadrille (c.1953)
Med: SSAA
Txt: Lewis Carroll
Dur: 2'
Pub: unpubl.
Mss: NYPL

107 Bauer, Marion
Mass in G minor (1902)
Med: SATB, org
Txt: LU
Dur: 14'
Mss: LC

108 Bauer, Marion
The thinker, Op. 35 (1938)
Med: SATB
Src: Grove

109 Bauer, Marion
Three noëls, Op. 22 (c.1930)
Med: SSA, pno
Txt: see below
Dur: 10'
Pub: AP Schmidt
Mss: LC
   Tryste noël (Louise Imogen Guiney)
   I sing of a maiden (anon.)
   Lullay! lullay! lytel child (anon.)

110 Bauer, Marion
Wenn ich rufe zu dir, Herr, mein Gott, Op. 3 (c.1903)
Med: SSA, S solo, pno or org

Txt: Ps. 28
Dur: 4'
Pub: Leipzig: Gebrüder Hug
Src: WmAmMus

111 Bergsma, William
Black salt, black provender (1946)
Med: SATB, 2 pno
Txt: Louise Bogan
Dur: 7'
Pub: unpubl.
Mss: LC

112 Bergsma, William
Confrontation (1963)
Med: SATB, M solo, pno or orch
Txt: Book of Job
Dur: 26'
Pub: Galaxy
Mss: LC

113 Bergsma, William
In a glass of water before retiring
(c.1947)
Med: TB, pno
Txt: Stephen Vincent Benét
Dur: 4'
Pub: C Fischer
N.B. Also arr. for SATB with S solo.

114 Bergsma, William
Let true love among us be (c.1950)
Med: 2-part, any voicing, pno
Txt: anon. 13th cent., adapt. Nancy Nickerson
Dur: 4'30"
Pub: C Fischer
Rev: *Musical America* 70 (Aug, 1950) p28; *Music News* 43 (Apr, 1951) p25

115 Bergsma, William
On the beach at night (1946)
Med: SATB
Txt: Walt Whitman

Dur: 5'
Pub: C Fischer

116 Bergsma, William
Praise (c.1959)
Med: SATB, org
Txt: George Herbert
Dur: 2'
Pub: Galaxy

117 Bergsma, William
*Riddle me this: answer: the cow, the
egg, the snow* (1957)
Med: SATB
Txt: not indicated
Dur: 1'30"
Pub: Galaxy

118 Bergsma, William
*The sun, the soaring eagle, the
turquoise prince, the god* (1968)
Med: SATB; brass and perc, pno and
perc., or pno only
Txt: Bernardino de Sahagún
Dur: 10'
Pub: Galaxy
Rev: *ASCAP* 2/3 (1968) p33
N.B. Includes speaking parts in Aztec.

119 Bergsma, William
Wishes, wonders, portents, charms
(c.1979)
Med: SATB, soli, fl, hp, pno, perc,
opt. harmonica
Txt: trad. and Sir Walter Scott, Walt
Whitman, Herman Melville
Dur: 27'
Pub: Galaxy

120 Bernstein, Leonard
Chichester psalms (1965)
Med: SATB, boy solo, 3 tpt, 3 tbn, 2
hp, perc, str
Txt: Ps. 2:1-4; Ps. 23:100; Ps. 104:2;
Ps. 131; Ps. 133:1

Dur: 18'30"
Pub: G Schirmer
Mss: LC
Rev: *Hi-Fidelity/Musical America* 17
(Aug, 1967) pMA21; *Musica* 22/
5 (1968) p352; *Musical Times* 108
(Aug, 1967) p722; *Performing Right*
43 (Oct, 1965) p21-3
Bib: B76, 78, 125
N.B. The composer prefers boys' voices
to sing the SA parts.

121 Bernstein, Leonard
Choruses from "The lark" (1955)
Med: SATB div, drum, bells
Txt: Jean Anouilh, adapt. Lillian
Hellman
Dur: 17'
Pub: G Schirmer
Bib: B76, 78

122 Bernstein, Leonard
Hashkivenu (1945)
Med: SATB, cantor, org
Txt: liturgical Hebrew
Dur: 10'
Pub: M Witmark
Mss: LC

123 Bernstein, Leonard
A little Norton lecture (1973)
Med: TTBB
Txt: e.e. cummings
Pub: unpubl.
Src: Grove

124 Bernstein, Leonard
The lonely men of Harvard (1957)
Med: TTBB, orch
Txt: Alan J. Lerner
Dur: 3'
Pub: unpubl.
Mss: LC

125 Bernstein, Leonard
Mass: a theatre piece for singers, players, and dancers (1971)
Med: SATB, choir of street people, boy choir, celebrant; 2 orch: strings and two organs; and brass, woodwinds, electric gtr and kybds; dancers
Txt: LU, others
Dur: 1hr, 40'
Pub: G Schirmer
Rev: *ADEM* 9/4 (1973) p154
American Choral Review 14/3 (1972) p137-9
Arts Reporting Service 2 (Sept 2, 1971) p4, and 3 (Feb 19, 1973) p3
ASCAP 5/3 (1972) p5
Billboard 85 (July 28, 1973) p49
Bühne 179 (Aug, 1973) p10
Christian Science Monitor July 20, 1972, p8
Crescendo International 20 (Dec, 1981) p3
Heterophonia 4/21 (1971) p18
Hi-Fidelity/Musical America 21 (Dec, 1971) pMA10-11 and 22 (Feb, 1972) pMA68-76
Inter-American Music Review 81 (July-Oct, 1971) p13-18
International Musician 70 (Oct, 1971) p3ff
Melos/NZ 2/4 (1976) p281-4
Music (AGO) 5 (Dec, 1971) p4ff, and 6 (Aug, 1972) p19ff
Music and Musicians 20 (March, 1972) p5
Music Educators Journal 58 (Nov, 1971) p16, and 60 (Nov, 1973) p26-8
Music Journal 30 (April, 1972) p23ff
Musica 25/6 (1971) p575
Musical Times 112 (Dec, 1971) p192-3
Musicians and Artists 4/5 (1971-72) p13-14
Musikhandel 22/7 (1971) p328
Musik und Bildung 6 (June, 1974) p374-80
Neue Musikzeitung 20/6 (1971) p29, and 22/5 (1972) p2
Neue Zeitschrift für Musik 132 (Nov, 1971) p615, and 6-7 (June-July, 1982) p75-6
New Yorker 48 (July 8, 1972) p58
Nuova Rivista Musicale Italiana 5/6 (1971) p1064
Oesterreichische Musikzeitschrift 26 (Dec, 1971) p713, and 36 (April, 1981) p50-1
Oper und Konzert 19/3 (1981) p27
Opera 32 (May, 1981) p501-3; 37 (Aug, 1986) p982-3; and 40 (June, 1989) p686-9
Opera News 36 (Oct, 1971) p20-1, 46 (July, 1981), p33, and 53 (Nov, 1988), p60-1
Opernwelt 8 (Aug, 1973) p34-6, and 22 (April, 1981) p45
Ovation 10 (May, 1989) p45
Pan Pipes 64/2 (1972) p8-14
Rolling Stone 95 (Nov 11, 1971) p8 and 102 (Feb 17, 1972) p54
Sacred Music 99/1 (1972) p3-8; 100/1 (1973) p33-6; and 100/4 (1973), p32
Saturday Review 55 (Sept 25, 1971) p74-5 and 55 (Dec 25, 1971) p55
Schweizeriche Musikzeitung 121/3 (1981), p187-8
Stereo Review 27 (Dec, 1971) p28 and 28 (March, 1972) p28
Tempo 103 (1972), p57-8

Time 98 (Sept 20, 1971), p41-3
Variety 264 (Sept 15, 1971) p1ff,
74; (Sept 22, 1971), p1ff; (Oct
6, 1971) p2; and 265 (July 5,
1972) p2ff
Village Voice 26 (Sept 23, 1981)
p111-12 and 34 (Feb 7, 1989)
p80
Wall Street Journal, Sept 10, 1972,
p8
Washington Post, Sept 9, 1971
World 1 (Sept 12, 1972) p58ff
World of Music 13/4 (971) p80
Bib: B3, 43, 49, 51, 66, 78, 79, 80,
93, 107, 125, 156, 159, 173
Devotions before Mass
Kyrie
Hymn and psalm
Responsory: Alleluia
First Introit (Rondo)
Prefatory prayers
Thrice-triple canon
Second Introit
In nomine patris
Prayer for the congregation
Epiphany
Confession
Confiteor
Trope: "I don't know"
Trope: "Easy"
Meditation No. 1 (orch)
Gloria
Gloria tibi
Gloria in excelsis
Trope: "Half of the people"
Trope: "Thank you"
Meditation No. 2 (orch)
Epistle
Gospel-sermon: "God said"
Credo
Credo in unum
Trope: "Non credo"
Trope: "Hurry"
Trope: "World without end"
Trope: "I believe in God"

Meditation No. 3
Offertory
The Lord's prayer
Our Father...
Trope: "I go on"
Sanctus
Agnus Dei
Fraction: "Things get broken"
Pax: Communion ("Secret songs")

126 Bernstein, Leonard
Missa brevis (c.1988)
Med: SATB
Txt: LU
Dur: 9'30"
Pub: NY: Jalni Publ.
Rev: *Tempo* 165 (June, 1988) p60

127 Bernstein, Leonard
Olympic hymn (1981)
Med: SATB, orch
Pub: G Schirmer
Src: Grove
Rev: *Musikhandel* 32/7 (1981) p350

128 Bernstein, Leonard
Symphony No. 3 (Kaddish) (1963,
rev. 1980)
Med: SATB, boys' choir, S solo, nar,
orch
Txt: composer, after trad. Hebrew
Dur: 30'
Pub: G Schirmer
Mss: copy of holograph in LC
Rev: *American Music Digest* 1/5 (1970)
p20
Bib: B76, 77, 159

129 Bernstein, Leonard
Warm-up (c.1970)
Med: SSATTTTBB
Txt: composer
Dur: 4'
Pub: G Schirmer

Rev: *ASCAP* 4/1 (1970) p31; *Music
    Journal* 28 (Jan, 1970) p12
N.B. Later incorporated into *Mass*.

130 Bernstein, Leonard
Yigdal (1950)
Med: SATB, pno
Txt: liturgical Hebrew
Src: Grove

131 Binkerd, Gordon
And viva sweet love (1949, rev.
    1956)
Med: TTBB, pno four hands
Txt: e.e. cummings
Dur: 11'
Pub: BH

132 Binkerd, Gordon
Autumnal flowers (1968)
Med: SATB
Txt: J. Very
Src: Grove

133 Binkerd, Gordon
Ave Maria (1963)
Med: SATB
Txt: LU
Dur: 2'
Pub: BH

134 Binkerd, Gordon
The beautiful changes (1964)
Med: SSAA
Txt: Richard Wilbur
Dur: 7'
Pub: BH

135 Binkerd, Gordon
A birthday (c.1951)
Med: SATB
Txt: Christina Rossetti
Dur: 3'
Pub: BH

136 Binkerd, Gordon
Browning choruses (1976)
Med: SATB
Txt: Elizabeth B. Browning
Dur: 3'
Pub: BH

137 Binkerd, Gordon
Chimes (1978)
Med: SA, bell-lyra
Txt: composer
Dur: 4'30"
Pub: BH
N.B. Also arr. for male voices.

138 Binkerd, Gordon
Choral strands (c.1977)
Med: SATB or STB
Txt: see below
Dur: 9'30"
Pub: BH
    Last light (Rudy Shackelford; also arr.
        for TTBB)
    The city child (Alfred Lord Tennyson)
    O darling room (Tennyson; S solo)
    What does the woman want? (com-
        poser)

139 Binkerd, Gordon
The Christ child (c.1977)
Med: SATB, S solo, pno
Txt: G.K. Chesterton
Dur: 3'
Pub: BH

140 Binkerd, Gordon
A Christmas caroll (c.1970)
Med: SATB div
Txt: Robert Herrick
Dur: 15'
Pub: BH

141 Binkerd, Gordon
Christmas Day (c.1973)
Med: SATB

Txt: Christina Rossetti
Dur: 2'
Pub: BH

142 Binkerd, Gordon
Compleynt, compleynt (c.1969)
Med: SATB
Txt: Ezra Pound
Dur: 10'
Pub: BH

143 Binkerd, Gordon
Confitebor tibi (c.1968)
Med: SATB
Txt: LU
Dur: 2'
Pub: BH

144 Binkerd, Gordon
Dakota day (1985)
Med: SATB, fl, ob, clar, hp
Txt: Alfred Lord Tennyson
Src: Grove

145 Binkerd, Gordon
Dum medium silentium (1960)
Med: TTBB
Txt: LU
Dur: 4'
Pub: BH

146 Binkerd, Gordon
The ebb and flow (c.1967)
Med: SATB
Txt: Edward Taylor
Dur: 4'
Pub: BH
Bib: B94

147 Binkerd, Gordon
Eternite (c.1971)
Med: SSATB
Txt: Robert Herrick
Dur: 6'
Pub: BH

148 Binkerd, Gordon
Feast of St. Francis of Assisi: gradual and alleluia (1964, 1969)
Med: SA or TB, org
Txt: Ps. 36
Dur: 4'
Pub: BH

149 Binkerd, Gordon
For unknown soldiers (1990)
Med: TTBB div, pno
Txt: see below
Dur: 6'30"
Pub: Samizdat Publications
    Folksong (Rainer Maria Rilke)
    The sunset of the year (anon.)

150 Binkerd, Gordon
From your throne, O Lord: gradual (c.1968)
Med: unison, org
Txt: Ps. 79
Dur: 5'30"
Pub: BH

151 Binkerd, Gordon
Hope is the thing with feathers (1956)
Med: SSA
Txt: Emily Dickinson
Pub: BH
Src: Paulin

152 Binkerd, Gordon
Houses at dusk (1984)
Med: 4 choruses, male voices, pno
Txt: Henry W. Longellow, Hilaire Belloc, F.G. Halleck, trad.
Src: Grove

153 Binkerd, Gordon
Infant joy (1959)
Med: SSAA
Txt: William Blake
Dur: 2'
Pub: BH

154 Binkerd, Gordon
It is not the tear (1989)
Med: SSAA, pno
Txt: Thomas Moore
Dur: 4'
Pub: Samizdat Publications

155 Binkerd, Gordon
The lamb (c.1971)
Med: SATB
Txt: William Blake
Dur: 3'
Pub: BH

156 Binkerd, Gordon
Let my prayer come as incense: gradual
(c.1968)
Med: TB, org
Txt: Ps. 140
Dur: 4'
Pub: BH

157 Binkerd, Gordon
Liebeslied (1958)
Med: TTBB
Txt: Rainer Maria Rilke
Pub: BH
Src: Paulin

158 Binkerd, Gordon
The Lord is king (n.d.)
Med: SATB, org
Txt: Ps. 93
Dur: 9'
Pub: CF Peters

159 Binkerd, Gordon
Minnedienst (1982)
Med: TTBB
Txt: trad. German
Pub: BH
Src: Paulin

160 Binkerd, Gordon
The mistletoe (1989)
Med: SSA, pno
Txt: A.D. Graves
Dur: 3'30"
Pub: Samizdat Publications

161 Binkerd, Gordon
My soul, there is a country (c.1973)
Med: SATB
Txt: Henry Vaughan
Dur: 4'
Pub: BH

162 Binkerd, Gordon
Nativitas est hodie (c.1966)
Med: SATB
Txt: LU
Dur: 5'
Pub: BH

163 Binkerd, Gordon
Never weather-beaten sail (c.1973)
Med: SATB
Txt: Thomas Campion
Dur: 2'30"
Pub: BH
N.B. From *Songs of farewell.*

164 Binkerd, Gordon
Nocturne (c.1969)
Med: SATB div, cello
Txt: William Carlos Williams
Dur: 11'
Pub: BH

165 Binkerd, Gordon
Now our meeting's over (c.1982)
Med: SATB
Txt: trad.
Dur: 4'
Pub: BH

166 Binkerd, Gordon
Omnes gentes (c.1968)
Med: SATB
Txt: LU
Dur: 3'
Pub: BH

167 Binkerd, Gordon
On the king's highway (1978–79)
Med: 1–3 part children's voices, S solo,
    ch. orch
Txt: James Stephens
Dur: 2'
Pub: BH
Mss: AMC
    Pater noster
    Little things
    Hesperus
    The white swan

168 Binkerd, Gordon
On the shortness of human life
    (c.1966)
Med: SATB
Txt: William Cowper
Dur: 3'
Pub: BH

169 Binkerd, Gordon
Promises like pie-crust (c.1978)
Med: SATB div
Txt: Christina Rossetti and Dante
    Gabriel Rossetti
Dur: 5'
Pub: BH

170 Binkerd, Gordon
Psalm 23 (c.1972)
Med: SATB, T solo, org
Txt: Ps. 23
Dur: 5'30"
Pub: BH

171 Binkerd, Gordon
Psalm 93 (c.1961)
Med: SATB, org
Txt: Ps. 93
Dur: 3'
Pub: CF Peters

172 Binkerd, Gordon
Quasi modo (c.1973)
Med: SATB
Txt: LU
Dur: 6'30"
Pub: BH

173 Binkerd, Gordon
The recommendation (c.1967)
Med: SATB
Txt: Richard Crashaw
Dur: 6'
Pub: BH

174 Binkerd, Gordon
Remember now thy creator (c.1967)
Med: SATB, S solo, org
Txt: Ecclesiastes
Dur: 10'
Pub: BH

175 Binkerd, Gordon
Requiem for soldiers lost in ocean
    transports (1984)
Med: SATB
Txt: Herman Melville
Dur: 9'
Pub: BH

176 Binkerd, Gordon
Salutis humanæ sator (c.1970)
Med: SATB
Txt: LU
Dur: 4'30"
Pub: BH

177 Binkerd, Gordon
Scapulis suis (1960)
Med: SSAA
Txt: Ps. 91
Pub: AMP
Src: Paulin

178 Binkerd, Gordon
A Scotch mist (1977)
Med: TTBB
Txt: Robert Burns
Dur: 7'
Pub: BH
　　Wilt thou be my dearie
　　Clout the caudron
　　Ay waukin O

179 Binkerd, Gordon
Songs from "The silver tassie" (1971)
Med: TBB, pno
Txt: Sean O'Casey
Dur: 7'
Pub: BH

180 Binkerd, Gordon
Song of praise and prayer (1972)
Med: unison children, kybd
Txt: William Cowper
Dur: 2'30"
Pub: BH

181 Binkerd, Gordon
Song of songs (c.1981)
Med: SATB, hn, pno
Txt: Wilfred Owen
Dur: 7'
Pub: BH

182 Binkerd, Gordon
Songs to poems of Elinor Wylie (1985–87)
Med: SSAA, Bar solo, pno
Txt: Elinor Wylie
Dur: 8'

Pub: Samizdat Publications
　　The lover
　　Little elegy
　　Velvet shoes
　　Sunset on the spire

183 Binkerd, Gordon
Sorrow hath a double voice (1978)
Med: unison choir, S or T solo, hp
Txt: Christina Rossetti
Dur: 4'
Pub: BH

184 Binkerd, Gordon
Sung under the silver umbrella (1978)
Med: SSA, pno
Txt: see below
Dur: 17'30"
Pub: BH
　　The Christ child (G.K. Chesterton)
　　Song of innocence (William Blake)
　　An evening falls (James Stephens)
　　The merry man of Paris (Stella Mead)
　　Child's song (Thomas Moore)
　　White fields (Stephens)

185 Binkerd, Gordon
There is a garden in her face (1972)
Med: TBB, pno
Txt: Thomas Campion
Dur: 3'
Pub: BH

186 Binkerd, Gordon
They lie at rest (1971)
Med: TBB
Txt: Christina Rossetti
Dur: 2'30"
Pub: BH

187 Binkerd, Gordon
Third Mass of Christmas and octave day of Christmas (c.1967)
Med: SATB, org
Txt: Ps. 97:3, 4, 2; Hebrews 1:1, 2

Dur: 7'30"
Pub: BH

188 Binkerd, Gordon
Though your strangeness frets my heart
        (1977)
Med: TTBB
Txt: Thomas Campion
Dur: 5'
Pub: BH

189 Binkerd, Gordon
Three slumber songs (1982)
Med: SATB (*SA only)
Txt: composer
Dur: 7'
Pub: BH
Src: Paulin
    No. 2: Lullaby of the boat people★
    (other numbers not found)

190 Binkerd, Gordon
To Electra, Set 1 (1968)
Med: SATB (*SSAA)
Txt: Robert Herrick
Pub: BH
Src: Paulin
    Love looks for love★
    (other numbers not found)

191 Binkerd, Gordon
To Electra, Set 2 (c.1972)
Med: SATB div, ST soli
Txt: Robert Herrick
Dur: 25'
Pub: BH
    A conjuration; to Electra
    Let not thy tombstone
    A vision to Electra

192 Binkerd, Gordon
To thy happy children (Institutional
        canons) (c.1971)
Med: SATB
Txt: composer

Dur: 3'30"
Pub: BH

193 Binkerd, Gordon
Two Salieri canons (1978)
Med: TTB
Txt: Alfred Lord Tennyson; trad.
    German
Pub: BH
Src: Paulin
    Milton
    Das Glockenspiel

194 Blitzstein, Marc
The airborne (1946)
Med: TTBB, TBar soli, monitor, orch
Txt: composer
Dur: 54'
Pub: unpubl.
Mss: State Historical Society, Madison,
    Wis.; copy in NYPL
Rev: *American Choral Review* 9/4 (1967)
    p48-9; New York *Post*, April 1,
    1946; New York *Times*, April 2,
    1946.
    Theory of flight
    Ballad of history and mythology
    Kittyhawk
    The airborne
    The enemy
    Threat and approach
    Ballad of the cities
    Morning poem
    Air force, Ballad of hurry-up
    Night music, Ballad of the bombardier
    Chorus of the rendezvous
    The open sky

195 Blitzstein, Marc
Cantatina (1935)
Med: SSA, perc
Txt: Walt Whitman, e.e. cummings
Src: Dox

196 Blitzstein, Marc
Children's cantata (1935)
Med: SATB
Pub: unpubl.
Src: Dox

197 Blitzstein, Marc
The condemned (1932)
Med: 4 choruses: TTBB, SSA, BB,
    TT; T solo, orch
Txt: composer
Dur: 3'
Pub: Arrow Music Press
Rev: *Village Voice* 34 (Oct 10, 1989) p82

198 (not used)

199 Blitzstein, Marc
This is the garden (1956)
Med: SATB, orch
Txt: composer
Dur: 18'
Pub: Chappell
Mss: copy of holograph in LC
Rev: *Musical America* 77 (Aug, 1958)
    p26; New York *Times*, May 6,
    1957, p24
    The Lex express
    I'm ten and you'll see
    Harlan Brown, killed in the street
    Hymie is a poop
    In twos
    San Gennaro

200 Bloch, Ernest
Adonai, Elohim (1924)
Med: SSAAB, orch
Txt: composer
Dur: 6'
Pub: G Schirmer
Mss: University of California at
    Berkeley; NYPL
N.B. From the composer's *Symphony
    Israel.*

201 Bloch, Ernest
*Anthem from "America: An epic
    rhapsody"* (1926)
Med: SATB (or SSA or TTBB), orch
Txt: not indicated
Dur: 48'
Pub: CC Birchard
Mss: University of California at Ber-
    keley
N.B. A symphony with choral ending;
    copy of published score in BPL
    has markings by S. Koussevitzky.

202 Bloch, Ernest
*Avodath hakodesh, a Sabbath morning
    service* (c.1934)
Med: SATB, Bar solo (incidental SA
    soli), org or orch
Txt: liturgical Hebrew; Eng. text by
    David Stevens
Dur: 49'
Pub: CC Birchard
Mss: University of California at Berkeley;
    copy of holograph in LC
Rev: *Music and Musicians* 27 (Nov,
    1978) p18ff; *Musical Times* 90 (Dec,
    1949) p450; *Schweizeriche Musik-
    zeitung* 114/2 (1974) p100-1; *Village
    Voice* 25 (Nov 26, 1980) p74
Bib: B21, 22, 67, 121, 124, 185
N.B. Also known as *Sacred service.*

C

203 Cadman, Charles W.
At dawning, Op. 29, No. 1
    (c.1920)
Med: SSA, pno
Txt: Nelle Richmond Eberhart
Dur: 2'
Pub: Ditson
N.B. Originally for solo voice; also arr.
    for SAB.

204   Cadman, Charles W.
The babe is here of Mary born
   (c.1925)
Med: SSA, pno
Txt: Nelle Richmond Eberhart
Dur: 3'
Pub: J Fischer

205   Cadman, Charles W.
The blizzard, Op. 45 (c.1908)
Med: TTBB, kybd
Txt: Nelle Richmond Eberhart
Dur: 6'30"
Pub: G Schirmer

206   Cadman, Charles W.
The brooklet came from the mountain
   (1910?)
Med: SATB, A solo, pno
Txt: Henry W. Longfellow
Dur: 5'
Pub: G Schirmer
Mss: NYPL

207   Cadman, Charles W.
The builder, Op. 78, No. 1 (c.1924)
Med: TTBB, pno
Txt: James W. Foley
Dur: 3'30"
Pub: H Flammer
N.B. Originally for solo voice; also arr.
   for SAB, SATB, SSA and SA
   (boys' voices).

208   Cadman, Charles W.
By his side (c.1932)
Med: TTBB
Txt: Forrest Barnes
Dur: 5'
Pub: NY: W. Maxwell; copy in LC

209   Cadman, Charles W.
By the Skeena River (n.d.)
Med: SATB, pno

Txt: Nelle Richmond Eberhart
Dur: 4'
Pub: Ginn and Co.
Mss: NYPL

210   Cadman, Charles W.
The call of the lark (c.1934)
Med: SSA
Txt: Mary V. Holloway
Dur: 2'
Pub: Presser

211   Cadman, Charles W.
The call of the river (n.d.)
Med: SATB
Txt; Nelle Richmond Eberhart
Dur: 4'
Pub: Ginn and Co.
Mss: NYPL

212   Cadman, Charles W.
Candle light (c.1936)
Med: SSA, pno
Txt: Lee Shipley
Dur: 2'30"
Pub: Presser

213   Cadman, Charles W.
Chinese flower fête, Op. 48, No. 1
   (c.1909)
Med: SSA
Txt: Nelle Richmond Eberhart
Dur: 3'
Pub: Ditson

214   Cadman, Charles W.
Clear the way (c.1946)
Med: SA (boys), pno
Txt: Charles Mackay
Dur: 2'
Pub: Lorenz
N.B. Originally for solo voice.

215 Cadman, Charles W.
"Come," says the drum (c.1931)
Med: TTBB, Bar solo, pno
Txt: Charles O. Roos
Dur: 4'
Pub: Ditson

216 Cadman, Charles W.
Conceited: an operatic burlesque (c.1941)
Med: TTBB, soli, pno
Txt: Henrietta Rees
Dur: 10'
Pub: NY: Concord Music; copy in LC

217 Cadman, Charles W.
Dawn in the wood (c.1933)
Med: SSAA, pno
Txt: Nelle Richmond Eberhart
Dur: 7'
Pub: HT FitzSimons

218 Cadman, Charles W.
Desert quest (c.1946)
Med: SATB
Txt: Nelle Richmond Eberhart
Dur: 4'
Pub: NY: Edwin H. Morris; copy in LC

219 Cadman, Charles W.
Drinking song (n.d.)
Med: TTBB
Txt: Forrest Barnes
Dur: 3'
Pub: unpubl.
Mss: NYPL

220 Cadman, Charles W.
Eastward in Eden (c.1928)
Med: SATB, A solo, org
Txt: not indicated
Dur: 5'
Pub: H Flammer

221 Cadman, Charles W.
Egyptian bridal procession, Op. 48, No. 3 (c.1910)
Med: SSAA, pno
Txt: Nelle Richmond Eberhart
Dur: 3'30"
Pub: Presser

222 Cadman, Charles W.
The far horizon (c.1934)
Med: SATB, SBar soli, pno
Txt: Juanita E. Roos
Dur: 12'
Pub: CC Birchard

223 Cadman, Charles W.
The father of waters (c.1928)
Med: SATB
Txt: Nelle Richmond Eberhart
Dur: 40'
Pub: Ditson
Introduction
The creative spirits
Itaska the source
Father of all running waters
The discovery
The lament of deSoto's men
The song of the Indian corn
The French explorers
Song of the voyagers
The nations of the earth are gathering here
Farewell of the Indian mothers
Love
The first white lovers
The cry of devastation
Night song to the Mississippi
Full moon in Louisiana
Mississippi
The spirit of freedom

224 Cadman, Charles W.
Fickle (c.1925)
Med: SSA, pno
Txt: Nelle Richmond Eberhart

Dur: 3'
Pub: J Church

225 Cadman, Charles W.
La fiesta (c.1935)
Med: SSA, A solo, pno
Txt: Nelle Richmond Eberhart
Dur: 7'
Pub: Galaxy

226 Cadman, Charles W.
*From the land of sky-blue waters,
Op. 45, No. 1* (c.1934)
Med: SA, pno
Txt: Nelle Richmond Eberhart
Dur: 2'
Pub: White-Smith; copy in LC, NYPL
Mss: NYPL
N.B. Originally for solo voice; also arr.
for SATB, SSA.

227 Cadman, Charles W.
Give unto the Lord (c.1926)
Med: SATB, org
Txt: biblical
Dur: 4'30"
Pub: H Flammer

228 Cadman, Charles W.
Glory (c.1930)
Med: SATB, pno
Txt: Edward Lynn
Dur: 4'
Pub: Ricordi

229 Cadman, Charles W.
The hidden song (c.1920)
Med: SATB, pno
Txt: Blanche Barbette Gibson
Dur: 3'
Pub: White-Smith; copy in LC

230 Cadman, Charles W.
Homeward bound (c.1929)
Med: TTBB, B solo, pno

Txt: Warner van Valkenburg
Dur: 3'30"
Pub: H Flammer

231 Cadman, Charles W.
The house of joy (c.1935)
Med: 2-part treble vv, pno
Txt: Nelle Richmond Eberhart
Dur: 16'
Pub: Ditson

232 Cadman, Charles W.
A hymn of brotherhood (n.d.)
Med: SATB
Txt: Nelle Richmond Eberhart
Dur: 2'30"
Pub: unpubl.
Mss: NYPL

233 Cadman, Charles W.
The hymn triumphant (c.1935)
Med: SATB, S(or T)B soli, org
Txt: Elsie Long
Dur: 5'
Pub: Presser

234 Cadman, Charles W.
In the pride of May (c.1912)
Med: SATB div
Txt: Thomas Weelkes
Dur: 3'
Pub: White-Smith; copy in LC

235 Cadman, Charles W.
An Indian love charm (c.1932)
Med: SATB, soli, pno
Txt: Sarah Grames Clark
Dur: 20'
Pub: Willis Music
N.B. "For junior and senior high
schools."

236 Cadman, Charles W.
*Indian mountain song, Op. 48, No.
2* (c.1909)

Med: SSAA, pno
Txt: Nelle Richmond Eberhart
Dur: 2'30"
Pub: Ditson

237 Cadman, Charles W.
Instructions to a lady's maid (An Elizabethan plaint) (c.1931)
Med: SSAA
Txt: Helena Munn Redewill
Dur: 6'
Pub: Galaxy

238 Cadman, Charles W.
Little land of heart's desire, Op. 74 (c.1922)
Med: TTBB, pno
Txt: Ethelyn Bourne Borland
Dur: 4'
Pub: White-Smith; copy in NYPL
Mss: NYPL

239 Cadman, Charles W.
The maid of the mist (c.1930)
Med: SSA, T solo, pno
Txt: John Proctor Mills
Dur: 4'
Pub: Ditson

240 Cadman, Charles W.
The master of the forge (c.1934)
Med: TTBB, pno
Txt: Edward Lynn
Dur: 5'
Pub: H Flammer

241 Cadman, Charles W.
A mighty vulcan: hymn of Pittsburgh (c.1915)
Med: TTBB, Bar solo, org, opt. anvil
Txt: composer?
Dur: 5'
Pub: White-Smith; copy in LC

242 Cadman, Charles W.
Naranoka (Friend of peace) (c.1940)
Med: SATB, SBarB soli
Txt: George Murray Brown
Dur: 18'
Pub: CC Birchard

243 Cadman, Charles W.
Nile water (c.1940)
Med: SATB, Bar solo, pno
Txt: Nelle Richmond Eberhart
Dur: 6'
Pub: Ditson
Mss: NYPL

244 Cadman, Charles W.
No blackout (c.1951)
Med: SSA, pno
Txt: Marie Joy Mills
Dur: 4'
Pub: Kjos

245 Cadman, Charles W.
Out of Main Street (c.1926)
Med: SSA, S solo, pno
Txt: Nelle Richmond Eberhart
Dur: 4'
Pub: J Fischer
Mss: NYPL

246 Cadman, Charles W.
Pageant of Colorado (1927?)
Med: TTBB, SATB soli, boys' voices, orch
Txt: Lillian White Spencer
Dur: 25'
Pub: Denver Music Week Assoc.; copy in NYPL
Mss: NYPL

247 Cadman, Charles W.
Peace rests upon the hills of God (New world anthem) (c.1920)
Med: SATB, pno
Txt: Corinne B. Dodge

Dur: 2'30"
Pub: White-Smith; copy in LC

248 Cadman, Charles W.
The prayer of the great chief (c.1929)
Med: TTBB, Bar solo, pno
Txt: Elsie Long
Dur: 3'
Pub: White-Smith; copy in LC

249 Cadman, Charles W.
The psalm of praise (c.1928)
Med: SATB, A solo, org
Txt: Ps. 113
Dur: 3'
Pub: White-Smith; copy in LC

250 Cadman, Charles W.
The rainbow waters whisper (c.1957)
Med: SSA, pno
Txt: Nelle Richmond Eberhart
Dur: 3'30"
Pub: White-Smith; copy in LC
Mss: NYPL

251 Cadman, Charles W.
A red bird sang in a green, green tree
    (c.1947)
Med: SSAA
Txt: Helen Louise Shaffer
Dur: 3'
Pub: NY: Edward Schuberth; copy in
    LC
Mss: NYPL

252 Cadman, Charles W.
The rose of Jericho (c.1925)
Med: SSA, pno
Txt: Doris Smith
Dur: 2'30"
Pub: J Fischer

253 Cadman, Charles W.
The sacrifice of the Ayran rose (c.1927)
Med: TTBB, Bar solo, pno

Txt: Doris Smith
Dur: 4'30"
Pub: Ditson

254 Cadman, Charles W.
Snowflakes at my window (c.1936)
Med: SSA, pno
Txt: Francesca Falk Miller
Dur: 3'
Pub: HT FitzSimons

255 Cadman, Charles W.
A song of the air (c.1937)
Med: TTBB
Txt: Nelle Richmond Eberhart
Dur: 4'30"
Pub: J Fischer
Mss: NYPL
N.B. Originally for solo voice.

256 Cadman, Charles W.
Spring ecstasy (n.d.)
Med: SSA, pno
Txt: Nelle Richmond Eberhart
Dur: 4'
Pub: unpubl.?
Mss: NYPL

257 Cadman, Charles W.
Spring hymn for Aphrodite (c.1925)
Med: SATB div, pno
Txt: Nelle Richmond Eberhart
Dur: 3'
Pub: J Fischer
Mss: NYPL

258 Cadman, Charles W.
Stars of the morning (c.1929)
Med: SATB, S or T solo, kybd
Txt: Elsie Long
Dur: 3'30"
Pub: White-Smith; copy in LC

259 Cadman, Charles W.
The sum of love, Op. 29, No. 2
  (1905?)
Med: SATB
Txt: Bertha Reynolds McDonald
Dur: 1'
Pub: Ditson
Mss: NYPL

260 Cadman, Charles W.
Sunlit ways: in the XVIII century
  style (1938?)
Med: SATB
Txt: Nelle Richmond Eberhart
Dur: 5'
Pub: HW Gray
Mss: NYPL

261 Cadman, Charles W.
The sunset trail, Op. 69 (c.1920)
Med: SATB, Bar solo, pno
Txt: Gilbert Moyle
Dur: 30'
Pub: White-Smith; copy in NYPL
Mss: NYPL
N.B. "An operatic cantata depicting
the struggles of American Indians
against the edict of the United
States Government restricting
them to prescribed reservations."

262 Cadman, Charles W.
The thunder god's child, Op. 78
  (c.1923)
Med: SSA, pno
Txt: not indicated
Dur: 2'
Pub: White-Smith; copy in LC

263 Cadman, Charles W.
The tree of hope (c.1951)
Med: SATB
Txt: Grace Osburn Wharton

Dur: 4'
Pub: Kjos

264 Cadman, Charles W.
Trees in the rain (c.1947)
Med: SSA, pno
Txt: Betty Davis
Dur: 3'
Pub: J Fischer
Mss: NYPL

265 Cadman, Charles W.
The vision of Sir Launfal (c.1910)
Med: TTBB, TBar soli, pno and org
Txt: James Russell Lowell
Dur: 24'
Pub: G Schirmer
Mss: NYPL
  Prologue
  Summer
  Winter

266 Cadman, Charles W.
The winds of March (c.1934)
Med: SSATTB
Txt: Nelle Richmond Eberhart
Dur: 4'
Pub: HT FitzSimons

267 Cadman, Charles W.
The wish (c.1913)
Med: SSA, opt. vn and cello
Txt: Nelle Richmond Eberhart
Dur: 3'
Pub: White-Smith; copy in LC

268 Carpenter, John Alden
The home road (c.1917)
Med: SATB or unison, pno
Txt: composer
Dur: 1'30"
Pub: G Schirmer
N.B. Originally for solo voice; also arr.
for SSA.

269   Carpenter, John Alden
Skyscrapers (1923-24)
Med: ST chorus, orch
Txt: composer and Robert Edmund
Dur: 27'
Pub: G Schirmer
Mss: LC (with performance markings by Carpenter)
Bib: B5, 118
N.B.   A ballet with choral ending. The copy of the printed score in BPL has markings in the hand of S. Koussevitzsky.

270   Carpenter, John Alden
Song of David (1951)
Med: SSAA, solo cello, orch
Src: Grove

271   Carpenter, John Alden
Song of faith (c.1932, rev. 1936)
Med: 4-part children's, men's or women's voices, nar, orch
Txt: composer
Dur: 11'
Pub: G Schirmer
Mss: LC

272   Carpenter, John Alden
Song of freedom (1941)
Med: unison chorus, orch
Txt: Morris H. Martin
Dur: 5'
Pub: G Schirmer
Mss: LC
N.B.   A march for orchestra, with opt. choral ending; also arr. for band.

273   Carter, Elliott
The bridge (1937)
Txt: Hart Crane
Dur: unfinished
Src: Dox

274   Carter, Elliott
The defense of Corinth (1941)
Med: TTBB, speaker, pno four hands
Txt: François Rabelais
Dur: 17'
Pub: Mercury Music
Mss: LC
Rev: *Musical America* 70 (Aug, 1950) p29; *Music News* 42 (Sept, 1950) p19; MLA *Notes* 7 (June, 1950) p442-3
Bib: B190

275   Carter, Elliott
Emblems (1947)
Med: TTBB, pno
Txt: Allen Tate
Dur: 16'
Pub: NY: Music Press
Mss: LC

276   Carter, Elliott
The harmony of morning (1944)
Med: SSAA, ch. orch, pno
Txt: Mark van Doren
Dur: 8'30"
Pub: AMP
Mss: LC
Rev: *Musical America* 75 (June, 1955) p28; MLA *Notes* 12 (June, 1955) p496
Bib: B190

277   Carter, Elliott
Harvest home (1937)
Med: SATB
Txt: Robert Herrick
Pub: unpubl.
Src: Grove
Rev: *Tempo* 167 (Dec, 1988) p4, 9-10

278   Carter, Elliott
Heart not so heavy as mine (c.1939)
Med: SATB
Txt: Emily Dickinson
Dur: 4'

Pub: AMP
Rev: *Music News* 41 (July, 1949) p17

279 Carter, Elliott
Let's be gay (1937)
Med: SSAA
Txt: John Gay
Dur: unfinished
Mss: LC

280 Carter, Elliott
Musicians wrestle everywhere (1945)
Med: SSATB, opt. strings
Txt: Emily Dickinson
Dur: 6'30"
Pub: Mercury Music
Rev: *Music Review* 10 (Feb, 1949) p75
Bib: B190

281 Carter, Elliott
Tarantella (1936)
Med: TTBB, pno four hands
Txt: Ovid
Dur: 8'
Pub: AMP
N.B. Accompaniment originally for chamber orchestra.

282 Carter, Elliott
To music (c.1955)
Med: SATB
Txt: Robert Herrick
Dur: 7'
Pub: Peer Intl.
Mss: copy in NYPL
Rev: MLA *Notes* 13 (Mar, 1956) p348
Bib: B190
N.B. Later withdrawn by the composer; originally included in a set of *Twelve madrigals*.

283 Carter, Elliott
Tom and Lily (1934)
Med: SATB, 4 soli, ch. orch
Src: Grove

N.B. Also listed as an opera; later withdrawn by the composer.

284 Chihara, Paul
Ave Maria — Scarborough fair (c. 1972)
Med: TTB div
Txt: LU, trad.
Dur: 6'
Pub: CF Peters

285 Chihara, Paul
Magnificat (c.1967)
Med: SSSAAA
Txt: LU
Dur: 3'30"
Pub: Summy-Birchard

286 Chihara, Paul
Missa carminum brevis ("Folk song Mass") (c.1975)
Med: SATB dbl choir
Txt: LU, trad.
Dur: 15'
Pub: CF Peters
Rev: *Music Journal*, 34 (March, 1976), p41.
Bib: B51
   Kyrie — Sally gardens
   Gloria
      Et in terra pax
      Domine Deus
      Qui tollis
   Sanctus — Willow Song
   Benedictus — The houlihan
   Agnus Dei — I once loved a boy

287 Chihara, Paul
The 90th Psalm (c.1970)
Med: SATB (12-part), org, opt. brass quartet
Txt: Ps. 90
Dur: 10'
Pub: Shawnee Press

288 Converse, Frederick
The answer of the stars (1919, rev. 1932)
Med: SATB, S solo, orch
Txt: M.A. DeWolfe Howe
Dur: 8'
Pub: CC Birchard

289 Converse, Frederick
Arise, shine O Zion (c.1928)
Med: SATB, S solo, org
Txt: biblical
Dur: 7'
Pub: C Fischer

290 Converse, Frederick
Covenant (c.1918)
Med: SATB
Txt: Cordelia Brooks Fenno
Dur: 1'
Pub: CC Birchard

291 Converse, Frederick
The flight of the eagle (1930)
Med: SATB, Bar solo, orch
Txt: Cordelia Brooks Fenno
Dur: 20'
Pub: CC Birchard

292 Converse, Frederick
I will praise thee, O Lord (c.1924)
Med: SATB, S solo, org, pno, 2 tpt, 3 tbn
Txt: Ps. 9
Dur: 10'
Pub: CC Birchard

293 Converse, Frederick
In a tropic garden (c.1930)
Med: SSAA, pno
Txt: Frederick James Hill
Dur: 3'
Pub: Boston: Riker, Brown, Wellington; copy in LC

294 Converse, Frederick
Jeanne d'Arc (1906?)
Med: SATB, orch
Txt: not indicated
Dur: unfinished
Mss: NYPL
Src: NYPL

295 Converse, Frederick
Job, Op. 24 (c.1907)
Med: SATB div, STBB soli, orch
Txt: Book of Job, arr. John Hays Gardiner and John Albert Macy
Dur: 60'
Pub: HW Gray
Rev: Worcester (Mass.) *Evening Gazette,* Oct. 3, 1907, p1, 7.

296 Converse, Frederick
Land of Romance (c.1930)
Med: SSAA, pno
Txt: Frederick James Hill
Dur: 2'30"
Pub: Boston: Riker, Brown, Wellington; copy in LC

297 Converse, Frederick
Laudate Dominum (c.1906)
Med: TTBB, org, 2 tpt, 4 tbn
Txt: Book of Psalms
Dur: 5'
Pub: Boston Music Co.

298 Converse, Frederick
The masque of St. Louis (c.1914)
Med: TB, pno
Txt: Percy MacKaye
Dur: 18'
Pub: HW Gray

299 Converse, Frederick
The peace pipe (c.1915)
Med: SATB div, Bar solo, orch
Txt: Henry W. Longfellow

Dur: 30'
Pub: CC Birchard

300 Converse, Frederick
The pirate (c.1930)
Med: TTBB, pno
Txt: Frederick James Hill
Dur: 4'
Pub: Boston: Riker, Brown, Wellington; copy in LC

301 Converse, Frederick
Serenade, Op. 25 (c.1908)
Med: TTBB, ST soli, fl, hp, str
Txt: John Macy
Dur: 16'
Pub: HW Gray

302 Copland, Aaron
Las agachadas (1942)
Med: SATB div
Txt: trad. Spanish
Dur: 10'
Pub: BH

303 Copland, Aaron
Canticle of freedom (1955, rev. 1965)
Med: SATB, orch
Txt: John Barbour
Dur: 13'
Pub: BH
Mss: LC
Rev: *American Choral Review* 10/3 (1968) p135; MLA *Notes* 13 (June, 1956) p529-30
Bib: B199

304 Copland, Aaron
Five kings (1938)
Med: SATB, soli, clar, tpt, perc, 2 vln, vla, cello, bass, org
Txt: William Shakespeare
Dur: 20'
Pub: BH
Mss: LC; copy in NYPL

N.B. Incidental music to a series of Shakespeare's plays adapted by Orson Welles.

305 Copland, Aaron
Four motets (1921)
Med: SATB
Txt: biblical
Dur: see below
Pub: BH
  Help us, O Lord (3')
  Thou, O Jehovah, abideth forever (2'30")
  Have mercy on us, O Lord (3'45")
  Sing ye praises to our king (2'30")

306 Copland, Aaron
The house on the hill (1925)
Med: SSAA
Txt: Edwin Arlington Robinson
Dur: 5'
Pub: EC Schirmer
Mss: LC

307 Copland, Aaron
An immortality (1925)
Med: SSA, pno
Txt: Ezra Pound
Dur: 5'
Pub: EC Schirmer
Mss: LC

308 Copland, Aaron
In the beginning (1947)
Med: SATB, M solo
Txt: Genesis 1:1-2, 7
Dur: 17'
Pub: BH
Mss: LC; copy of holograph in BPL
Rev: *Music and Letters* 35 (Jan, 1954) p77
Bib: B109, 199

309 Copland, Aaron
Into the streets May first (1934)
Med: unison, pno
Txt: A. Hayes
Src: Grove

310 Copland, Aaron
Lark (1938)
Med: SATB, Bar solo
Txt: Genevieve Taggard
Dur: 5'
Pub: EC Schirmer
Mss: LC

311 Copland, Aaron
Old American songs (1950s)
Med: various arrangements (see below)
Txt: trad.
Dur: 3'-5' each
Pub: BH
Rev: MLA *Notes* 9 (Sept, 1952) p649–
50 and 13 (June, 1956) p529–30
Bib: B199
   Set One
      The boatman's dance (SATB,
       TTBB)
      The dodger (TB)
      Long time ago (SATB)
      Simple gifts (SA, TB)
      I bought me a cat (SSA, TBB)
   Set Two
      The little horses (SA, SSA,TBB)
      Zion's walls (SATB, TTBB)
      Golden willow tree (SATB)
      At the river (SA, SSA, SATB,
       TTBB)
      Ching-a-ring-chaw (SSAA, SATB,
       TTBB)

312 Copland, Aaron
The promise of living (c.1954)
Med: SATBB, pno duet
Txt: Horace Everett
Dur: 6'30"
Pub: BH

Mss: LC
Rev: MLA *Notes* 13 (June, 1956) p529
Bib: B199
N.B. From his opera *The tender land*.

313 Copland, Aaron
Song of the guerrillas (1943)
Med: TTBB, Bar solo, pno
Txt: Ira Gershwin
Dur: 3'
Pub: BH
Bib: B199
N.B. From the film score *North star*.

314 Copland, Aaron
Stomp your foot (c.1954)
Med: SATB, pno duet
Txt: Horace Everett
Dur: 5'
Pub: BH
Mss: LC
Rev: MLA *Notes* 13 (June, 1956) p529
Bib: B199
N.B. From his opera *The tender land*.

315 Copland, Aaron
What do we plant? (1935)
Med: SA, pno
Txt: Henry Abbey
Dur: 4'
Pub: BH

316 Copland, Aaron
Younger generation (1943)
Med: SATB, pno
Txt: Ira Gershwin
Dur: 2'
Pub: BH
Bib: B199
N.B. From the film score *North star*.

317 Cowell, Henry
Air held her breath (1946)
Med: SATB
Txt: Abraham Lincoln

Dur: 3'
Pub: Music Press

318 Cowell, Henry
American muse (1943)
Med: SA, pno
Txt: Stephen Vincent Benét
Dur: 7'
Pub: Music Press, Inc.; copy in NYPL
Bib: B72
    American muse
    Swift runner
    Immensity of wheel

319 Cowell, Henry
Atlantis (1926)
Med: SATB, soli, orch
Txt: not indicated; composer?
Dur: 20'
Pub: unpubl.
Mss: LC
N.B. A ballet.

320 Cowell, Henry
Ballad of the two mothers (1949)
Med: SSATBB
Txt: Elizabeth Harold
Dur: 6'30"
Pub: Peer Intl.
Rev: MLA *Notes* 8 (Mar, 1951) p404

321 Cowell, Henry
Banners (1942)
Med: SATB, winds, perc, str
Txt: not indicated
Dur: 20'
Pub: unpubl.
Mss: LC

322 Cowell, Henry
The coming of light (1938)
Med: SSAA
Txt: Dora Hagemeyer

Dur: 3'30"
Pub: H Flammer
Mss: LC

323 Cowell, Henry
The creator (1963)
Med: SATB div, SATB soli, orch
Txt: Gavrül R. Derzhavin
Dur: 15'
Pub: unpubl.
Mss: LC

324 Cowell, Henry
Day, evening, night, morning (1950)
Med: TTTBBB (falsettos or boys'
    voices ad lib.)
Txt: Paul Laurence Dunbar
Dur: 11'
Pub: Peer Intl.
Rev: MLA *Notes* 8 (June, 1951) p571-2

325 Cowell, Henry
Do, do, do is C, C, C (1948)
Med: children, pno
Txt: composer
Dur: 6'
Pub: Peer Intl.
Src: Grove

326 Cowell, Henry
Do you doodle as you dawdle? (1948)
Med: SATB, pno, opt. drums
Txt: composer?
Dur: 4'
Pub: CF Peters

327 Cowell, Henry
Edson hymns and fuging tunes
    (c.1963)
Med: SATB div
Txt: Lewis Edson, Jr., *The Social
    Harmonist* (1801)
Dur: various
Pub: AMP

328 Cowell, Henry
Evensong at brookside: a father's lullaby (1948)
Med: TTBB, T solo
Txt: composer
Dur: 3'
Pub: Peer Intl.
Rev: MLA *Notes* 8 (Mar, 1951) p404

329 Cowell, Henry
Fire and ice (1943)
Med: TTBB, band
Txt: Robert Frost
Dur: 3'
Pub: Boston Music Co.
Mss: LC

330 Cowell, Henry
The golden harp (1952)
Med: 4-part boys' chorus
Txt: trad.
Pub: unpubl.
Src: Grove

331 Cowell, Henry
Hail, mills! (c.1943)
Med: SSA, pno
Txt: L. Seltzer
Pub: unpubl.
Src: Grove

332 Cowell, Henry
Hamlet (Incidental music) (n.d.)
Med: TTBB, winds, perc, str, pno
Txt: William Shakespeare
Dur: 10'
Pub: unpubl.
Mss: LC

333 Cowell, Henry
...if he pleases (1955)
Med: SATB div, boys or children, orch
Txt: Edward Taylor
Dur: 12'

Pub: CF Peters
Mss: LC; copy in NYPL
Bib: B55

334 Cowell, Henry
The Irish girl (c.1945)
Med: SATB
Txt: P.W. Joyce
Dur: 2'
Pub: BMI

335 Cowell, Henry
The Irishman lilts (c.1945)
Med: SATB, pno
Txt: composer
Dur: 2'
Pub: BMI

336 Cowell, Henry
The light of peace (1917)
Med: SATB, pno
Txt: biblical
Dur: 4'
Pub: unpubl.

337 Cowell, Henry
Lilting fancy (1949)
Med: SSAA
Txt: not indicated
Dur: 3'30"
Pub: NY: Merrymount Press
Mss: LC

338 Cowell, Henry
The lily's lament (c.1948)
Med: SSA div, pno
Txt: Alan Lomax
Dur: 3'30"
Pub: EB Marks
Rev: *Musicology* 2 (Apr, 1949) p315

339 Cowell, Henry
Luther's carol for his son (1948)
Med: TTBB
Txt: Martin Luther

Dur: 3'
Pub: Leeds Music

340 Cowell, Henry
Maker of day (1914)
Med: SATB, ABar soli, timp, pno
Src: Grove

341 Cowell, Henry
The morning cometh (1937)
Med: SATB
Txt: F. Chalmers Furnes
Dur: 3'
Pub: Mercury Music

342 Cowell, Henry
Mountain tree (1952)
Med: SATB
Txt: Dora Hagemeyer
Pub: unpubl.
Src: Grove

343 Cowell, Henry
O salutaris (1913)
Med: SATB, pno
Txt: LU
Dur: 3'
Pub: unpubl.

344 Cowell, Henry
Psalm 121 (1953)
Med: SATB
Txt: Ps. 121
Dur: 3'
Pub: AMP

345 Cowell, Henry
The road leads into tomorrow (1947)
Med: SATB div, opt. pno
Txt: Dora Hagemeyer
Dur: 4'
Pub: AMP
Mss: copy in NYPL
Rev: *Musicology* 2 (Apr, 1949) p315
N.B. Originally for solo voice.

346 Cowell, Henry
Song for a tree (1950)
Med: SSA, opt. pno
Txt: Dora Hagemeyer
Dur: 1'30"
Pub: CC Birchard

347 Cowell, Henry
Spring at summer's end (1938?)
Med: SSA
Txt: Dora Hagemeyer
Dur: 3'
Pub: Peer Intl.
Rev: MLA *Notes* 10 (June, 1953) p493

348 Cowell, Henry
Supplication: processional (1962)
Med: unison, 2 tpt, 2 tbn, org, opt.
        timp
Txt: composer
Dur: 3'30"
Pub: CF Peters

349 Cowell, Henry
Sweet was the song the Virgin sung
        (1948)
Med: SATB, pno
Txt: trad.
Dur: 3'
Pub: AMP
Mss: LC

350 Cowell, Henry
A thanksgiving psalm (1956)
Med: TTBB, orch
Txt: *Dead Sea Scrolls*, trans. Millar
        Burrows
Dur: 6'
Pub: AMP
Mss: LC
Rev: *Hi-Fidelity/Musical America* 17
        (Mar, 1967) pMA16

351 Cowell, Henry
To a white birch (1950)
Med: SATB
Txt: Dora Hagemeyer
Dur: 4'
Pub: HW Gray

352 Cowell, Henry
To America (1946)
Med: SATB div
Txt: Dora Hagemeyer
Dur: 3'
Pub: AMP

353 Cowell, Henry
The tree of life (1955)
Med: SATB
Txt: Edward Taylor
Dur: 3'
Pub: Christ-Janer, Albert. *American Hymns Old and New*. NY: Columbia University Press, 1980.

354 Cowell, Henry
Ultimo actio (1964)
Med: SATB
Txt: José de Diego, trans. Joseph Machlis
Dur: 4'
Pub: AMP

355 Cowell, Henry
Union of voices (1954-6?)
Med: SSA div
Txt: not indicated
Dur: 2'30"
Pub: unpubl.

356 Cowell, Henry
The wave of D... (c.1914)
Med: 3vv, pno
Dur: unfinished
Src: Grove

357 Cowell, Henry
With choirs divine (1952)
Med: SSA
Txt: J.T. Shotwell
Pub: unpubl.
Src: Grove

358 Creston, Paul
Calamus, Op. 104 (1972)
Med: SSATTBB, pno or brass and perc
Txt: Walt Whitman
Dur: 12'
Pub: G Schirmer
N.B. Originally for men's voices.

359 Creston, Paul
The celestial vision, Op. 60 (1954)
Med: TTBB
Txt: Dante, Walt Whitman, Bhagavad Gita
Dur: 15'
Pub: Shawnee Press
Mss: LC

360 Creston, Paul
Cindy (c.1953)
Med: SATB, pno
Txt: trad.
Dur: 4'
Pub: Presser

361 Creston, Paul
Dedication, Op. 22 (c.1965)
Med: SATB, kybd
Txt: Arturo Giovanetti
Dur: 3'45"
Pub: Shawnee Press

362 Creston, Paul
Hyas Illahee, a corosymfonic suite (1969)
Med: SATB, orch
Txt: arbitrary syllables and Indian words

Dur: 16'30"
Pub: EC Kirby
N.B. Earlier title: *The Northwest.*

363 Creston, Paul
Isaiah's profecy, a Christmas oratorio,
     Op. 80 (1962)
Med: SATB, pno
Txt: Book of Isaiah
Dur: 30'
Pub: Franco Colombo
Mss: LC

364 Creston, Paul
The lambs to the lamb, Op. 47
     (1950)
Med: SSA, kybd
Txt: Martha Nicholson Kemp
Dur: 2'
Pub: C Fischer
Mss: LC

365 Creston, Paul
Leaves of grass, Op. 100 (1970)
Med: SATB, pno
Txt: Walt Whitman
Dur: 15'
Pub: G Schirmer
     One's self I sing
     I believe
     Reconciliation
     Smile, O voluptuous earth
     The most jubilant song

366 Creston, Paul
Lillium regis (c.1959)
Med: SATB, pno
Txt: Francis Thompson
Dur: 7'
Pub: G Ricordi

367 Creston, Paul
Mass of the angels (1966)
Med: SATB, org
Txt: LU

Dur: 8'
Pub: J Fischer

368 Creston, Paul
Missa "Adoro te," Op. 54 (1952)
Med: unison, SA or TB, org
Txt: LU
Dur: 12'
Pub: J Fischer

369 Creston, Paul
Missa "cum jubilo," a liturgical-concert
     Mass, Op. 97 (1972)
Med: SATB, and org, pno, or str
Txt: LU
Dur: 14'
Pub: Joseph Boonin; EC Kerby
Rev: *ASCAP* 4/1 (1970) p31
Bib: B51, 218

370 Creston, Paul
Missa solemnis, Op. 44 (1949)
Med: TTBB, orch
Txt: LU
Dur: 15'
Pub: Mills Music
Mss: LC
N.B. Also arr. for SATB.

371 Creston, Paul
None lives forever, Op. 92 (c.1968)
Med: SSA, kybd
Txt: Rabindranath Tagore
Dur: 13'
Pub: C Fischer
Rev: *ASCAP* 2/3 (1968) p35
N.B. Sometimes indicated as Op. 91.

372 Creston, Paul
Now thank we all our God, Op. 88
     (c.1966)
Med: SATB, cong, org
Txt: after Johann Crüger
Dur: 3'
Pub: J Fischer

373 Creston, Paul
O come let us sing: Thanksgiving anthem, Op. 119 (c.1982)
Med: SATB, org
Txt: Ps. 92, 95, 96
Dur: 6'
Pub: San Diego: Music Graphics Press

374 Creston, Paul
Praise the Lord, Op. 72 (c.1958)
Med: SATB
Txt: Book of Psalms
Dur: 2'30"
Pub: Ricordi

375 Creston, Paul
Prayer of thanksgiving (c.1953)
Med: SATB
Txt: Netherlands folk song
Dur: 3'30"
Pub: J Fischer

376 Creston, Paul
Prodigal, Op. 115 (c.1982)
Med: SATB, pno
Txt: Renato M. Getti
Dur: 5'
Pub: G Schirmer

377 Creston, Paul
Three chorales from Tagore, Op. 11 (1936)
Med: TTBB
Txt: Rabindranath Tagore
Dur: 7'
Pub: G Schirmer
N.B. Also arr. for SATB
Thou hast made me endless
Here is thy footstool
Where the mind is without fear

378 Creston, Paul
Two motets, Op. 45 (c.1950)
Med: TTBB, org

Txt: biblical
Dur: 8'
Pub: G Schirmer
Mss: LC
Adoro te devote
Salve regina

379 Creston, Paul
Way up on Old Smoky (c.1953)
Med: SATB, pno
Txt: trad.
Dur: 3'
Pub: Presser

D

380 Dello Joio, Norman
Adieu, Mignonne, when you are gone (1954)
Med: SSA, pno
Txt: Owen Meredith, Earl of Lytton
Dur: 3'30"
Pub: C Fischer
Mss: LC

381 Dello Joio, Norman
As of a dream (1978)
Med: SATB, SABar soli, nar, orch, opt. dancers
Txt: Walt Whitman
Dur: 21'
Pub: AMP

382 Dello Joio, Norman
The bluebird (1950)
Med: SATB, pno
Txt: Joseph Machlis
Dur: 5'
Pub: C Fischer
Rev: MLA *Notes* 10 (June, 1953) p493;
Music and Letters 34 (July, 1953) p269

383 Dello Joio, Norman
A Christmas carol (1960)
Med: SATB, pno
Txt: G.K. Chesterton
Dur: 3'
Pub: EB Marks

384 Dello Joio, Norman
Come to me, my love (1972)
Med: SATB, pno
Txt: Christina Rossetti
Dur: 3'
Pub: EB Marks

385 Dello Joio, Norman
Evocations (1970)
Med: SATB, orch
Txt: see below
Dur: 32'
Pub: EB Marks
    Visitants at night (Robert Hillyer)
    Promise of spring (Richard Hovey)

386 Dello Joio, Norman
A fable (1946)
Med: SATB, pno
Txt: Vachel Lindsay
Dur: 6'
Pub: C Fischer

387 Dello Joio, Norman
The holy infant's lullaby (1961)
Med: SATB, pno four hands, opt. orch
Txt: trad., arr. by composer
Dur: 3'30"
Pub: EB Marks

388 Dello Joio, Norman
Hymns without words (1980)
Med: SATB, orch
Txt: arbitrary syllables
Dur: 8'
Pub: AMP

389 Dello Joio, Norman
I dreamed of a city invincible (1984)
Med: SATB, SBar soli, kybd
Txt: Walt Whitman
Dur: 4'30"
Pub: AMP

390 Dello Joio, Norman
A jubilant song (1945)
Med: SATB, pno
Txt: Walt Whitman
Dur: 6'
Pub: G Schirmer

391 Dello Joio, Norman
Leisure (1981)
Med: SATB, pno
Src: Grove

392 Dello Joio, Norman
Love songs at parting (c.1984)
Med: SATB, pno
Txt: composer
Dur: 12'
Pub: AMP
    When you and I were young
    I put memories to rest
    We sang a joyful song
    Adieu, my love

393 Dello Joio, Norman
Madrigal (1947)
Med: SATB, pno
Txt: Christina Rossetti
Dur: 4'
Pub: C Fischer

394 Dello Joio, Norman
*Mass in honor of the Blessed Virgin
    Mary* (1975)
Med: 3-part choir, cantor, cong, org,
    opt. brass
Txt: LU

Dur: 19'
Pub: AMP

395 Dello Joio, Norman
Mass in honor of the Eucharist (1976)
Med: SATB, cantor, cong, brass
Txt: LU
Dur: 26'
Pub: AMP
Rev: *BMI* (Spring, 1976) p32-3; *Diapason* 67 (Jan, 1976) p13; *MusicAGO* 10 (Feb, 1976), p21; *School Musician* 50 (March, 1979), p19.
Bib: B51, 147, 212

396 Dello Joio, Norman
Mass of Hope (1969)
Med: SATB, org, 3 tpt, 3 tbn, tuba
Txt: LU
Dur: 21'
Pub: EB Marks
Rev: *American String Teacher* 20/1 (1970) p35; *BMI* (March, 1970), p5; *Diapason* 61 (Feb, 1970) p10; *School Musician* 41 (Jan, 1970) p35.
Bib: B51, 147, 212

397 Dello Joio, Norman
The mystic trumpeter (c.1945)
Med: SATB, STBar soli, hn
Txt: after Walt Whitman
Dur: 12'
Pub: G Schirmer

398 Dello Joio, Norman
Nativity: a Christmas canticle for the child (c.1990)
Med: SATB, soli, orch
Txt: William Gibson
Dur: 35'
Pub: AMP

Rev: *Central Opera* 28/1-2 (1987-88) p14; *Symphony Magazine* 38/5 (1987) p30

399 Dello Joio, Norman
Notes from Tom Paine (c.1975)
Med: SATB, pno
Txt: Thomas Paine
Dur: 6'
Pub: AMP
Rev: *BMI* (Spring, 1971) p32-3; *Variety* 278 (Apr 23, 1975) p47ff

400 Dello Joio, Norman
O sing unto the Lord (1958)
Med: TBB, org
Txt: Ps. 98
Dur: 4'
Pub: C Fischer

401 Dello Joio, Norman
Of crows and clusters (c.1972)
Med: SATB, pno
Txt: Vachel Lindsay
Dur: 8'
Pub: EB Marks

402 Dello Joio, Norman
The poet's song (1973)
Med: SATB, pno
Txt: Alfred Lord Tennyson
Dur: 4'
Pub: AMP

403 Dello Joio, Norman
Prayers of Cardinal Newman (1960)
Med: SATB, pno or org
Txt: John Henry Cardinal Newman
Dur: 4'
Pub: C Fischer

404 Dello Joio, Norman
A proclamation: let us sing a new song (c.1990)
Med: SATB, pno or band

Txt: biblical, arr. composer
Dur: 14'
Pub: Presser

405 Dello Joio, Norman
Proud music of the storm (1967)
Med: SATB, brass, org
Txt: Walt Whitman
Dur: 15'
Pub: EB Marks
Rev: *BMI* (Feb, 1968) p18–19; *Diapson* 59 (Jan, 1968) p8; *Hi-Fidelity/ Musical America* 59 (Feb, 1968) pMA23; *Music Journal* 26 (Jan, 1968) p4; *National Music Council Bulletin* 28/2 (1968) p20; *The Strad* 78 (Feb, 1968) p403

406 Dello Joio, Norman
A psalm of David (1950)
Med: SATB, orch
Txt: Ps. 50, other biblical
Dur: 27'
Pub: C Fischer
Rev: *Diapason* 42 (June, 1951) p22; MLA *Notes* 8 (June, 1951) p571; *Music and Letters* 32 (Oct, 1951) p388–9; *Music News* 43 (June, 1951) p25; *Music Review* 14 (Aug, 1953) p250; *Musical America* 71 (Dec, 1951) p30

407 Dello Joio, Norman
Psalm of peace (1972)
Med: SATB, tpt, hn, kybd
Txt: Book of Psalms
Dur: 16'
Pub: EB Marks

408 Dello Joio, Norman
The psalmist's meditation (1979)
Med: SATB, kybd
Txt: Book of Psalms
Dur: 10'
Pub: AMP

409 Dello Joio, Norman
Sing a song universal (c.1987)
Med: SATB, pno
Txt: composer
Dur: 9'
Pub: AMP

410 Dello Joio, Norman
Somebody's coming (c.1953)
Med: SATB, pno
Txt: Barbara Anderson
Dur: 4'
Pub: C Fischer
N.B. From his opera *The tall Kentuckian*.

411 Dello Joio, Norman
Song of affirmation (1953)
Med: SATB, S solo, nar, orch
Txt: Stephen Vincent Benét
Dur: 42'
Pub: C Fischer
Rev: *Choral Guide* 7 (May, 1954) p30–1; MLA *Notes* 11 (Sept, 1954) p10; *Music Clubs Magazine* 33 (Jan, 1954) p29; *Musical America* 75 (Jan 1, 1955) p32; *Musical Courier* 148 (Nov 15, 1953) p26
N.B. Earlier title: *Symphony for voices and orchestra*.

412 Dello Joio, Norman
Song of the open road (1952)
Med: SATB div, tpt, pno
Txt: Walt Whitman
Dur: 10'
Pub: C Fischer
Rev: *Music and Letters* 34 (July, 1953) p269; *Musical Courier* 34 (Apr 15, 1953) p34

413 Dello Joio, Norman
Song's end (1963)
Med: SSA, pno
Txt: John Payne

Dur: 4'30"
Pub: EB Marks

414 Dello Joio, Norman
Songs of Walt Whitman (1966)
Med: SATB, Bar solo, orch
Txt: Walt Whitman
Dur: 25'
Pub: EB Marks
    I sit and look out upon the world
    The dalliance of eagles
    Tears
    Take our hand, Walt Whitman

415 Dello Joio, Norman
Sweet sunny (c.1953)
Med: SATB, pno
Txt: Barbara Anderson
Dur: 4'
Pub: C Fischer
N.B. From his opera *The tall Kentuckian.*

416 Dello Joio, Norman
Three songs of Chopin (1964)
Med: SATB, orch
Txt: trans. Harold Heiberg
Dur: 14'
Pub: EB Marks
    The lovers
    The ring
    The wish

417 Dello Joio, Norman
To St. Cecilia (1958)
Med: SATB, pno or brass ensemble
Txt: John Dryden
Dur: 15'
Pub: C Fischer

418 Dello Joio, Norman
Vigil strange (1941)
Med: SATB, pno
Txt: Walt Whitman
Dur: 5'
Pub: NY: Weaner-Levant; copy in LC

419 Dello Joio, Norman
Years of the modern (1968)
Med: SATB, brass, perc
Txt: Walt Whitman
Dur: 16'
Pub: EB Marks
Rev: *BMI* (June, 1968) p18

420 Dett, Nathaniel
The chariot jubilee (c.1919)
Med: SATB, T solo, and org, pno or
    orch
Txt: composer?
Dur: 14'
Pub: J Church

421 Dett, Nathaniel
Don't be weary, traveler (c.1931)
Med: SSATBB
Txt: trad.
Dur: 4'30"
Pub: Presser
Bib: B140

422 Dett, Nathaniel
Don't you weep no more, Mary
    (c.1930)
Med: SATB
Txt: trad.
Dur: 4'
Pub: G Schirmer

423 Dett, Nathaniel
Drink to me only with thine eyes
    (c.1933)
Med: SATB
Txt: Ben Jonson
Dur: 4'
Pub: J Fischer

424 Dett, Nathaniel
Gently, Lord, O gently lead us
    (c.1924)
Med: SATB

Txt: from a hymn
Dur: 7'30"
Pub: J Church

425 Dett, Nathaniel
Go not far from me, O God (c.1933)
Med: SSATTB, Bar solo
Txt: trad.
Dur: 4'30"
Pub: J Fischer

426 Dett, Nathaniel
Hampton! My home by the sea
    (c.1914)
Med: SATB
Txt: composer
Dur: 1'30"
Pub: copy in NYPL

427 Dett, Nathaniel
Heavenly union (c.1941)
Med: SATB, T or Bar solo
Txt: trad.
Dur: 6'
Pub: Mills Music

428 Dett, Nathaniel
I'll never turn back no more (c.1917)
Med: SATB
Txt: trad.
Dur: 4'
Pub: J Fischer
Mss: holograph in NYPL
Rev: *American Organist* 32 (May, 1949)
    p146

429 Dett, Nathaniel
Juba (c.1934)
Med: SATB
Txt: composer
Dur: 7'
Pub: Summy-Birchard
Bib: B140
N.B. From the suite *In the bottoms*.

430 Dett, Nathaniel
Let us cheer the weary traveler (c.1926)
Med: SATB
Txt: trad.
Dur: 4'
Pub: J Church

431 Dett, Nathaniel
Listen to the lambs (c.1936)
Med: SATB, S solo
Txt: composer
Dur: 4'30"
Pub: G Schirmer
Bib: B140
N.B. Also arr. for SSA.

432 Dett, Nathaniel
Music in the mine: an unaccompanied
    folk-song scena (c.1916)
Med: SATB, T solo
Txt: trad.
Dur: 7'30"
Pub: G Schirmer

433 Dett, Nathaniel
O Mary, don't you weep (c.1919)
Med: SATB
Txt: trad.
Dur: 4'
Pub: CC Birchard

434 Dett, Nathaniel
The ordering of Moses (c.1937)
Med: SATB, SATBB soli, nar, orch
Txt: biblical and trad. folk lore
Dur: 45'
Pub: J Fischer
Rev: *Central Opera* 20/1 (1977–78) p1;
    Cincinnati Enquirer, May 8, 1937,
    p1, 8.
Bib: B140, 187, 227

435 Dett, Nathaniel
Rise up, shepherd, and follow (c.1936)

Med: SATB, S solo, pno
Txt: trad.
Dur: 3'
Pub: J. Fischer
N.B. Also arr. for TTBB.

436   Dett, Nathaniel
Sit down, servant, sit down (c.1936)
Med: SATB, T solo, pno
Txt: trad.
Dur: 4'30"
Pub: G Schirmer

437   Dett, Nathaniel
Somebody's knocking at your door
(c.1932)
Med: SATB, pno
Txt: trad.
Dur: 7'
Pub: Presser

438   Dett, Nathaniel
Wasn't that a mighty day? (c.1953)
Med: SATBB
Txt: trad.
Dur: 3'30"
Pub: G Schirmer

439   Dett, Nathaniel
Weeping Mary (c.1918)
Med: SATB
Txt: trad.
Dur: 4'30"
Pub: J Fischer

440   Diamond, David
All in green my love went riding
(c.1950)
Med: SSA
Txt: e.e. cummings
Dur: 3'
Pub: Southern Music
Rev: MLA *Notes* 8 (June, 1951) p172

441   Diamond, David
Amen and hallelujah (n.d.)
Med: SATB
Src: composer

442   Diamond, David
Chorale (c.1950)
Med: SATB div
Txt: James Agee
Dur: 7'
Pub: Southern Music
Rev: MLA *Notes* 7 (Sept, 1950) p634

443   Diamond, David
Cradle song (1991)
Med: TTBB
Src: composer

444   Diamond, David
The glory is fallen out of the sky
(c.1950)
Med: SSA
Txt: e.e. cummings
Dur: 2'
Pub: Southern Music

445   Diamond, David
Let us all take to singing (c.1951)
Med: TTBB
Txt: Herman Melville
Dur: 3'30"
Pub: Southern Music
Rev: MLA *Notes* 9 (Dec, 1951)
     p172-3

446   Diamond, David
The martyr (c.1951)
Med: TTBB
Txt: Herman Melville
Dur: 3'
Pub: Southern Music
Rev: MLA *Notes* 9 (Dec, 1951)
     p172-3
N.B. Text concerns Lincoln's death.

447   Diamond, David
Mizmor L'David (1951)
Med: SATB, cantor, org or orch
Txt: liturgical Hebrew
Dur: various short pieces
Pub: Mills Music

448   Diamond, David
Ode to the morning of Christ's nativity (n.d.)
Med: SATB
Src: composer

449   Diamond, David
Paris this April sunset (1937)
Med: SA, cello, bass
Txt: e.e. cummings
Pub: unpubl.
Src: Grove

450   Diamond, David
Prayer for peace (1960)
Med: SATB
Txt: trad.
Dur: 2'30"
Pub: Southern Music

451   Diamond, David
A secular cantata (1976)
Med: SATB, MTBar soli, ch. orch, org
Txt: James Agee
Dur: 35'
Pub: G Schirmer
Rev: *Variety* 286 (Feb 9, 1977) p120

452   Diamond, David
A song for Shabuoth (1935)
Med: children's choir, pno
Src: Grove

453   Diamond, David
This is the garden (1935)
Med: SATB
Txt: not indicated; biblical?

Dur: 5'
Pub: C Fischer

454   Diamond, David
This sacred ground (1962)
Med: SATB, children, Bar solo, orch
Txt: Abraham Lincoln
Dur: 16'30"
Pub: Southern Music
Rev: *Musical America* 84 (Jan, 1964) p70

455   Diamond, David
Three madrigals (c.1965)
Med: SATB
Txt: James Joyce
Dur: 4'30"
Pub: Southern Music

456   Diamond, David
To music: choral symphony (c.1969)
Med: SATB, TB soli, orch
Txt: see below
Dur: 20'
Pub: Southern Music
Rev: *InterAmerican Music Bulletin* 78 (July-Oct, 1970) p98; *Hi-Fidelity/ Musical America* 20 (Apr, 1970) pMA17-18; *Music Educators Journal* 56 (Mar, 1970) p23; *Music Journal* 28 (Apr, 1970) p70-1
Invitation to music (J. Masefield)
Symphonic affirmation
Dedication (H.W. Longfellow)
Bib: B120

457   Diamond, David
Two anthems (1955)
Med: SATB
Txt: biblical
Dur: 2'30"
Pub: Southern Music
To thee, O Lord
Why the fuss?

458 Diamond, David
Warning (c.1973)
Med: SATB, tubular bells
Txt: James Agee
Dur: 4'
Pub: Elkan-Vogel

459 Diamond, David
Why? (1992)
Med: TTBB, str orch, pno, perc
Src: composer

460 Diamond, David
Young Joseph (c.1947)
Med: SSA, kybd or str
Txt: Thomas Mann
Dur: 7'
Pub: NY: Music Press

461 Diemer, Emma Lou
All the world's a dream (1991)
Med: SATB, organ
Txt: Walt Whitman
Dur: 4'
Pub: Santa Barbara Music Publishing

462 Diemer, Emma Lou
Alleluia (1959)
Med: SSA
Txt: "Alleluia"
Dur: 3'
Pub: C Fischer

463 Diemer, Emma Lou
Alleluia! Christ is risen! (1964)
Med: SATB, org, tpt
Txt: biblical
Dur: 4'
Pub: H Flammer

464 Diemer, Emma Lou
And in the last days (1966)
Med: SATB, org
Txt: biblical

Dur: 5'
Pub: Augsburg

465 Diemer, Emma Lou
The angel Gabriel (1959)
Med: SATB, kybd
Txt: not indicated
Dur: 3'
Pub: C Fischer

466 Diemer, Emma Lou
Anthem of faith (1966)
Med: SATB, org
Txt: New Testament
Dur: 4'
Pub: G Schirmer

467 Diemer, Emma Lou
As a hart longs (1959)
Med: SATB
Txt: Ps. 42
Dur: 4'
Pub: HW Gray

468 Diemer, Emma Lou
At a solemn musick (c.1970)
Med: SATB
Txt: John Milton
Dur: 8'
Pub: BH

469 Diemer, Emma Lou
Awake my glory (1976)
Med: SATB, opt. gtr
Txt: biblical
Dur: 4'
Pub: Hope

470 Diemer, Emma Lou
Away delights (1979)
Med: TTBB
Txt: not indicated
Dur: 3'
Pub: Alexander Broude

471 Diemer, Emma Lou
A babe is born (1965)
Med: SATB, brass quartet, tamb
Txt: biblical
Dur: 6'
Pub: Sacred Music Press

472 Diemer, Emma Lou
Before the paling of the stars (1957)
Med: SATB, org
Txt: biblical
Dur: 4'
Pub: Elkan-Vogel

473 Diemer, Emma Lou
The bells (1959)
Med: SATB, pno four hands
Txt: not indicated
Dur: 4'
Pub: BH

474 Diemer, Emma Lou
Blessed are you (1969)
Med: SATB, opt. gtr
Txt: biblical
Dur: 4'
Pub: C Fischer

475 Diemer, Emma Lou
California madrigals (1976)
Med: SATB, pno
Pub: C Fischer
Src: composer

476 Diemer, Emma Lou
The call (1976)
Med: SATB, str, perc
Pub: G Schirmer
Src: composer

477 Diemer, Emma Lou
Cantata for Palm Sunday (1963)
Med: SATB, org
Txt: Henry Vaughan
Dur: 15'

Pub: unpubl.
Src: composer

478 Diemer, Emma Lou
Caprice (c.1988)
Med: SATB, pno
Txt: Helen Skinner Adamson
Dur: 7'
Pub: C Fischer

479 Diemer, Emma Lou
Choral responses for worship (1989)
Med: SATB, kybd
Txt: liturgical
Dur: various short pieces
Pub: Sacred Music Press

480 Diemer, Emma Lou
Choruses on freedom (1975)
Med: SATB, str, pno, perc
Txt: not indicated
Dur: 18'
Pub: unpubl.
Src: composer

481 Diemer, Emma Lou
Christ the Lord is risen today (1987)
Med: SATB, cong, 3 tpt, org
Txt: biblical
Dur: 4'
Pub: Sacred Music Press

482 Diemer, Emma Lou
Christmas cantata (1988)
Med: SATB, children, soli, readers, org,
    pno, perc, opt. gtr, and synthe-
    sizer
Txt: Dorothy Diemer Hendry
Dur: 45'
Pub: Sacred Music Press

483 Diemer, Emma Lou
A Christmas carol (1959)
Med: SSA, pno
Txt: not indicated

Dur: 3'30"
Pub: C Fischer

484 Diemer, Emma Lou
Christmas madrigals (1988)
Med: SATB, 3 tpt, 3 tbn
Txt: see below
Dur: 12'
Pub: copy in AMC
  The Christmas tree (Peter Cornelius)
  Blow, blow thou winter wind
  (William Shakespeare)
  On Christmas eve (Sir Walter Scott)
  Sweet dreams, form a shade (William
  Blake)
  Make we joy now in this feast (anon.,
  15th cent.)

485 Diemer, Emma Lou
Clap your hands (c.1984)
Med: SATB, org
Txt: Ps. 47
Dur: 6'30"
Pub: C Fischer

486 Diemer, Emma Lou
Come hither, you that love (c.1974)
Med: SSA, fl, pno
Txt: John Fletcher
Dur: 1'30"
Pub: EB Marks

487 Diemer, Emma Lou
Communion service (1982)
Med: SATB, cong, nar, org
Txt: *Lutheran Book of Worship*
Dur: 60'
Pub: unpubl.
Src: composer

488 Diemer, Emma Lou
Counting-out rhyme (1983)
Med: SSAA
Txt: not indicated

Dur: 3'
Pub: Plymouth Music Co.

489 Diemer, Emma Lou
Dance, dance my heart (1967)
Med: SATB, org, perc
Pub: C Fischer
Src: composer

490 Diemer, Emma Lou
Eleven limericks by Lear (1990)
Med: SSAA
Txt: Edward Lear
Dur: 7'
Pub: C Fischer

491 Diemer, Emma Lou
A feast for Christmas (1988)
Med: SATB, brass quintet or pno
Txt: William Blake
Dur: 10'
Pub: Santa Barbara Music
  Publishing

492 Diemer, Emma Lou
For ye shall go out with joy (1967)
Med: SATB, pno
Txt: biblical
Dur: 5'
Pub: C Fischer
Mss: composer

493 Diemer, Emma Lou
Four carols (1961)
Med: SATB, pno
Txt: trad.
Dur: 8'
Pub: Elkan-Vogel
Mss: composer
N.B. Also arr. for SSA, unaccompanied.

494 Diemer, Emma Lou
Fragments from the Mass (c.1961)
Med: SSAA
Txt: LU

Dur: 6'
Pub: Hal Leonard

495 Diemer, Emma Lou
From this hour, freedom (1976)
Med: SATB, str, perc
Pub: G Schirmer
Src: composer

496 Diemer, Emma Lou
Glory to God (1988)
Med: SATB, kybd
Txt: Dorothy Diemer Hendry
Dur: 3'
Pub: Sacred Music Press

497 Diemer, Emma Lou
God is love (1982)
Med: SATB div, tape
Txt: 1 John 4:13-21
Dur: 7'30"
Pub: Arsis Press

498 Diemer, Emma Lou
Hast thou not known (1984)
Med: SATB, kybd
Txt: biblical
Dur: 3'
Pub: Roger Dean

499 Diemer, Emma Lou
Honor to thee (1957)
Med: SATB, kybd
Txt: Dorothy Diemer Hendry
Dur: 4'15"
Pub: HW Gray

500 Diemer, Emma Lou
How majestic is thy name (1957)
Med: unison vv, pno
Txt: biblical
Dur: 3'
Pub: HW Gray

501 Diemer, Emma Lou
I sing! (1992)
Med: SATB, kybd
Txt: Robert Herrick
Dur: 4'
Pub: Hinshaw

502 Diemer, Emma Lou
I stand beside the manger stall (1959)
Med: SATB, kybd
Txt: not indicated
Dur: 3'
Pub: C Fischer

503 Diemer, Emma Lou
I will extol you (1988)
Med: SATB, kybd
Txt: Ps. 145
Dur: 5'
Pub: Augsburg

504 Diemer, Emma Lou
I will give thanks (1959)
Med: SATB, org
Txt: biblical
Dur: 4'
Pub: Sacred Music Press

505 Diemer, Emma Lou
Invocation (1985)
Med: SATB, orch
Txt: May Sarton
Dur: 7'
Pub: C Fischer

506 Diemer, Emma Lou
Is it a dream? (1992)
Med: SATB, kybd
Txt: Walt Whitman
Dur: 3'
Pub: Santa Barbara Music Publishing

507 Diemer, Emma Lou
Joy to the world (1976)
Med: SAB, pno

Txt: Isaac Watts
Dur: 4'30"
Pub: Agape Music Press

508 Diemer, Emma Lou
Laughing song (1974)
Med: SATB, pno four hands
Txt: William Blake
Pub: Shawnee Press
Src: composer

509 Diemer, Emma Lou
The Lord is mindful (1979)
Med: SATB, kybd
Txt: biblical
Dur: 4'
Pub: Hinshaw

510 Diemer, Emma Lou
The Lord is my light (1977)
Med: SATB, kybd
Txt: Ps. 27
Dur: 4'
Pub: Hinshaw

511 Diemer, Emma Lou
The Lord's prayer (1985)
Med: SATB, tape
Txt: biblical
Dur: 5'
Pub: Broadman Press

512 Diemer, Emma Lou
Madrigals three (1971)
Med: SATB, pno
Txt: see below
Dur: 9'
Pub: C Fischer
Mss: composer
  Come, O come my life's delight
  (Thomas Campion)
  Daybreak (John Donne)
  It was a lover and his lass (William
  Shakespeare)

513 Diemer, Emma Lou
The magnificat (c.1963)
Med: SSA, kybd
Txt: Gospel of Luke
Dur: 5'
Pub: Piedmont Music

514 Diemer, Emma Lou
Mary's lullaby (1959)
Med: SSA, pno
Txt: not indicated
Dur: 3'
Pub: BH

515 Diemer, Emma Lou
Men are fools that wish to die (1974)
Med: SATB
Pub: American Book Company
Src: composer

516 Diemer, Emma Lou
More madrigals (1984)
Med: SATB
Txt: Dorothy Diemer Hendry
Pub: Santa Barbara Music Publishing
Src: composer

517 Diemer, Emma Lou
Noel—rejoice and be merry (1959)
Med: SATB, kybd
Txt: trad.
Dur: 4'
Pub: C Fischer

518 Diemer, Emma Lou
Now the spring has come again (1961)
Med: SATB, pno
Txt: *Piae cantiones*
Dur: 7'
Pub: BH
Mss: composer

519 Diemer, Emma Lou
O come let us sing unto the Lord
(1960)

Med: SATB, pno
Txt: Ps. 95, 96
Dur: 6'
Pub: C Fischer
Mss: composer

520 Diemer, Emma Lou
O give thanks to the Lord (1959)
Med: SATB, org
Txt: Ps. 67
Dur: 4'
Pub: Franco Colombo

521 Diemer, Emma Lou
O Shenandoah (1959)
Med: TTBB, pno
Txt: trad.
Dur: 4'
Pub: C Fischer

522 Diemer, Emma Lou
O to make the most jubilant song
(1971)
Med: SATB, pno
Txt: Walt Whitman, Alfred Lord
Tennyson
Dur: 8'
Pub: C Fischer
Mss: composer

523 Diemer, Emma Lou
O to praise God again (1972)
Med: SATB
Txt: biblical
Dur: 4'
Pub: C Fischer

524 Diemer, Emma Lou
Outburst of praise (1961)
Med: SATB, kybd
Txt: not indicated
Dur: 4'
Pub: Presser

525 Diemer, Emma Lou
Peace cantata (1986)
Med: SATB, nar, org, brass, timp
Txt: not indicated
Dur: 25'
Pub: unpubl.
Src: composer

526 Diemer, Emma Lou
Prairie spring (1983)
Med: SSAA
Txt: not indicated
Dur: 4'
Pub: Plymouth Music Co.

527 Diemer, Emma Lou
Praise of created things (c.1964)
Med: SATB, kybd
Txt: St. Francis of Assisi
Dur: 4'30"
Pub: Franco Colombo

528 Diemer, Emma Lou
Praise the Lord (c.1958)
Med: SATB, org
Txt: Ps. 150
Dur: 4'
Pub: HW Gray

529 Diemer, Emma Lou
Praise the Lord (1974)
Med: SATB, brass quintet, org, opt.
timp
Txt: Ps. 149
Dur: 7'
Pub: C Fischer
Mss: composer

530 Diemer, Emma Lou
Praise ye the Lord (1960)
Med: SATB, pno four hands
Txt: biblical
Dur: 5'
Pub: Shawnee Press

531   Diemer, Emma Lou
Proclaim the day (c.1964)
Med: SATB, org, brass
Txt: Dorothy Diemer Hendry
Dur: 4'
Pub: H Flammer

532   Diemer, Emma Lou
The prophecy (1968)
Med: SSAA, pno
Txt: biblical
Dur: 8'
Pub: BH
Mss: composer

533   Diemer, Emma Lou
Psalm 113 (1990)
Med: SATB, kybd
Txt: Ps. 113
Dur: 4'
Pub: C Fischer

534   Diemer, Emma Lou
Psalm 134 (1974)
Med: SATB
Txt: Ps. 134
Dur: 7'
Pub: Seesaw Music
Mss: composer

535   Diemer, Emma Lou
*Reasons briefly set down by th' auctor
        to persade euery one to learne to
        singe* (1990)
Med: TTBB, pno
Txt: William Byrd
Dur: 4'
Pub: unpubl.
Src: composer

536   Diemer, Emma Lou
Romance (1974)
Med: SATB, kybd
Pub: C Fischer
Src: composer

537   Diemer, Emma Lou
St. Chrysostom cantata (1957)
Med: SATB, SATB soli, orch
Txt: Ps. 95, 96, 100, 119; Romans; 1
        John
Dur: 40'
Pub: unpubl.
Mss: composer

538   Diemer, Emma Lou
The sea (1987)
Med: SATB div, fl, clar, perc, pno, 2
        vln, vla, cello, bass
Txt: Pablo Neruda
Dur: 8'
Pub: copy in AMC

539   Diemer, Emma Lou
A service in music and poetry (1967)
Med: SATB, cong, soli, org, pno, perc
Txt: various poets
Dur: 60'
Pub: unpubl.
Src: composer

540   Diemer, Emma Lou
The shepherd to his love (1959)
Med: SSA, fl, pno
Txt: Christopher Marlowe
Dur: 1'30"
Pub: Hal Leonard

541   Diemer, Emma Lou
Sing a glory (1964)
Med: SATB, orch, band
Txt: Dorothy Diemer Hendry
Src: Grove

542   Diemer, Emma Lou
Sing, O heavens (1974)
Med: SATB
Txt: biblical
Dur: 5'
Pub: C Fischer
Mss: composer

543   Diemer, Emma Lou
So have I seen a silver swan (1974)
Med: SATB
Txt: not indicated
Dur: 3'
Pub: Gemini Press

544   Diemer, Emma Lou
Spring (1965)
Med: SATB, kybd
Pub: Heritage Music Press
Src: composer

545   Diemer, Emma Lou
A spring carol (1960)
Med: SATB, kybd
Pub: C Fischer
Src: composer

546   Diemer, Emma Lou
Strong Son of God (1976)
Med: SATB, kybd
Txt: biblical
Dur: 4'
Pub: Agape Music Press

547   Diemer, Emma Lou
Tell me dearest, what is love? (1979)
Med: SATB
Pub: Alexander Broude
Src: composer

548   Diemer, Emma Lou
There is a morn unseen (1991)
Med: SATB, S solo, orch
Txt: Emily Dickinson
Dur: 10'
Pub: Santa Barbara Music Publishing
Mss: composer

549   Diemer, Emma Lou
Thine, O Lord (1961)
Med: 2-part choir, pno
Txt: biblical

Dur: 3'
Pub: H Flammer

550   Diemer, Emma Lou
Three anniversary choruses (1970)
Med: SATB, orch
Txt: Ps. 101, 81; H. Timrod, A.
       Rutledge
Src: Grove
Rev: *Music Clubs Magazine* 50/3 (1970)
       p10.
       I will sing of mercy and judgement
       Sleep sweetly, sleep (Ode)
       Sing aloud unto God

551   Diemer, Emma Lou
Three choruses (1986)
Med: SATB, kybd
Txt: biblical
Dur: 7'
Pub: Hinshaw
       I will give thanks to the Lord
       Let thy steadfast love
       Sing praises to the Lord

552   Diemer, Emma Lou
Three hymn-anthems (1981)
Med: SATB, brass ensemble, org
Txt: trad. hymns
Dur: 8'
Pub: Hinshaw
       God of love and God of power
       The church's one foundation
       How firm a foundation

553   Diemer, Emma Lou
Three madrigals (1960)
Med: SATB, pno
Txt: William Shakespeare
Dur: 7'
Pub: BH
Mss: composer
       O mistress mine
       Take, O take those lips away
       Sigh no more ladies

554 Diemer, Emma Lou
Three poems by Alice Meynell (1976)
Med: SATB, woodwind quintet, perc,
    marimba, vibraphone, pno, org
Txt: Alice Meynell
Dur: 15'
Pub: unpubl.
Src: composer

555 Diemer, Emma Lou
Three poems of Ogden Nash (1960)
Med: TTB, pno
Txt: Ogden Nash
Dur: 6'
Pub: H Flammer

556 Diemer, Emma Lou
Three poems by Oscar Wilde (1984)
Med: SATB, kybd
Txt: Oscar Wilde
Dur: 8'
Pub: C Fischer

557 Diemer, Emma Lou
To him all glory give (1960)
Med: SATB, orch
Txt: Dorothy Diemer Hendry
Dur: 4'
Pub: Elkan-Vogel

558 Diemer, Emma Lou
The triumphal entry (1963)
Med: SATB, org
Txt: Henry Vaughan
Dur: 15'
Pub: unpubl.
Mss: composer

559 Diemer, Emma Lou
Verses from the Rubáiyát (1967)
Med: SATB
Txt: Omar Khayyám
Dur: 12'
Pub: BH
Mss: composer

560 Diemer, Emma Lou
Weep no more (c.1979)
Med: SSA
Txt: John Fletcher
Dur: 2'30"
Pub: Alexander Broude

561 Diemer, Emma Lou
What child is this? (1989)
Med: SATB, kybd
Txt: William Dix
Dur: 3'
Pub: Sacred Music Press

562 Diemer, Emma Lou
When in man's music (1976)
Med: SATB, kybd
Txt: not indicated
Dur: 4'
Pub: Augsburg

563 Diemer, Emma Lou
Why so pale and wan? (1971)
Med: SATB
Src: composer

564 Diemer, Emma Lou
Wild nights! wild nights! (1978)
Med: SATB, pno
Txt: Emily Dickinson
Dur: 4'
Pub: Hinshaw

565 Diemer, Emma Lou
Winds of spring (1966)
Med: unison vv, kybd
Txt: not indicated
Dur: 3'
Pub: Shawnee Press

566 Druckman, Jacob
Antiphonies I, II, III (1963)
Med: SATB dbl choir
Txt: Gerard Manley Hopkins
Dur: 12'

Pub: BH
Rev: *Hi-Fidelity/Musical America* 26 (Nov, 1976) pMA24

567 Druckman, Jacob
Dance of the maidens (1965)
Med: SATB, org, perc
Pub: unpubl.
Src: Grove

568 Druckman, Jacob
Four madrigals (1958)
Med: SATB
Txt: see below
Dur: 7'
Pub: Presser
    Shake off your heavy trance (Francis Beaumont)
    The faery beam upon you (Ben Jonson)
    Death, be not proud (John Donne)
    Corina's going a Maying (Robert Herrick)

569 Druckman, Jacob
Hymnus referamus (1965)
Med: SATB, org, perc
Txt: Book of Psalms
Pub: unpubl.
Src: Grove

570 Druckman, Jacob
Psalm 84 (1965)
Med: SATB, org, perc
Txt: Ps. 84
Pub: unpubl.
Src: Grove

571 Druckman, Jacob
Sabbath eve service (Shir Shel Yakov) (1967)
Med: SATB, T solo, org
Txt: liturgical Hebrew
Dur: 20'
Pub: BH

572 Druckman, Jacob
The simple gifts (1954)
Med: SATB, pno
Txt: trad. Shaker
Src: Grove

573 Druckman, Jacob
Vox humana (1983)
Med: SATB, SATBar soli, orch
Txt: Greek and Latin text, unidentified
Dur: 30'
Pub: BH
Rev: *ASCAP* (Fall, 1984) p60; *Ovation* 4 (Feb, 184) p17ff; *Symphony Magazine* 34/5 (1983) p27

E

574 Erb, Donald
Christmas greetings (c.1968)
Med: children, brass ensemble, rhythm band
Txt: anon.
Dur: 3'
Pub: Ann Arbor: University Microfilms
Mss: copy of holograph in LC

575 Erb, Donald
Cummings cycle (1963)
Med: SATB, orch
Src: Grove

576 Erb, Donald
Fallout (1964)
Med: SATB, nar, str quartet, pno
Src: Grove

577 Erb, Donald
God love you now (1971)
Med: SATB, speaker, assorted inst., reverberation device
Txt: Thomas McGrath

Dur: 9'
Pub: Merion Music

578 Erb, Donald
Kyrie (1965)
Med: SATB, perc, pno, tape
Txt: LU
Dur: 3'
Pub: Presser
Rev: *BMI* (Oct, 1967) p22; *Choral Journal* 12/7 (Mar, 1972), p23; MLA *Notes* 29 (1973) p567-8; *New Records* 31 (Jan, 1971) p13-14
Bib: B57, 61

579 Erb, Donald
N 1965 (1965)
Med: SATB, vla, cello, bass, pno
Src: Grove

580 Erb, Donald
New England's prospect (1974)
Med: triple choir, children, nar, orch
Txt: Thomas Jefferson, Anne Bradford, William Lloyd Garrison, William Carlos Williams
Pub: Presser
Mss: Presser
Src: Dox
Rev: Cincinnati *Enquirer*, May 18, 1974.

F

581 Farwell, Arthur
After the battle (1917)
Med: unison, pno
Txt: composer
Dur: 2'
Pub: G Schirmer

582 Farwell, Arthur
Breathe on us, breath of God (c.1918)
Med: SATB, pno
Txt: anon.
Dur: 2'
Pub: J Church

583 Farwell, Arthur
Build thee more stately mansions, Op. 10, No. 1 (1901)
Med: SATB
Txt: Oliver Wendell Holmes
Src: Grove

584 Farwell, Arthur
Caliban choruses, Op. 47 (1915)
Med: SATB, pno
Txt: William Shakespeare, adapt. Percy MacKaye
Dur: 20'
Pub: G Schirmer

585 Farwell, Arthur
Cathedral scene (1929)
Med: SATB
Src: Farwell

586 Farwell, Arthur
The Christ child's Christmas tree, Op. 41 (1913)
Med: SATB
Src: Grove

587 Farwell, Arthur
Defenders (1920)
Med: SATB, pno
Txt: composer
Dur: 2'
Pub: J Church

588 Farwell, Arthur
Five songs for community chorus, Op. 57 (1920)
Med: SATB, SSAA, or TTBB
Src: Farwell
We will be free
On a summer morning

Sing, brother, sing
Another time for singin'
Sing a while longer

589   Farwell, Arthur
Four Indian songs, Op. 102 (1937)
Med: SATB
Txt: trad.
Dur: 14'
Pub: G Schirmer
  Navajo war dance No. 1
  The old man's love song
  Pawnee horses
  The mother's vow

590   Farwell, Arthur
Grace for Christmas (n.d.)
Med: SATB
Txt: Gertrude Farwell
Dur: 4'
Pub: unpubl.
Mss: LC

591   Farwell, Arthur
Hosanna (c.1918)
Med: SATB, S solo, pno
Txt: composer
Dur: 3'
Pub: J Church

592   Farwell, Arthur
Hymn to liberty, Op.35 (1910)
Med: SATB, pno
Txt: composer
Dur: 3'
Pub: Wa-wan Press; copy in LC
Rev: *Musical America* 14/10 (1911) p5

593   Farwell, Arthur
Joy! brothers, joy! (c.1916)
Med: SATB, pno
Txt: composer
Dur: 2'
Pub: G Schirmer

594   Farwell, Arthur
Kéramos (The potter's wheel), Op. 28 (1907)
Med: SATB, ST soli, pno
Txt: Henry W. Longfellow
Dur: 4'
Pub: NY: Remick Music; copy in LC
Rev: MLA *Notes* 11 (Dec, 1953) p145

595   Farwell, Arthur
The lamb, Op. 88 (1930)
Med: SATB, SATB soli
Txt: William Blake
Src: Grove

596   Farwell, Arthur
March! march!, Op. 49 (c.1916)
Med: unison, pno
Txt: composer
Dur: 2'
Pub: G Schirmer

597   Farwell, Arthur
Mountain song, Op. 90 (1931)
Med: SATB, orch
Txt: composer
Dur: 1 hr, 12'
Pub: unpubl.
Mss: LC

598   Farwell, Arthur
O captain! my captain! Op. 34 (1918)
Med: SATB
Txt: Walt Whitman
Dur: 8'
Pub: J Church

599   Farwell, Arthur
The old man's love song, Op. 32, No. 3 (1908)
Med: SATB
Src: Farwell

600   Farwell, Arthur
Our country, Op. 81 (1929)
Med: SATB
Src: Farwell

601   Farwell, Arthur
Our country's prayer (1919)
Med: SATB, pno
Txt: Carl Roppel
Dur: 2'
Pub: J Church
N.B. Originally for solo voice.

602   Farwell, Arthur
La primavera, Op. 56a (1920)
Med: SATB
Src: Farwell

603   Farwell, Arthur
Soldier, soldier (c.1920)
Med: SATB, Bar solo, pno
Txt: composer
Dur: 12'
Pub: J Church

604   Farwell, Arthur
*Symphonic song on "Old Black Joe,"
Op. 67* (1923)
Med: audience, orch
Txt: Stephen Foster
Src: Grove

605   Farwell, Arthur
Two choruses (c.1945)
Med: SATB
Src: Farwell
      One world
      America's vow

606   Farwell, Arthur
Two choruses, Op. 111 (1946)
Med: 8 vv
Src: Grove
      Navajo war dance No. 2
      Indian scene

607   Farwell, Arthur
Up and away (c.1919)
Med: 2 vv
Src: Farwell

608   Farwell, Arthur
Watchword (1918)
Med: SATB, pno
Txt: Bishop Arthur Cleveland Cooke
Dur: 2'
Pub: J Church

609   Felciano, Richard
Alleluia to the heart of (the) matter
   (1976)
Med: SATB, org
Txt: composer, after Pierre Teilhard
      de Chardin
Dur: 4'
Pub: unpubl.
Src: composer
Bib: B129

610   Felciano, Richard
*Antiphon and benediction (Canticle of
   Zachary)* (1968)
Med: unison vv, org
Txt: biblical
Dur: 4'
Pub: EC Schirmer

611   Felciano, Richard
Benedictio nuptalis (c.1972)
Med: unison, org
Txt: Book of Psalms
Dur: 4'30"
Pub: EC Schirmer

612   Felciano, Richard
The captives (1965)
Med: SATB, orch
Txt: Thomas Merton
Dur: 10'
Pub: EC Schirmer

613   Felciano, Richard
Christ became obedient unto death (1966)
Med: 3 equal vv
Txt: biblical
Dur: 1'30"
Pub: WLSM

614   Felciano, Richard
A Christmas madrigal (1964)
Med: SATB, brass, perc
Txt: medieval Latin, English
Dur: 3'
Pub: EC Schirmer

615   Felciano, Richard
Communion service (1961)
Med: 2-part mixed choir, org
Txt: liturgical
Dur: 8'
Pub: HW Gray

616   Felciano, Richard
The eyes of all look hopefully to you (c.1970)
Med: SSA or TTB, org
Txt: Ps. 144
Dur: 3'
Pub: EC Schirmer

617   Felciano, Richard
First Sunday of Passiontide: lesson chants (c.1967)
Med: SA or TB
Txt: liturgical
Dur: 2'30"
Pub: WLSM
    Gradual: Rescue me from my enemies
    Tract: Much have they oppressed me
    from my youth

618   Felciano, Richard
Four poems from the Japanese (1964)
Med: SSA, 5 hp, 2 perc
Txt: trans. K. Rexroth
Dur: 4'30"
Pub: unpubl.

619   Felciano, Richard
From Sion, perfect in beauty (1966)
Med: 2 equal vv, org
Txt: biblical
Dur: 2'
Pub: WLSM

620   Felciano, Richard
From your throne, O Lord (1966)
Med: 3 equal vv, org
Txt: biblical
Dur: 3'
Pub: WLSM

621   Felciano, Richard
Give thanks to the Lord (1968)
Med: unison vv, org
Txt: biblical
Dur: 1'30"
Pub: EC Schirmer

622   Felciano, Richard
Hosanna to the Son of David (1966)
Med: 3 equal vv
Txt: biblical
Dur: 6'
Pub: WLSM

623   Felciano, Richard
Hymn of the universe (1973)
Med: SAB, electronic sounds
Txt: Pierre Teilhard de Chardin
Dur: 3'45"
Pub: EC Schirmer

624   Felciano, Richard
The Lord is near (1966)
Med: 3 equal vv, org
Txt: biblical
Dur: 1'30"
Pub: WLSM

625   Felciano, Richard
*Lullaby on a Christmas chorale: Von
   Himmel hoch* (1952)
Med: unison treble vv, str
Txt: *Geistliche Lieder* (Leipzig, 1539)
Dur: 2'
Pub: EC Schirmer

626   Felciano, Richard
Mad with love (1981)
Med: SATB, org, handbells
Txt: Catherine of Siena
Src: Grove

627   Felciano, Richard
Madrigals from William Shakespeare
   (1956)
Med: SATB
Txt: William Shakespeare
Dur: 6'
Pub: EC Schirmer
   Tell me, where is fancy bred
   Take, O take those lips away
   Fye on sinful fantasy!

628   Felciano, Richard
Mass (1967)
Med: SATB, ch. orch, org, tape
Txt: LU
Dur: unfinished
Pub: unpubl.

629   Felciano, Richard
*Missa brevis in honorem Sancti
   Dominici* (1952)
Med: STB, org
Txt: LU
Dur: 13'
Pub: Paris: *Les editions musicales de la
   schola cantorum*
Src: composer

630   Felciano, Richard
None who waits for you (1966)
Med: 2 equal vv, org
Txt: biblical
Dur: 2'
Pub: WLSM

631   Felciano, Richard
*O Lord, I have heard your hearing
   and was afraid* (1967)
Med: 3 equal vv
Txt: biblical
Dur: 5'
Pub: WLSM

632   Felciano, Richard
*Out of sight (The ascension that
   nobody saw)* (1971)
Med: SATB, org, tape
Txt: various, including biblical pas-
   sages
Dur: 4'
Pub: EC Schirmer

633   Felciano, Richard
The passing of Enkidu (1973, rev.
   1975)
Med: SATB, pno four hands, tape
Txt: composer, after H. Mason
Src: Grove

634   Felciano, Richard
Pentecost Sunday (1967)
Med: unison male vv, org, tape
Txt: Ps. 103:30
Dur: 3'
Pub: WLSM
N.B.   Score calls for unusual vocal
   techniques.

635   Felciano, Richard
Psalm 150 (1968)
Med: SATB, org
Txt: Ps. 150

Dur: 2'
Pub: EC Schirmer

636   Felciano, Richard
Pshelly's psalm (1964)
Med: SATB
Txt: not indicated
Dur: 2'
Pub: EC Schirmer

637   Felciano, Richard
Rescue me from my enemies (1967)
Med: 2 equal vv
Txt: biblical
Dur: 2'30"
Pub: WLSM

638   Felciano, Richard
The seasons (1978)
Med: SATB div, SSA soli
Txt: composer
Dur: 14'30"
Pub: EC Schirmer

639   Felciano, Richard
Sic transit (1970)
Med: SAB, org, tape, light sources
Txt: St. Francis, John F. Kennedy,
Martin Luther King
Dur: 4'
Pub: EC Schirmer
Rev: *Diapason* 62 (Apr, 1971) p14;
Music (AGO) 4 (July, 1970) p31ff;
Music Journal 28 (Sept, 1970) p73
Bib: B129, 170

640   Felciano, Richard
Signs (1971)
Med: SATB, tape, 1-3 filmstrip pro-
jectors
Txt: Buckminster Fuller, Pierre Teil-
hard de Chardin, Jean-François
Revel, Gospel of Luke
Dur: 4'
Pub: EC Schirmer

641   Felciano, Richard
Songs for the darkness and light (1970)
Med: 3 equal vv
Txt: biblical
Dur: 5'
Pub: WLSM
I will sing to the Lord
My friend has a vineyard
Give ear, O heavens
As the hind longs for running waters

642   Felciano, Richard
Stars (1951)
Med: SATTBB
Txt: Robert Frost
Dur: 6'
Pub: unpubl.
Src: composer

643   Felciano, Richard
Susani: a carousel for Christmas
(1974)
Med: SATB, org, perc, tape
Txt: trad. German
Dur: 7'
Pub: EC Schirmer

644   Felciano, Richard
Te Deum (1974)
Med: SATB, SATB and boy soli, org,
pno, perc
Txt: LU
Dur: 14'
Pub: EC Schirmer
Rev: *Diapason* 65 (July, 1974) p6

645   Felciano, Richard
This is the day (1968)
Med: SAB, org, opt. bells
Txt: biblical
Dur: 2'30"
Pub: unpubl.
Src: composer

646   Felciano, Richard
3 in 1 in 3 (1971)
Med: SATB dbl choir, org, tape
Txt: composer?
Dur: 8'30"
Pub: EC Schirmer

647   Felciano, Richard
A tweedle ding dong dub a dub trilogy
(1964)
Med: children, 2 perc
Txt: Mother Goose and William
       Shakespeare
Dur: 6'
Pub: EC Schirmer
       Tweedledum and tweedledee
       Full fathom five
       Rub-a-dub-dub

648   Felciano, Richard
Two hymns to howl by (1963)
Med: unison vv
Txt: Allen Ginsburg
Dur: 2'
Pub: EC Schirmer

649   Felciano, Richard
Two public pieces (1972)
Med: unison, electronic sounds
Txt: see below
Dur: 4'
Pub: EC Schirmer
       The not-yet flower (a crisis of growth)
       (St. John)
       Cosmic festival (Elizabeth Browning,
       R.W. Emerson, W. Whitman)

650   Felciano, Richard
Unison Mass (1966)
Med: unison choir or cong, org
Txt: LU
Dur: 9'
Pub: EC Schirmer

651   Felciano, Richard
Were you there? (1986)
Med: SATB
Txt: trad.
Dur: 4'
Pub: EC Schirmer

652   Felciano, Richard
Windows in the sky (1975)
Med: SATB, org, tape
Txt: trad.
Dur: 5'
Pub: unpubl.
Src: composer

653   Felciano, Richard
Words of St. Peter (1965)
Med: SATB, org, tape
Txt: Book of Peter
Dur: 3'
Pub: WLSM

654   Felciano, Richard
Yours is princely power (1966)
Med: STTB, org, opt. Zimbelstern
Txt: biblical
Dur: 2'30"
Pub: WLSM

655   Feldman, Morton
Chorus and instruments No. 1
(c.1963)
Med: SATB, hn, perc, celesta, vln,
       cello, bass
Txt: no text
Dur: 8'
Pub: CF Peters

656   Feldman, Morton
Chorus and instruments, No. 2
(c.1967)
Med: SATB, chimes, tuba
Txt: no text
Dur: 7'
Pub: CF Peters

657 Feldman, Morton
Chorus and orchestra No. 1 (c.1978)
Med: SATB, S solo, hn, perc, celesta,
vln, cello, bass
Txt: no text
Dur: 15'
Pub: Universal Edition
Rev: *Music and Musicians* 21 (Apr,
1973) p62-3; *Neue Musikzeitung*
22 (Aug-Sept, 1973) p29; *Neue
Zeitschrift für Musik* 133 (Nov,
1972) p663

658 Feldman, Morton
Chorus and orchestra No. 2 (1972)
Med: 3 choirs, S solo, orch
Txt: no text
Dur: 15'
Pub: European-American

659 Feldman, Morton
Christian Wolff in Cambridge (1963)
Med: SATB div
Txt: no text
Dur: indeterminate (3'-6')
Pub: CF Peters

660 Feldman, Morton
Rothko chapel (c.1973)
Med: SATB, SA soli, perc, str
Txt: no text
Dur: 30'
Pub: Universal Edition
Rev: *Hi-Fidelity/Musical America* 20
(Dec, 1970) pMA27; *Music and
Musicians* 21 (Apr, 1973) p68;
Musical Times (114/4 (Feb, 1973)
p163-4; *Musicians and Artists* 5/4
(1972) p21-2; *Neue Zeitschrift für
Musik* 133 (Apr, 1972) p217;
World of Music 14/3 (1972) p79
Bib: B167

661 Feldman, Morton
The swallows of Salangan (1960)
Med: SSAATB, 4 fl, alto fl, 5 tpt, 2
tuba, 2 vibraphones, 2 pno, 7
celli
Txt: no text
Dur: indeterminate
Pub: CF Peters
Rev: *Hi-Fidelity/Musical America* 22
(Dec, 1970) pMA27; *Melos/Neue
Zeitschrift für Musik* 36 (Feb, 1969)
p82-3; *Musica* 23/1 (1969) p29;
Nuova Rivista Musica Italiana 4
(Sept-Oct, 1970) p919

662 Feldman, Morton
Voices and instruments (1972)
Med: I: SATB, 2 fl, Eng. hn, clar,
bsn, hn, timp, bass; II: SSA, fl,
cello, bass
Txt: no text
Dur: 11'
Pub: Universal Edition
Rev: *Neue Zeitschrift für Musik* 134/3
(1973) p67; *World of Music* 15/2
(1973) p67

663 Fine, Irving
The choral New Yorker (1944)
Med: see below, with pno
Txt: see below
Dur: 8'
Pub: C Fischer
Mss: LC
Prologue (P. Bacon) SATB, S solo
Scherzando (I. MacMeekin) SSAA,
SA soli
Concertante (David McCord) TBB
Epilogue (J. Falstaff) SATB, Bar soli

664 Fine, Irving
Clam chowder (n.d.)
Med: TBB
Txt: David McCord

Dur: unfinished
Mss: LC

665 Fine, Irving
The hour-glass (1949)
Med: SATB div, 2 SA soli and TB soli
Txt: Ben Jonson
Dur: 18'
Pub: G Schirmer
Mss: LC
Rev: MLA *Notes* 9 (Dec, 1951) p173
      O to know to end as to begin
      Have you seen the white lily grow
      O do not wanton with those eyes
      Against jealousy
      Lament
      The hour-glass

666 Fine, Irving
Hymn "In gratio jubilo" (1949)
Med: SA, ch. orch
Txt: David McCord
Src: Grove

667 Fine, Irving
Hymn: Koussic piece (1949?)
Med: SSA, orch
Txt: Koussic
Dur: 3'
Pub: unpubl.
Mss: LC

668 Fine, Irving
McCord's menagerie; four vivariations
      (1957)
Med: TBB
Txt: David McCord
Dur: 7'
Pub: Mills Music
Mss: photocopy in LC
      Vultur gryphus
      Jerboa
      Mole
      Clam

669 Fine, Irving
An old song (1953)
Med: SATB
Txt: Yehoash, trans. Marie Syrkin
Dur: 4'
Pub: G Schirmer

670 Fine, Irving
A short alleluia (1945)
Med: SSAA
Txt: "Alleluia"
Dur: 3'
Pub: MCA Music

671 Fine, Irving
Three choruses from Alice in
      Wonderland (1942)
Med: see below, with pno
Txt: Lewis Carroll
Dur: 4'
Pub: M Witmark
N.B. Version with orchestra published
      in 1949.
      The lobster quadrille (SATB)
      Lullaby of the duchess (SSA)
      Father William (TBB)

672 Fine, Irving
Three choruses from Alice in
      Wonderland (1953)
Med: SSA, S solo, pno
Txt: Lewis Carroll
Dur: 8'
Pub: G Schirmer
      The knave's letter
      The white knight's song
      Beautiful soup

673 Fine, Irving
Voices of freedom (Battle hymn of the
      republic) (1944)
Med: SATB, solo voice, orch
Txt: Julia Ward Howe
Dur: 4'

Pub: unpubl.
Mss: LC

674 Fine, Vivian
A guide to the life expectancy of a rose
(1956?)
Med: SATB dbl choir, fl, clar, vln,
    cello, hp
Txt: S.R. Tilley
Dur: 14'
Pub: unpubl.?
Mss: NYPL, with performance mark-
    ings in hand of composer.

675 Fine, Vivian
Meeting for equal rights, 1866 (1975)
Med: SATB, MB soli, nar, orch with
    large perc
Txt: not indicated
Dur: 25'
Pub: copy in AMC
Mss: copy in NYPL
Rev: *Hi-Fidelity/Musical America* 26
    (Aug, 1976) pMA26-7; Long Is-
    land *Press,* May 21, 1976.
N.B. Score calls for three spatially sep-
    arated performing ensembles
    drawn from the forces listed; also
    calls for unusual vocal techniques.

676 Fine, Vivian
Morning (1962)
Med: SATB, nar, kybd
Txt: Henry D. Thoreau
Dur: 7'
Pub: Shaftsbury, Vt.: Catamount Fac-
    simile Ed.
Mss: composer

677 Fine, Vivian
Oda a las ranas (1980)
Med: SSA, fl, ob, cello, perc
Txt: Pablo Neruda
Src: Grove

678 Fine, Vivian
Pæan (1969)
Med: SA, T solo, 6 tpt, 6 tbn
Txt: John Keats
Dur: 12'
Pub: Shaftsbury, Vt.: Catamount
    Facsimile Ed.
Mss: composer
Src: WmAmMus

679 Fine, Vivian
*The passionate shepherd to his love
    and her reply* (1938)
Med: SSA
Txt: Christopher Marlowe and Sir
    Walter Raleigh
Src: Grove

680 Fine, Vivian
Psalm 13 (1953)
Med: SSA, Bar solo, kybd
Txt: Ps. 13
Src: Grove

681 Fine, Vivian
Sounds of the nightingale (1971)
Med: SSAA, S solo, 9 inst.
Txt: John Keats, R. Barnefield, et al.
Src: Grove

682 Fine, Vivian
Teish (1975)
Med: SATB (or eight soli), str quartet
Txt: trad. Zen
Dur: 30'
Pub: Shaftsbury, Vt.: Catamount
    Facsimile Ed.
Mss: copy in NYPL
    The stringless harp
    With the passing of winter
    Let the difference be even a tenth of
    an inch
    If people ask me what Zen is like
    The king of good memory

683 Fine, Vivian
Valedictions (1959)
Med: SATB, ST soli, fl, ob, clar, bsn, hn, tpt, str quartet
Txt: John Donne
Dur: 18'
Pub: Shaftsbury, Vt.: Catamount Facsimile Ed.
Mss: composer

684 Finney, Ross Lee
Earthrise (1978)
Med: SATB, AT soli, orch, taped voice
Txt: Lewis Thomas, Pierre Teilhard de Chardin
Dur: 30'
Pub: CF Peters
Mss: NYPL

685 Finney, Ross Lee
Edge of shadow (1959)
Med: SATB, pno
Txt: Archibald MacLeish
Dur: 19'
Pub: CF Peters
Mss: NYPL
Bib: B1, 24

686 Finney, Ross Lee
Immortal autumn (1952)
Med: SSATBB, org
Txt: Archibald MacLeish
Dur: 6'
Pub: unpubl.
Mss: copies in LC, NYPL

687 Finney, Ross Lee
The martyr's elegy (1967)
Med: SATB, S or T solo, orch
Txt: Percy Bysshe Shelley
Dur: 17'30"
Pub: CF Peters
Mss: NYPL
Bib: B1

688 Finney, Ross Lee
The nun's priest's tale (c.1977)
Med: SATB, soli, orch
Txt: Chaucer
Dur: 14'
Pub: CF Peters
Bib: B40

689 Finney, Ross Lee
Oh, bury me not on the lone prairie (1940)
Med: TTBB
Txt: trad.
Dur: 3'
Pub: Volkwein Bros.
Mss: copy in LC (in hand of Theodore M. Finney)
N.B. Also arr. for SSAA

690 Finney, Ross Lee
Pilgrim psalms (1945)
Med: SATB, SAT soli, kybd
Txt: Book of Psalms (Ainsworth)
Dur: 40'
Pub: C Fischer
Rev: *Diapason* 42 (June 1, 1951) p22; MLA *Notes* 8 (June, 1951) p570-1; *Music and Letters* 52 (Oct, 1951) p388-9; *Music Review* 14 (Aug, 1953) p250
Bib: B1, 40

691 Finney, Ross Lee
Pole star for this year (1939)
Med: SATB, AT soli, orch
Txt: Archibald MacLeish
Pub: unpubl.
Src: Grove

692 Finney, Ross Lee
The remorseless rush of time (1969)
Med: SATB, orch
Txt: composer, Joseph Conrad
Src: Grove

693 Finney, Ross Lee
Spherical madrigals (1947)
Med: SATB
Txt: see below
Dur: 12'
Pub: CF Peters
Bib: B24
> When all again these rare perfections
> met (Lord Herbert of Cherbury)
> All circling point (Richard Crashaw)
> His body an orb (John Dryden)
> On a round ball (John Donne)
> Nor doe I doubt (Crashaw)
> See how the arched earth does here
> (Andrew Marvell)

694 Finney, Ross Lee
Still are new worlds (1962)
Med: SATB, SATB soli, speaking
voice, orch, tape
Txt: Marjorie Hope Nicholson
Dur: 24'
Pub: CF Peters
Mss: NYPL
Bib: B1, 24, 40

695 Finney, Ross Lee
A stranger to myself (1962)
Med: TTTBBB, 2 tbn, timp
Txt: Albert Camus
Dur: 4'
Pub: unpubl.
Mss: composer
Src: Roberts

696 Finney, Ross Lee
Trail to Mexico (1941)
Med: TTBB
Txt: trad.
Pub: Volkwein Bros.
Src: Grove

697 Finney, Ross Lee
When the curtain of the night (1940)
Med: TTBB/SSAA

Txt: Ogle
Pub: Volkwein Bros.
Src: Grove

698 Foss, Lukas
Adon olom (c.1951)
Med: SATB, cantor, org
Txt: liturgical Hebrew
Dur: 4'
Pub: G Schirmer

699 Foss, Lukas
American cantata (1976)
Med: SATB dbl choir, T solo, orch
Txt: Arieh Sachs and composer, from Walt
Whitman, Henry D. Thoreau, et al.
Dur: 37'
Pub: BH
Mss: copy in NYPL
Rev: *American Choral Review* (July,
1978) p17–18; *Choral Journal* 17/
2 (Oct, 1976) p22; *National Music
Council Bulletin* 36/1 (1976) p32;
Oesterreichische Musikzeitschrift 33
(Jan, 1978) p49; *Variety* 289 (Dec
7, 1977) p72; *Village Voice* 23
(Jan 2, 1978) p64
> Prologue
> Earth, water, air
> Love
> Money (Scherzo)
> Trial and error

700 Foss, Lukas
*And then the rocks on the mountain
began to shout* (1978)
Med: SATB
Txt: arbitrary syllables
Dur: 8'
Pub: C Fischer

701 Foss, Lukas
Behold! I build an house (1950)
Med: SATB, kybd
Txt: biblical

Dur: 8'
Pub: Mercury Music
Rev: MLA *Notes* 8 (Mar, 1951)
p492-3

702 Foss, Lukas
Cantata dramatica (1940)
Med: SATB, T solo, orch
Src: Grove
N.B. Later withdrawn by the composer.

703 Foss, Lukas
De profundis (1982)
Med: SATB
Src: Grove

704 Foss, Lukas
Fragments of Archilochos (1965)
Med: 4 choirs, opt. large choir; Countertenor solo, male and female speakers, mandolin, gtr, perc
Txt: Archilochos, trans. Guy Davenport
Dur: 12'
Pub: B Schott; C Fischer
Rev: *American Choral Review* 9/3 (1967) p26-8; *Hi-Fidelity/Musical America* 17 (Apr, 1967) pMA12; *Music Journal* 25 (Mar, 1967) p97
Bib: B10

705 Foss, Lukas
Geod (1969)
Med: opt. SATB or boy soprano, orch, folk inst.
Txt: no text
Dur: 25' - 75'
Pub: B Schott; C Fischer
Bib: B65

706 Foss, Lukas
Lamdeni (Teach me) (1973)
Med: see below, with "plucked and beaten sounds (any mixture), all amplified if possible"

Txt: 12th cent. Hebrew
Dur: 9'
Pub: Editions Salabert
Rev: *Das Orchester* 22 (Apr, 1974) p245-7
Baruch hagever (TTBB)
Wa-eda mah (SSAA)
Mi al har horev (SATB)

707 Foss, Lukas
A parable of death (c.1953)
Med: SATB, T solo, nar, orch
Txt: Rainer Maria Wilke, trans. Anthony Hecht
Dur: 32'
Pub: C Fischer
Rev: *Christian Science Monitor*, March 25, 1954; *Music and Letters* (Jan, 1955) p100; *Musical America* 74 (Nov 15, 1954) p24; *Musical Courier* 149 (May 15, 1954) p41; *Musical Quarterly* 39 (1953) p595.
Bib: B145

708 Foss, Lukas
The prairie (1944)
Med: SATB, SATB soli, orch
Txt: Carl Sandburg
Dur: 60'
Pub: G Schirmer
Rev: New York *Times*, May 16, 1944.
I was born on the prairie
Dust of men
They are mine
When the red and white men met
In the dark of a thousand years
Cool prayers
O prairie girls
Songs hidden in eggs
To-morrow

709 Foss, Lukas
Psalms (c.1957)
Med: SATB, 2 pnos

Txt: Ps. 121:1-2; Ps. 95:64; Ps. 98:1, 4, 6; Ps. 23:1-3
Dur: 13'
Pub: C Fischer
Mss: copy in NYPL
Rev: MLA *Notes* 16 (Dec, 1958) p151

710 Foss, Lukas
Three airs for Frank O'Hara's angel (1972)
Med: SSA dbl choir, S solo, male speaker, inst.
Txt: V. Lang and Frank O'Hara
Dur: 10'
Pub: Editions Salabert
Rev: *World of Music* 15/2 (1973) p67

711 Foss, Lukas
We sing (1941)
Med: children's vv, pno, drums
Src: Grove
N.B. Later withdrawn by the composer.

G

712 Gaburo, Kenneth
Ad te, Domine (c.1958)
Med: SATB
Txt: LU
Dur: 2'
Pub: WLSM

713 Gaburo, Kenneth
Alas! alack! (c.1976)
Med: SA, children
Txt: composer
Dur: 3'
Pub: Lingua Press
  Hi!
  Lone
  The huntsmen
  Alas! alack!

714 Gaburo, Kenneth
Antiphony II: 1962 (1962?; c.1976)
Med: SATB, S solo, tape
Txt: Cavafy
Dur: 12'
Pub: Lingua Press

715 Gaburo, Kenneth
Antiphony III: 1963: Pearl white moments (1963)
Med: SATB, tape
Txt: Virginia Hommel Gaburo
Dur: 20'
Pub: Lingua Press
Rev: *American Choral Review* 9/3 (1967) p37-8; *Musical Quarterly* 53/2(1967) p249-50

716 Gaburo, Kenneth
Ave Maria (c.1965)
Med: SATB
Txt: LU
Dur: 3'
Pub: WLSM

717 Gaburo, Kenneth
December 8 (1967)
Med: male vv
Txt: word sounds
Dur: 4'
Src: NYPL

718 Gaburo, Kenneth
The flow of [u] (c.1976)
Med: SAB
Txt: no text
Dur: 25'
Pub: Lingua Press

719 Gaburo, Kenneth
Humming, including some notes from a mostly bad year, 1954-5 (1955)
Med: SATB

Txt: no text
Dur: 4'
Pub: Lingua Press

720 Gaburo, Kenneth
Lætantur cæli (c.1966)
Med: SATB
Txt: LU
Dur: 3'30"
Pub: WLSM

721 Gaburo, Kenneth
Mass (1958)
Med: TB
Txt: LU
Dur: 7'
Pub: WLSM; Lingua Press

722 Gaburo, Kenneth
Never 1: 4 groups of male voices
    (1966)
Med: TTBB
Txt: text consists of subsounds of the
    word "never"
Dur: 8'
Pub: Lingua Press

723 Gaburo, Kenneth
Psalm (c.1965)
Med: SATB
Txt: Ps. 31:1
Dur: 2'
Pub: WLSM

724 Gaburo, Kenneth
Terra tremuit (c.1967)
Med: SATB
Txt: LU
Dur: 3'
Pub: WLSM

725 Gaburo, Kenneth
Three dedications to Lorca (1953)
Src: Grove

726 Gaburo, Kenneth
Two madrigals (1950)
Med: SATB
Txt: Walter de la Mare
Dur: 6'
Pub: Lingua Press
Mss: NYPL
    Snow
    Willow

727 Giannini, Vittorio
A canticle of Christmas (1956)
Med: SATB, Bar solo, orch, opt. brass
    choir
Txt: Gospel of Luke
Dur: 23'
Pub: Ricordi
Mss: copy in NYPL
Rev: *Moravian Music* 2/1-2 (1958) p1ff

728 Giannini, Vittorio
Canticle of the martyrs (c.1959)
Med: SATB, Bar solo, orch
Txt: not indicated
Dur: 15'
Pub: HW Gray; Broude Bros.

729 Giannini, Vittorio
The harvest (c.1961)
Med: SATB, pno
Txt: not indicated
Dur: 12'
Pub: Ricordi

730 Giannini, Vittorio
Hosanna (n.d.)
Med: SATB
Txt: LU
Dur: 4'
Pub: HW Gray

731 Giannini, Vittorio
Lament for Adonis (1940)
Med: SSAA
Txt: Bion, trans. John A. Symonds

Dur: 10'
Pub: Ricordi
Mss: Manhattan School of Music

732 Giannini, Vittorio
Madrigale no. 1 (c.1930)
Med: SATB, pno or str quartet
Txt: Francesco Petrarca, trans. Frederick H. Martens
Dur: 6'
Pub: Ricordi

733 Giannini, Vittorio
Mass (n.d.)
Med: TTBB, org
Src: Grove

734 Giannini, Vittorio
Primavera (1933)
Med: "cantata"
Src: Grove

735 Giannini, Vittorio
Requiem (1937)
Med: SATB, soli, orch
Txt: LU
Dur: 70'
Pub: Universal Edition

736 Giannini, Vittorio
Resurrection (n.d.)
Med: SATB, pno
Src: Grove

737 Giannini, Vittorio
Stabat mater (1920)
Med: SATB, orch
Txt: LU
Src: Grove

738 Giannini, Vittorio
Tell me, oh blue, blue sky (c.1938)
Med: SSA, pno
Txt: not indicated

Dur: 3'
Pub: Ricordi

739 Giannini, Vittorio
Three devotional motets (c.1960)
Med: SATB, org
Txt: biblical, arr. composer
Dur: 3'-4' each
Pub: Ricordi
    Christmas
    Good Friday
    Easter

740 Giannini, Vittorio
Two madrigals (c.1966)
Med: SSA, pno, fl, ob
Txt: see below
Dur: 9'
Pub: Franco Colombo
    The passionate shepherd to his love
        (Christopher Marlowe)
    The nymph's reply to the shepherd
        (Sir Walter Raleigh)

741 Grainger, Percy
Anchor song (1899, rev. 1921)
Med: TTBB, pno
Txt: Rudyard Kipling
Dur: 4'
Pub: B Schott

742 Grainger, Percy
At twilight (1900-09)
Med: SATB, T solo, pno
Txt: not indicated
Dur: 8'
Pub: B Schott

743 Grainger, Percy
Australian up-country song (1928)
Med: SSATB
Txt: trad. Australian
Dur: 2'
Pub: G Schirmer

744   Grainger, Percy
The ballad of the "Bolivar" (1901)
Med: TTBB, orch, banjos
Txt: Rudyard Kipling
Dur: 6'
Pub: B Schott

745   Grainger, Percy
The beaches of Lukannon (1898, rev. 1941)
Med: SATB, str orch, opt harmonium
Txt: Rudyard Kipling
Dur: 3'
Pub: B Schott

746   Grainger, Percy
The bride's tragedy (1908-9)
Med: SATB, band
Txt: Algernon Charles Swinburne
Dur: 13'
Pub: B Schott

747   Grainger, Percy
Brigg fair (c.1911)
Med: SATB, T solo
Txt: English folk song
Dur: 3'
Pub: B Schott

748   Grainger, Percy
Danny Deever (1903, rev. 1924)
Med: TTBB dbl choir, orch
Txt: Rudyard Kipling
Dur: 5'
Pub: B Schott

749   Grainger, Percy
Dollar and a half a day (1909)
Med: TTBB
Txt: trad.
Dur: 7'30"
Pub: G Schirmer

750   Grainger, Percy
The fall of the stone (1904, rev. 1923)
Med: SATB, 2 vla, 3 celli, brass, 2 hn, 2 bsn; opt. Eng. hn, euphonium, harmonium, pno
Txt: Rudyard Kipling
Dur: 3'30"
Pub: B Schott

751   Grainger, Percy
Father and daughter (1909)
Med: SATB dbl choir, 5 male soli, str, brass, perc, mandolin and gtr band
Txt: composer, after Scandinavian folk songs
Dur: 13'
Pub: B Schott

752   Grainger, Percy
Harvest hymn (1905, rev. 1932)
Med: unison vv, pno four hands
Txt: not indicated
Dur: 4'
Pub: G Schirmer

753   Grainger, Percy
The hunter in his career (1904, rev. 1929)
Med: TTBB, 2 pnos
Txt: William Chappell
Dur: 5'
Pub: B Schott

754   Grainger, Percy
Hunting song on the Seeonee pack (1899, rev. 1922)
Med: TTBB
Txt: composer
Dur: 2'30"
Pub: B Schott

755   Grainger, Percy
I'm seventeen come Sunday (1905)
Med: SATB, brass band

Txt: trad.
Dur: 11'
Pub: B Schott

756 Grainger, Percy
The immovable "do" (or, The cyphering "C") (1939)
Med: SATB, org or orch
Txt: arbitrary syllables
Dur: 6'
Pub: G Schirmer
Bib: B196

757 Grainger, Percy
The Inuit (1902)
Med: SATB
Txt: Rudyard Kipling
Dur: 2'30"
Pub: B Schott

758 Grainger, Percy
Irish tune from County Derry (1911)
Med: SATB
Txt: no text
Dur: 2'30"
Pub: B Schott; G Schirmer
N.B. Also arr. for SSA or TBB, with band or winds.

759 Grainger Percy
The lads of Wamphray (1904)
Med: TTBB, 2 pnos, orch
Txt: Sir Walter Scott
Dur: 12'
Pub: G Schirmer
Bib: B196

760 Grainger, Percy
The lost lady found (1910)
Med: STBB, orch
Txt: trad.
Dur: 2'30"
Pub: B Schott
Bib: B196

761 Grainger, Percy
The love song of the Har Dyl (1901, rev. 1958)
Med: unison women's vv, ch. ensemble
Txt: Rudyard Kipling
Dur: 5'
Pub: unpubl.
Src: Balough

762 Grainger, Percy
Love verses (1900, rev. 1931)
Med: SATB, AT soli, ch. orch
Txt: Song of Solomon
Dur: 8'
Pub: Oxford

763 Grainger, Percy
Marching song of democracy (1901, rev. 1917)
Med: SATB, orch, org
Txt: arbitrary syllables
Dur: 14'
Pub: G Schirmer; Universal Edition

764 Grainger, Percy
Marching tune (1905)
Med: SATB, brass band
Txt: trad.
Dur: 4'
Pub: B Schott

765 Grainger, Percy
Mary Thomson (n.d.)
Med: SATB
Txt: trad. British
Dur: 4'
Pub: unpubl.
Mss: LC

766 Grainger, Percy
The merry wedding (1915)
Med: SATB, 9 soli, orch, opt. org
Txt: composer, from Scandinavian folk songs

Dur: 16'
Pub: Ditson; Oxford

767   Grainger, Percy
Morning song in the jungle (1905)
Med: SATB
Txt: Rudyard Kipling
Dur: 4'
Pub: B Schott

768   Grainger, Percy
Mowgli's song against the people (1903)
Med: SATB, ob, vln, 2 vla, 3 celli, bass, harmonium, pno; opt. ob II, Eng. hn
Txt: Rudyard Kipling
Dur: 7'
Pub: B Schott

769   Grainger, Percy
My dark haired girl (1900)
Med: SATB
Txt: trad.
Dur: 3'
Pub: unpubl.
Mss: LC

770   Grainger, Percy
Near Woodstock town (1903)
Med: SATB
Txt: trad. British
Dur: 3'
Pub: unpubl.
Mss: LC

771   Grainger, Percy
Night-song in the jungle (c.1925)
Med: TTBB
Txt: Rudyard Kipling
Dur: 2'
Pub: B Schott

772   Grainger, Percy
O gin I were where Gowrie rins (1900)
Med: SATB, S solo, pno
Txt: trad. Scottish
Dur: 4'
Pub: unpubl.
Src: Balough

773   Grainger, Percy
O mistress mine (1903)
Med: SATB
Txt: William Chappell
Dur: 3'30"
Pub: unpubl.
Src: Balough

774   Grainger, Percy
The only son (1947)
Med: SATB (opt.), S solo, 8-23 inst.
Txt: Rudyard Kipling
Dur: 4'
Pub: B Schott

775   Grainger, Percy
The peora hunt (1906)
Med: SATB; any combination of harmonium, pno, 2 bsns or 2 celli
Txt: Rudyard Kipling
Dur: 3'
Pub: B Schott
N.B. Also arr. for TTBB.

776   Grainger, Percy
The power of love (1922)
Med: S chorus, S solo, str, org, pnos
Txt: trad. British
Dur: 5'
Pub: unpubl.
Src: Balough

777   Grainger, Percy
Recessional (1929)
Med: SATB, opt. org

Txt: Rudyard Kipling
Dur: 3'30"
Pub: B Schott

778 Grainger, Percy
Red dog (1941)
Med: TTBB
Txt: Rudyard Kipling
Dur: 4'
Pub: B Schott
Mss: LC

779 Grainger, Percy
The running of Shindand (1903?)
Med: TTBB div
Txt: Rudyard Kipling
Dur: 2'30"
Pub: B Schott

780 Grainger, Percy
The rhyme of the three sailors (1901)
Med: TTBB
Txt: Rudyard Kipling
Dur: 5'
Pub: unpubl.
Mss: LC

781 Grainger, Percy
Sailor's chanty (1901)
Med: TTBB, pno
Txt: Arthur Conan Doyle
Dur: 3'30"
Pub: unpubl.
Src: Balough

782 Grainger, Percy
Scotch strathspey and reel (ca. 1925)
Med: TTBB, 16 inst. or pno
Txt: trad. Scottish
Dur: 6'
Pub: G Schirmer

783 Grainger, Percy
The sea-wife (1905)
Med: SATB, pno duet

Txt: Rudyard Kipling
Dur: 3'30"
Pub: B Schott

784 Grainger, Percy
Shallow brown (1910, rev. 1925)
Med: unison, pno
Txt: trad.
Dur: 4'
Pub: G Schirmer

785 Grainger, Percy
Sir Eglamore (1904)
Med: SATB dbl choir, band
Txt: Stafford Smith, *Musica antiqua*
Dur: 8'
Pub: B Schott

786 Grainger, Percy
Soldier, soldier (1908)
Med: SSATB, 6 soli
Txt: Rudyard Kipling
Dur: 4'
Pub: B Schott

787 Grainger, Percy
A song of Vermeland (1903)
Med: SSATB
Txt: trad. Swedish
Dur: 4'
Pub: Vincent Music Co.
Mss: LC

788 Grainger, Percy
There was a pig went out to dig
    (1905, rev. 1910)
Med: SSAA (women or children)
Txt: trad.
Dur: 7'
Pub: G Schirmer

789 Grainger, Percy
Thou gracious power (1903, rev.
    1951)
Med: SATB

Txt: Oliver Wendell Holmes
Dur: 4'
Pub: unpubl.
Mss: LC

790 Grainger, Percy
The three ravens (1902)
Med: SATB, Bar solo, 5 clar, org
Txt: trad.
Dur: 5'
Pub: B Schott
Rev: *Music Teacher* 29 (Oct, 1950) p485

791 Grainger, Percy
Tiger-tiger (1905)
Med: TTBB
Txt: Rudyard Kipling
Dur: 2'
Pub: B Schott

792 Grainger, Percy
To Wolcott Balestier (1901)
Med: TTBB, org
Txt: Rudyard Kipling
Dur: 4'
Pub: unpubl.
Src: Balough

793 Grainger, Percy
Tribute to Foster (1914, rev. 1931)
Med: SATB, 5 soli, musical glasses,
    pno and orch, or 2 pnos
Txt: composer, after Stephen Foster
Dur: 14'
Pub: G Schirmer

794 Grainger, Percy
The two corbies (1909)
Med: TTBB
Txt: Sir Walter Scott
Dur: 4'
Pub: unpubl.
Src: Balough

795 Grainger, Percy
Two sea chanties (c.1984)
Med: TTBB, Bar solo
Txt: trad.
Dur: 5'
Pub: CF Peters
    Shenandoah
    Stormy

796 Grainger, Percy
Two Welsh fighting songs (1904)
Med: SATB dbl choir, gtr and drums
Txt: William Duthie
Dur: 7'30"
Pub: G Schirmer
    The camp
    The march of the men of Harlech

797 Grainger, Percy
*We have fed our sea for a thousand
    years* (1904, rev. 1926)
Med: SATB, brass, opt. str
Txt: Rudyard Kipling
Dur: 6'30"
Pub: B Schott

798 Grainger, Percy
The widow's party (1906, rev. 1926)
Med: TTBB, ch. orch
Txt: Rudyard Kipling
Dur: 8'
Pub: B Schott

799 Grainger, Percy
Willow, willow (1902-11, rev. 1960)
Med: unsion male vv, hp or pno, str
Txt: William Chappell
Dur: 4'
Pub: unpubl.
Src: Balough

800 Grainger, Percy
The wrath of Odin (1903, rev. 1947)
Med: SATB dbl choir, pno
Txt: Henry W. Longfellow

Dur: 7'
Pub: unpubl.
Src: Balough

801 Grainger, Percy
Ye banks and braes o'bonnie Doon
(1901)
Med: children, women's, men's or
mixed voices, org or band
Txt: Robert Burns
Dur: 2'30"
Pub: B Schott

H

802 Hanson, Howard
Centennial ode (1950)
Med: SATB, Bar solo, nar, orch
Txt: J.R. Slater
Src: Grove

803 Hanson, Howard
The cherubic hymn, Op. 37 (1950)
Med: SATB, orch
Txt: St. John Chrysostom
Dur: 20'
Pub: C Fischer
Mss: Eastman School of Music; copy
in NYPL
Rev: MLA *Notes* 7 (June, 1950) p442-
4; *Music Clubs Magazine* 30 (Oct,
1950) p24; *Musical America* 70
(Aug, 1950) p28; *Musical Courier*
142 (June, 1950) p6
Bib: B34

804 Hanson, Howard
Heroic elegy, Op. 28 (1927)
Med: SATB, orch
Txt: textless
Mss: Eastman School of Music
Src: Grove

805 Hanson, Howard
How excellent thy name (1952)
Med: SATB, org
Txt: Ps. 8:1, 3-6
Dur: 4'
Pub: C Fischer
Mss: holograph of SSAA version in
LC, under "O Lord, how
excellent thy name"
N.B. Originally for SSAA.

806 Hanson, Howard
Hymn for the pioneers (1938)
Med: TTBB
Txt: E.W. Olson
Dur: 4'30"
Pub: J Fischer

807 Hanson, Howard
The lament for Beowulf, Op. 25
(c.1909)
Med: SATB, orch
Txt: Anglo-Saxon epic, trans. William
Morris and A.J. Wyatt
Dur: 18'
Pub: C Fischer; CC Birchard
Mss: Eastman School of Music; copy
in NYPL
Bib: B34, 109

808 Hanson, Howard
Lumen in Christo (1974)
Med: SATB, orch
Txt: Isaiah 60:2-3; 9:2; LU
Src: Grove
N.B. Also arr. for SSAA, pno.

809 Hanson, Howard
The mystic trumpeter (1970)
Med: SATB, nar, orch
Txt: Walt Whitman
Dur: 8'
Pub: C Fischer
Mss: copy in NYPL

Rev: *ASCAP* 4/2 (1970) p31; *Pan Pipes* 63/2 (1971) p34–5

810 Hanson, Howard
New land, new covenant (c.1976)
Med: SATB dbl choir, SBar soli, nar, ch. orch; opt. children's choir
Txt: compiled by Howard C. Kee, from Bible, colonial American writings, 17–18th cent. hymns, T.S. Eliot
Dur: 25'
Pub: C Fischer
Mss: AMC; copy in NYPL
Rev: *ASCAP* 8/1 (1976) p34–9; *Choral Journal* 16/8 (1976) p36; *Hi-Fidelity/Musical America* 26 (Aug, 1976) pMA28
  Creation and fall
  New exodus, new covenant (1620)
  The great awakening (1750)
  New order of the ages (1776)
  Renewing the covenant (1976)

811 Hanson, Howard
North and west, Op. 22 (1923)
Med: opt. chorus, orch
Txt: textless
Pub: unpubl.
Mss: Eastman School of Music
Src: Grove

812 Hanson, Howard
A prayer for the Middle Ages (c.1976)
Med: SATB div
Txt: anon. 8th cent., adapt. James Francis Cooke
Dur: 4'
Pub: C Fischer

813 Hanson, Howard
Psalm 121 (1968)
Med: TTBB, Bar solo, orch
Txt: Ps. 121
Dur: 5'30"

Pub: C Fischer
N.B. Also arr. for SATB, 1969.

814 Hanson, Howard
Psalm 150 (1965)
Med: TTBB
Txt: Ps. 150
Dur: 4'30"
Pub: C Fischer
Mss: NYPL
N.B. Also arr. for SATB, 1969.

815 Hanson, Howard
A sea symphony (Symphony No. 7) (1977)
Med: SATB, orch
Txt: Walt Whitman
Dur: 17'
Pub: C Fischer
Rev: *Music Educators Journal* 64 (Nov, 1977) p75–6; *National Music Council Bulletin* 37/1 (1977) p33; *School Musician* 49 (Oct, 1977) p52

816 Hanson, Howard
Song of democracy, Op. 44 (1956)
Med: SATB div, band or orch
Txt: Walt Whitman
Dur: 12'
Pub: C Fischer
Bib: B34
N.B. Also arr. for TTBB.

817 Hanson, Howard
Song of human rights, Op. 49 (1963)
Med: SATB, orch
Txt: Preamble of the Universal Declaration of Human Rights
Dur: 12'
Pub: C Fischer

818 Hanson, Howard
Songs from "Drum taps" (c.1935)
Med: SATB, Bar solo, orch

Txt: Walt Whitman
Dur: 18'
Pub: J Fischer
    Beat! beat! drums!
    By the bivouac's fitful flame
    To thee, old cause

819   Hanson, Howard
Streams in the desert (1969)
Med: SATB div, orch
Txt: Isaiah 35
Dur: 12'
Pub: C Fischer
Bib: B34

820   Harbison, John
Ave Maria (c.1991)
Med: SSAA
Txt: LU
Dur: 2'30"
Pub: AMP

821   Harbison, John
Ave verum corpus (c.1991)
Med: SSATB, opt. str
Txt: LU
Dur: 5'
Pub: AMP

822   Harbison, John
Five songs of experience (1971)
Med: SATB, SATB soli, str quartet, perc
Txt: William Blake
Dur: 20'
Pub: AMP
    Introduction
    Earth's answer
    Ah! sunflower
    The voice of the ancient band
    A divine image

823   Harbison, John
The flight into Egypt (1986)
Med: SATB, SBar soli, orch and org

Txt: Matthew 3:13-23
Dur: 14'
Pub: AMP
Rev: *American Choral Review* 30/1
    (1988) p18-20; *Central Opera* 27/
    4 (1987) p56 and 28/4 (1988)
    p37; *Choral Journal* 28/1 (1987)
    p31; MLA *Notes* 46/2 (1989)
    p14-15; *Musical America* 107/5
    (1987) p45
N.B. Winner of the 1987 Pulitzer Prize
    in music.

824   Harbison, John
Flower-fed buffaloes (1976)
Med: SATB div, Bar solo, clar, sax,
    vln, cello, bass, pno, perc
Txt: see below
Dur: 22'
Pub: AMC
Mss: LC
Rev: *National Music Council Bulletin* 37/
    2 (1978) p22
    Preamble
    The flower-fed buffaloes (Vachel
    Lindsay)
    Enrich my resignation (Hart Crane)
    Depths (Michael Fried)
    Above the Pate Valley (Lindsay)
    The aramanth (Gary Snyder)

825   Harbison, John
Music (1966)
Med: SATB
Txt: Percy Bysshe Shelley
Src: Grove

826   Harbison, John
Nunc dimittis (1980)
Med: TB, pno
Txt: Luke 2: 25-35
Dur: 5'
Pub: AMP

827   Harris, Roy
America, we love your people (1975)
Med: SSATB, band
Txt: composer
Src: Grove

828   Harris, Roy
Bicentennial symphony (1976)
Txt: U.S. Constitution, Abraham Lin-
        coln, composer
Src: Grove

829   Harris, Roy
The bird's counting song (c.1945)
Med: SATB
Txt: trad.
Dur: 3'
Pub: Belwin-Mills

830   Harris, Roy
*Black is the color of my true love's
        hair* (1942)
Med: SATB
Txt: trad.
Dur: 2'
Pub: Belwin-Mills

831   Harris, Roy
Blow the man down (1946)
Med: SATB, ABar soli, orch
Txt: trad.
Dur: 10'
Pub: C Fischer

832   Harris, Roy
The brotherhood of man (1966)
Med: SATB, orch
Txt: Abraham Lincoln
Src: Grove

833   Harris, Roy
Challenge (1940)
Med: SATB, B solo, orch
Txt: composer, U.S. Constitution
Src: Grove

834   Harris, Roy
Choral symphony (1936)
Med: SATB, soli, orch
Txt: not indicated
Dur: unfinished
Pub: unpubl.
Mss: LC
Src: LC
N.B.   On cover: "Choral symphony
        never completed because of other
        commissions—this work was
        never commissioned."

835   Harris, Roy
Cindy (1949)
Med: SATB
Txt: trad.
Dur: 2'30"
Pub: C Fischer
Rev: MLA *Notes* 9 (June, 1952) p493

836   Harris, Roy
Easter motet (1942)
Med: unison vv, pno
Txt: biblical
Dur: 7'
Pub: G Schirmer

837   Harris, Roy
Folk fantasy for festivals (1955)
Med: SATB dbl choir (except where
        indicated below), soli, orch
Txt: trad., arr. composer
Dur: 50'
Pub: AMP
        My praise shall never end
        The weeping willow (SSAA)
        David slew Goliath
        The working man's pride (TTBB)
        Fun and nonsense parody

838   Harris, Roy
Folk-song symphony (1940)
Med: SATB, orch

Txt: trad., arr. composer
Dur: 42'
Pub: G Schirmer
Mss: LC (lacks third mvt.)
N.B. Also known as the composer's Symphony No. 4.
Welcome party
Western cowboy
Interlude
Mountaineer love song, or He's gone away
Interlude
Negro fantasy
Final

839   Harris, Roy
Freedom, toleration (1941)
Med: SATB
Txt: Walt Whitman
Dur: 4'
Pub: Belwin-Mills

840   Harris, Roy
Freedom's land (1941)
Med: SATB, org
Txt: Archibald MacLeish
Dur: 2'30"
Pub: Belwin-Mills
N.B. Also arr. for SSA, TTBB; originally for solo voice.

841   Harris, Roy
He's gone away (1939)
Med: SSATB, SBar soli
Txt: trad., arr. composer
Dur: 4'30"
Pub: G Schirmer

842   Harris, Roy
The hustle with the muscle (1957)
Med: TTBB, band
Txt: composer
Src: Grove

843   Harris, Roy
If I had a ribbon bow (1949)
Med: SATB
Txt: trad.
Dur: 3'30"
Pub: C Fischer
Rev: MLA *Notes* 9 (June, 1952) p493

844   Harris, Roy
Jubilation (1964)
Med: SATB, SATB soli, brass ensemble, vibraphone, pno
Txt: "Alleluia"
Dur: 7'
Pub: unpubl.
Mss: composer
Src: Dox

845   Harris, Roy
Life of Christ (n.d.)
Med: SATB, cello, orch
Txt: not indicated
Dur: unfinished
Mss: LC
Src: LC

846   Harris, Roy
Li'l boy named David (1942)
Med: SATB
Txt: trad.
Dur: 4'
Pub: Mills Music

847   Harris, Roy
Mass (1948)
Med: male voices, org
Txt: LU
Dur: 20'
Pub: C Fischer
Bib: B26

848   Harris, Roy
Mi chomocho (Who is mighty?) (c.1951)

Med: SATB, T or Bar solo, org
Txt: LU
Dur: 7'
Pub: C Fischer

849 Harris, Roy
Psalm 150 (1957)
Med: SATB
Txt: Ps. 150
Dur: 6'
Pub: Golden (Colo.) Music
Mss: LC

850 Harris, Roy
Railroad man's ballad (1940)
Med: SATB, orch
Txt: T. Lawrence
Src: Grove

851 Harris, Roy
A red bird in a green tree (c.1940)
Med: SATB
Txt: trad.
Dur: 3'
Pub: Belwin-Mills

852 Harris, Roy
Red Cross hymn (1951?)
Med: SATB, band
Txt: composer
Src: Grove

853 Harris, Roy
Rock of ages (1939)
Med: SATB, orch
Txt: trad. hymn
Dur: 7'
Pub: Belwin-Mills

854 Harris, Roy
Sammy's fighting sons (1944?)
Med: SSAA, TTBB, orch
Txt: composer
Src: Grove

855 Harris, Roy
Sanctus (1934)
Med: SATB
Txt: LU
Dur: 2'
Pub: G Schirmer

856 Harris, Roy
A song for occupations (1934)
Med: SATB div
Txt: Walt Whitman
Dur: 18'
Pub: G Schirmer
Mss: LC

857 Harris, Roy
Sons of Uncle Sam (1942)
Med: unison vv, pno
Txt: not indicated
Dur: 5'
Pub: Belwin-Mills

858 Harris, Roy
The story of Noah (1934)
Med: SATB div
Txt: after John Jacob Niles
Dur: 5'
Pub: G Schirmer

859 Harris, Roy
Symphony for voices (c.1939)
Med: SATB div
Txt: Walt Whitman
Dur: 12'
Pub: G Schirmer
 Song of all seas, all ships
 Tears
 Inscription

860 Harris, Roy
Symphony No. 10 (1965)
Med: SATB, brass, 2 pno, perc
Txt: Abraham Lincoln and composer
Dur: 5'
Pub: G Schirmer

861   Harris, Roy
Take the sun and keep the stars
   (1944)
Med: unison vv, band
Txt: composer
Src: Grove

862   Harris, Roy
They say that Susan has no heart for
   learning (1947)
Med: SSA, pno
Txt: composer
Dur: 3'
Pub: AMP

863   Harris, Roy
To thee, old cause (1941)
Med: SATB
Txt: Walt Whitman
Dur: 4'
Pub: Belwin-Mills

864   Harris, Roy
Walt Whitman suite (1944)
Med: SATB, str, 2 pno
Txt: Walt Whitman
Dur: 15'
Pub: Belwin-Mills

865   Harris, Roy
When Johnny comes marching home
   (1935)
Med: SATB
Txt: trad.
Dur: 8'
Pub: G Schirmer

866   Harris, Roy
Whether this nation (1971)
Med: SATB, band
Txt: composer, S. Harris, Archibald
   MacLeish
Src: Grove

867   Harris, Roy
Whitman triptych (1940)
Med: SSAA
Txt: Walt Whitman
Dur: 8'
Pub: G Schirmer
   I hear America singing
   An evening lull
   America

868   Harris, Roy
Work song (1942)
Med: SATB
Txt: trad.
Dur: 4'
Pub: Mills Music

869   Harris, Roy
Year that trembled (1941)
Med: SATB
Txt: Walt Whitman
Dur: 2'30"
Pub: Belwin-Mills

870   Harrison, Lou
Easter cantata (1966)
Med: SATB, soli, ch. orch
Txt: biblical
Pub: unpubl.
Src: Dox
   Sinfonia
   Aubade
   Chorale en rondeau
   Mary's song at the tomb
   Narrative
   Alleluia

871   Harrison, Lou
Four strict songs (1955)
Med: 8 Bar, 2 tbn, pno, hp, perc, str
Txt: composer
Dur: 40'
Pub: AMP

872 Harrison, Lou
Haiku (1968)
Med: unison vv, xiao, hp, perc
Txt: Kay Davis
Src: Grove

873 Harrison, Lou
Homage to Pacifica (1991)
Med: SATB, soli, gamelan
Txt: Mark Twain, Chief Seattle, composer
Src: Brunner (B31)

874 Harrison, Lou
A joyous procession and a solemn procession (1962)
Med: SATB, tbn, perc (4 tamb, 8 handbells, gong, bass drum)
Txt: no text
Dur: indeterminate (3'-10')
Pub: CF Peters
Mss: LC
Rev: MLA *Notes* 21/4 (1964) p609-10; *Musical America* 83 (Dec, 1963) p288

875 Harrison, Lou
La koro sutro (1972)
Med: SATB, gamelan, percussion orchestra
Txt: trad. Buddhist, trans. B. Kennedy
Src: Grove
Bib: B69

876 Harrison, Lou
Mass for St. Cecilia's Day (1986)
Med: unison vv, opt. org and hp
Txt: LU
Src: Brunner (B31)

877 Harrison, Lou
Mass to St. Anthony (1962)
Med: SATB, tpt, hp, str

Txt: LU
Dur: 20'
Pub: Peer Intl.
Mss: LC
Rev: *Musical Quarterly* (Oct, 1967) p566-8.
Bib: B51, 218, 219

878 Harrison, Lou
Novo odo (1963)
Med: TTBB, reciting chorus, orch
Txt: composer
Src: Grove

879 Harrison, Lou
Orpheus (from the singer to the dancer) (1969)
Med: SATB, T solo, perc
Pub: unpubl.
Src: Brunner (B31)

880 Harrison, Lou
Peace piece one (1968)
Med: unison vv, tbn, perc, 2 hp, org, str quintet
Txt: Metta Sutta
Dur: 6'
Pub: *Soundings* 3/4 (1972) p112-128.

881 Harrison, Lou
Scenes from Cavafy (1980)
Med: chorus and gamelan
Src: Brunner (B31)

882 Harrison, Lou
Soedjatmoko set (1989)
Src: Brunner (B31)

883 Harrison, Lou
Three songs (1985)
Med: TBB, pno, org, str
Txt: 2 Samuel 1:26, Walt Whitman

Pub: Peer Southern
Src: Brunner (B31)

884 Hovhaness, Alan
Ad lyram, Op. 143 (1955)
Med: SATB div, soli, orch
Src: Grove

885 Hovhaness, Alan
Adoration, Op. 221 (1968)
Med: SSAA/TTBB, SATB soli, orch
Src: Grove

886 Hovhaness, Alan
Alleluia, Op. 158 (1935, rev.1957)
Med: SATB, org
Txt: "Alleluia"
Dur: 3'30"
Pub: CF Peters

887 Hovhaness, Alan
Anabasis, Op. 141 (1953)
Med: SATB, SB soli, nar, org
Src: Grove

888 Hovhaness, Alan
And as they came down from the mountain, Op. 82 (c.1963)
Med: SATB, T solo
Txt: Mark 9:9
Dur: 4'
Pub: CF Peters

889 Hovhaness, Alan
Ave Maria, Op. 100a (1952)
Med: SSAA, 2 ob, 2 hn, hp
Src: Grove

890 Hovhaness, Alan
Behold, God is my help, Op. 26 (1940, rev. 1967)
Med: SATB, Bar solo, kybd
Txt: Ps. 54:1, 2, 4, 6
Dur: 5'
Pub: CF Peters

891 Hovhaness, Alan
The brightness of our noon, Op. 131 (1954)
Med: SATB
Txt: Judith Malina
Dur: 3'
Pub: CC Birchard
Mss: LC

892 Hovhaness, Alan
Cantate Domino, Op. 385 (1982?)
Src: Grove

893 Hovhaness, Alan
Easter anthem, Op. 18 (1937)
Med: SATB, S solo, org
Src: Grove

894 Hovhaness, Alan
Easter cantata, Op. 100, No. 3 (1953)
Med: SATB, S solo, ch. orch
Txt: composer
Dur: 20'
Pub: AMP
Rev: *Christian Science Monitor*, May 12, 1955.
   Prelude
   O Lord
   Mourn, mourn ye saints
   The Lord now is risen
   Jesus Christ is risen today

895 Hovhaness, Alan
Etchmiadzin: drama in six scenes, Op. 62 (1946)
Med: SATB, soli, orch
Txt: Zabelle Boyajian
Dur: 75'
Pub: privately publ. by composer in Boston
Mss: LC

896 Hovhaness, Alan
For the waters are come into my soul,
Op. 256, No. 2 (1973)
Med: TTBB
Txt: Ps. 69
Dur: 4'
Pub: Peer Intl.

897 Hovhaness, Alan
Four jashou sharagans (c.1944)
Med: SAB and SATB, org
Txt: trad. Armenian folk songs, arr.
composer
Dur: 4'30"
Pub: privately publ. by composer in
Boston; copy in LC

898 Hovhaness, Alan
From the ends of the earth, Op. 177
(1952)
Med: SATB, org
Src: Grove

899 Hovhaness, Alan
Fuji, Op. 182 (1960, later rev.)
Med: SSA, fl, hp, str
Txt: Yamabé Akahito
Dur: 13'
Pub: CF Peters
Mss: LC (several versions)
Rev: *Music Journal* 25 (May, 1967) p63

900 Hovhaness, Alan
Glory to God, Op. 124 (1954)
Med: SATB, SA soli, brass, perc, org
Txt: Luke 2:8-11, 13, 14
Dur: 14'
Pub: CF Peters

901 Hovhaness, Alan
Glory to man, Op. 167 (c.1959)
Med: SATB, org
Txt: John Lovejoy Elliott
Dur: 5'

Pub: CF Peters
Mss: LC

902 Hovhaness, Alan
God is our refuge and strength, Op.
359 (1981)
Med: SATB, orch
Txt: Ps. 46:1-5, 7
Dur: 6'
Pub: ABI (New York); copy in NYPL

903 Hovhaness, Alan
The God of glory thundereth, Op.
140 (1935, rev. 1960)
Med: SATB, S or T solo, org
Txt: Ps. 27, 117
Dur: 4'
Pub: CF Peters

904 Hovhaness, Alan
Hear my prayer, O Lord, Op. 149
(1935 as Op. 16; rev. 1960)
Med: SATB
Txt: Ps. 143
Dur: 4'
Pub: CF Peters

905 Hovhaness, Alan
The hermit bell-ringer of the tower,
Op. 256, No. 1 (1972)
Med: TTBB, B solo, fl, chimes
Txt: composer
Dur: 6' 30"
Pub: Peer Intl.

906 Hovhaness, Alan
I have seen the Lord, Op. 80 (1963)
Med: SATB, S solo, opt. tpt, org
Txt: John 20:11-16, 18
Dur: 5'
Pub: CF Peters

907 Hovhaness, Alan
I will lift up mine eyes, Op. 93
(1969)

Med: SATB, org; opt. boys' choir and
B solo
Txt: Ps. 121
Dur: 15'
Pub: CF Peters
Rev: *American Organist* 53 (Jan, 1970)
p7-8; *Diapason* 61 (Jan, 1970) p2

908 Hovhaness, Alan
I will rejoice in the Lord, Op. 42
(n.d.)
Dur: 15'
Pub: CF Peters
Rev: *American Organist* 53 (Jan, 1970)
p7-8; *Diapason* 61 (Jan, 1970) p2

908 Hovhaness, Alan
I will rejoice in the Lord, Op. 42
(n.d.)
Med: SATB, org
Txt: biblical
Src: Grove

909 Hovhaness, Alan
Immortality, Op. 134 (1960)
Med: SATB, S solo, org
Txt: Christian F. Gellert, trans. Frances
Cox
Dur: 3'
Pub: CF Peters

910 Hovhaness, Alan
*In the beginning was the word, Op.
206* (1963)
Med: SATB, AB soli, ch. orch
Txt: John 1:1-18
Dur: 27'
Pub: CF Peters

911 Hovhaness, Alan
Jesus, lover of my soul, Op. 53 (n.d.)
Med: SATB, solo, org
Src: Grove

912 Hovhaness, Alan
*Keep not thou silence, Op. 87, No.
3* (1951)
Med: SATB
Txt: Ps. 83:1
Dur: 3'
Pub: AMP
Mss: LC

913 Hovhaness, Alan
Lady of light, Op. 227 (c.1969)
Med: SATB, SBar soli, orch
Txt: composer
Dur: 36'
Pub: CF Peters

914 (not used)

915 Hovhaness, Alan
The leper king, Op. 219 (c.1967)
Med: TTBB, Bar solo, 3 fl, tpt, perc
Txt: composer
Dur: 33'
Pub: CF Peters
Mss: LC

916 Hovhaness, Alan
Let them praise the name of the Lord!
(c.1962)
Med: SATB, org
Txt: biblical
Dur: 2'
Pub: CF Peters

917 Hovhaness, Alan
Let us love one another, Op. 46
(1941, rev. 1968)
Med: SATB, T or Bar solo
Src: Grove

918 Hovhaness, Alan
Look toward the sea, Op. 158 (1957)
Med: SATB, Bar solo, tbn, org
Txt: 1 Kings 17, 18
Dur: 30'
Pub: CF Peters

919   Hovhaness, Alan
The Lord's prayer, Op. 35 (c.1965)
Med: SATB, org
Txt: Gospel of Matthew
Dur: 3'
Pub: CF Peters
Mss: LC

920   Hovhaness, Alan
Magnificat, Op. 157 (1958)
Med: SATB div, STB soli, orch
Txt: Luke 2
Dur: 33'
Pub: CF Peters
Mss: LC
Rev: *Musical America* 79 (May, 1959)
      p26
Bib: B111

921   Hovhaness, Alan
*Majnun Symphony, Symphony No.
      24, Op. 273* (c.1978)
Med: SATB, T solo, tpt, vln solo, str
Txt: Jami, trans. Ed. Fitzgerald
Dur: 25'
Pub: AMP
Rev: *Hi-Fidelity/Musical America* 24
      (May, 1974) pMA7; *Music Edu-
      cators Journal* 60 (Apr, 1974) p125
      Majnun
      Letters in the sand
      The distracted lover
      The sword-wind
      Majnun answered
      The beloved
      The celestial beloved
      Majnun's love song
      The mysterious beloved

922   Hovhaness, Alan
Make a joyful noise, Op. 105 (1967)
Med: SATB, T or Bar solo, 2 tpt, 2
      tbn, org
Txt: Book of Psalms
Dur: 17'

Pub: CF Peters
Rev: *BMI* (Apr, 1968) p19-20

923   Hovhaness, Alan
Make haste, Op. 86 (1961)
Med: SATB
Txt: Ps. 70:1
Dur: 2'
Pub: CF Peters

924   Hovhaness, Alan
Mesrob, Op. 98 (1952)
Med: SATB, SAB soli, 2 fl, 3 tpt,
      perc, hp, celesta
Txt: composer
Dur: 40'
Pub: unpubl.
Mss: LC

925   Hovhaness, Alan
Missa brevis, Op. 4 (c.1936)
Med: SATB, B soli, str, org
Txt: LU
Dur: 16'
Pub: CF Peters
Mss: copy in LC
Rev: *Diapason* 41/11 (Oct, 1950) p33.
Bib: B51

926   Hovhaness, Alan
Motets, Op. 87 (1951)
Med: SATB
Txt: see below
Dur: see below
Pub: AMP
      Why hast thou cast us off? (Ps. 74:1,
      21; 2'15")
      Unto thee, O God (Ps. 75:1; 1'15")
      Keep not thou silence (Ps. 83:1; 1'30")
      Praise ye the Lord (Ps. 106:1; 2')

927   Hovhaness, Alan
Motets, Op. 246 (1972)
Med: SATB, opt. org
Txt: see below

Dur: see below
Pub: CF Peters
    David wept for slain Absalom (biblical; 8')
    The word of our Lord shall stand forever (Isaiah 40; 5')
    Heaven: an echo anthem (George Herbert; 5'30")
    A rose tree blossoms (composer; 3')

928   Hovhaness, Alan
Motets, Op. 259 (c.1974)
Med: SATB
Txt: see below
Dur: see below
Pub: Broude Bros.
    Peace be multiplied (1 Peter 1:2; 2'20")
    God be merciful unto us (Ps. 67; 5')
    Wisdom (Eccl. 8:1, 9:17, 18; 2')

929   Hovhaness, Alan
Motets, Op. 268 (1973)
Med: SATB
Src: Grove
N.B. Four works.

930   Hovhaness, Alan
Motets, Op. 269 (1973)
Med: SATB
Src: Grove
N.B. Three works.

931   Hovhaness, Alan
O for a shout of sacred joy, Op. 161 (c.1958)
Med: SATB, org
Txt: colonial American hymn
Dur: 4'
Pub: CF Peters

932   Hovhaness, Alan
O God our help in ages past, Op. 137 (1963)
Med: SATB, org
Txt: Isaac Watts

Dur: 2'30"
Pub: CF Peters
Mss: LC

933   Hovhaness, Alan
O God, rebuke me not, Op. 28 (n.d.)
Med: SATB, org
Txt: biblical
Src: Grove

934   Hovhaness, Alan
O lady moon, Op. 139 (ca. 1962)
Med: SSA, clar, pno
Txt: Lafcadio Hearn
Dur: 4'
Pub: EB Marks

935   Hovhaness, Alan
O Lord, God of hosts, Op. 27 (1940, rev. 1967)
Med: SATB, kybd, opt. 2 tpt, 2 tbn
Txt: Ps. 89:8, 9, 11, 52
Dur: 5'
Pub: CF Peters

936   Hovhaness, Alan
O Lord, our Lord, Op. 23 (1937)
Med: SATB, B solo, org
Txt: biblical
Src: Grove

937   Hovhaness, Alan
On Christmas Eve a child cried out, Op. 337 (1981)
Med: SATB, fl, hp
Src: Grove

938   Hovhaness, Alan
Out of the depths I cry to you, Op. 142, No. 3 (1938, rev. 1960)
Med: SATB, org
Txt: Ps. 130
Dur: 3'
Pub: CF Peters

Mss: holograph of song in LC
N.B. Originally for solo voice.

939 Hovhaness, Alan
Praise the Lord with psaltery, Op. 222 (1968)
Med: SATB, orch
Txt: Ps. 33:2, 3; 146:1–2; 150:3, 6
Dur: 21'
Pub: CF Peters
Mss: LC
Rev: *BMI* (Mar, 1969) p13; *Hi-Fidelity/Musical America* 19 (Mar, 1969) pMA20; *International Music Bulletin* 72 (July, 1969) p69; *Music Journal* 27 (Feb, 1969) p85

940 Hovhaness, Alan
Praise ye the Lord, Op. 87, No. 4 (1951)
Med: SATB
Txt: Ps. 106:1
Dur: 2'
Pub: AMP
Mss: LC

941 Hovhaness, Alan
Protest and prayer, Op. 41 (1941)
Med: TTBB, T solo, kybd
Txt: composer
Dur: 4'
Pub: CF Peters

942 Hovhaness, Alan
Psalm 23 (c.1969)
Med: SATB, org or ch. orch
Txt: Ps. 23:1–3
Dur: 14'
Pub: CF Peters
N.B. Excerpted from the composer's Symphony No. 12.

943 Hovhaness, Alan
Psalm 23 (c.1969)
Med: SATB, org or fl, 2 tpt, hp, str
Txt: Ps. 23:5, 6

Dur: 7'
Pub: CF Peters

944 Hovhaness, Alan
Psalm 28, Op. 162 (1958)
Med: SATB
Txt: Ps. 28:1, 2, 9
Dur: 3'30"
Pub: CF Peters
Mss: LC

945 Hovhaness, Alan
Psalm 61, "From the end of the earth," Op. 187 (c.1961)
Med: SATB, org
Txt: Ps. 61:1–4
Dur: 3'30"
Pub: CF Peters

946 Hovhaness, Alan
Psalm 148, Op. 160, No. 1 (1958)
Med: SATB div, B solo, org
Txt: Ps. 148
Dur: 9'
Pub: CF Peters
Mss: LC

947 Hovhaness, Alan
Revelations of St. Paul, Op. 343 (1980)
Med: SATB, STBar soli, orch
Txt: Donald V.R. Thompson
Dur: 70'
Pub: Alexander Broude
Rev: *Hi-Fidelity/Musical America* 31 (June, 1981) pMA34-5; New York *Times,* Jan 29, 1981, pC14; *Symphony Magazine* 32/3 (1981) p39ff

948 Hovhaness, Alan
A simple Mass, Op. 282 (1977)
Med: unison choir, SATB soli, org
Txt: LU

Dur: 13'
Pub: AMP

949 Hovhaness, Alan
Sing aloud, Op. 68 (1951)
Med: SATB
Txt: Ps. 81
Dur: 2'
Pub: CF Peters
Mss: LC

950 Hovhaness, Alan
The stars, Op. 126 (1954)
Med: SATB, S solo, Eng. hn, celesta,
      hp, str
Txt: Henry D. Thoreau
Dur: 12'
Pub: unpubl.
Mss: copy of holograph in LC

951 Hovhaness, Alan
Symphony No. 12, "The Choral,"
      Op. 188 (c.1961)
Med: SATB, ch. orch
Txt: Ps. 23
Dur: 25'
Pub: CF Peters
Mss: LC
Rev: *Music Journal* 30 (Jan, 1972) p75
N.B. An excerpt from this work is
      published separately (see his *Psalm
      23*, No. 943, above).

952 Hovhaness, Alan
Teach me thy way, Op. 320 (1978)
Med: SSA
Src: Grove

953 Hovhaness, Alan
Thirtieth ode of Solomon, Op. 76
      (c.1949)
Med: SATB, Bar solo, tpt, tbn, str
Txt: Song of Solomon
Dur: 30'

Pub: CF Peters
Mss: LC, including preliminary sketches
Rev: New York *Times*, Mar 7, 1949.

954 Hovhaness, Alan
Three madrigals, Op. 258 (1972)
Med: SATB
Txt: Francis Bacon (no. 1), composer
Dur: 8'
Pub: Broude Bros.
      The pencil of the Holy Ghost
      My sorrow is my love
      They all laugh

955 Hovhaness, Alan
To the God who is in the fire, Op.
      146 (1956)
Med: TTBB, T solo, perc
Txt: *Sh'vet Upanishad*
Dur: 8'
Pub: CF Peters
Mss: copy in LC

956 Hovhaness, Alan
Transfiguration, Op. 82 (1950)
Med: SATB, T solo
Txt: Mark 9:2-9
Dur: 17'
Pub: CF Peters

957 Hovhaness, Alan
Triptych, Op. 100 (1952)
Med: voicing see below, with 2 ob, 2
      hn, hp, celesta, str
Txt: see below
Dur: see below
Mss: LC
Src: LC
Rev: *Christian Science Monitor*, May 12,
      1955.
      1a. Ave Maria (SSAA; LU; 3')
      1b. As on the night (S solo; George
      Wither; 16')
      2. The Beatitudes (SATB; Matthew
      5:1-12; 7')

3. Easter cantata (see separate listing above, No. 894)

958 Hovhaness, Alan
Unto thee, O God, Op. 87, No. 2 (1951)
Med: SATB
Txt: Ps. 75:1
Dur: 2'
Pub: AMP
Mss: LC

959 Hovhaness, Alan
The voice of the Lord, Op. 25 (1937)
Med: SATB, T solo, org
Src: Grove

960 Hovhaness, Alan
Watchman, tell us of the night, Op. 34b (c.1962)
Med: SATB, B solo, ob, clar, str or kybd
Txt: John Bowring
Dur: 5'
Pub: CF Peters
Mss: LC

961 Hovhaness, Alan
The waves unbuild the wasting shore, Op. 376 (1982?)
Med: SATB, T solo, org
Src: Grove

962 Hovhaness, Alan
The way of Jesus, Op. 279 (1974)
Med: SATB, STB soli, cong, 3 gtr, orch
Txt: drawn from Bible, et al.
Dur: 1 hr, 50'
Pub: Mount Tahoma Music Publ., copies in LC and Harvard
Rev: New York *Times*, Feb 23, 1975.

963 Hovhaness, Alan
Wind drum, Op. 183 (1962)

Med: unison vv, ch. orch
Src: Grove

964 Hovhaness, Alan
Why hast thou cast us off?, Op. 87, No. 1 (1951)
Med: SATB
Txt: Ps. 74:1, 21
Dur: 3'
Pub: AMP
Mss: LC

965 Hovhaness, Alan
Why hast thou forsaken me?, Op. 24 (1937)
Med: SATB, S solo, org
Txt: biblical
Src: Grove

I

966 Imbrie, Andrew
Drum taps (1960)
Med: SATB, orch
Txt: Walt Whitman
Src: composer

967 Imbrie, Andrew
Introit, gradual, and alleluia for All Saints' Day (1956)
Med: SATB, org
Txt: LU
Src: composer

968 Imbrie, Andrew
Let all the world (1971)
Med: SATB, brass, perc, org
Txt: George Herbert
Src: composer

969 Imbrie, Andrew
On the beach at night (1949)
Med: SATB, str orch
Txt: Walt Whitman

Dur: 12'
Pub: Shawnee Press

970   Imbrie, Andrew
Prometheus bound (1979)
Med: SATB dbl choir, STBar soli, orch
Txt: Aeschylus
Dur: 40'
Pub: unpubl.
Mss: University of California at Berkeley
Src: Dox
Rev: *American Choral Review*, 23/2 (April, 1981) p3-10.

971   Imbrie, Andrew
Psalm 42 (As the hart panteth) (1942)
Med: TTBB, org
Txt: Ps. 42:1-2, 5, 7-8, 11
Dur: 6'
Pub: CF Peters

972   Imbrie, Andrew
Requiem, in memoriam John H. Imbrie (1984)
Med: SATB, S solo, orch
Txt: LU, Wm. Blake, John Donne, George Herbert
Src: composer

973   Imbrie, Andrew
Song for St. Cecilia's Day (1981)
Med: SATB, brass ensemble, perc, fl, 2 vln, 2 pnos
Txt: John Dryden
Dur: 15'
Pub: unpubl.
Mss: University of California at Berkeley
Src: Dox
Rev: San Francisco *Chronicle*, June 4, 1982.

974   Imbrie, Andrew
Three songs (1965)
Med: SATB
Txt: see below
Dur: 12'
Pub: Shawnee Press
A wind has blown the rain away (e.e. cummings)
Love distills desire upon the eyes (Euripides)
The serpent (Theodore Roethke)

975   Imbrie, Andrew
Two Christmas carols (1955)
Med: male voices, pno
Src: composer
Quid petis, o fili?
In die nativitatis

J

976   Jacobi, Frederick
Ahavas Olom (1945)
Med: SATB, cantor, org
Txt: liturgical Hebrew
Dur: 2'30"
Mss: LC
Src: LC

977   Jacobi, Frederick
Ashrey Haish (1949)
Med: chorus, str
Txt: M. Zaira
Src: Grove

978   Jacobi, Frederick
Avrit le-Shabbat (Friday evening service No. 2) (1952)
Med: SATB, cantor, org
Txt: liturgical Hebrew
Dur: 30'
Pub: Transcontinental Music Publishers
Mss: LC

979   Jacobi, Frederick
Contemplation (1946)
Med: SATB, pno (opt. 2nd pno)
Txt: William Blake
Dur: 4'30"
Pub: EB Marks
Mss: LC
Rev: MLA *Notes* 10 (June, 1953) p493-4

980   Jacobi, Frederick
Fugue (1912?)
Med: SATB
Txt: no text
Dur: 3'
Pub: unpubl.
Mss: LC

981   Jacobi, Frederick
Kaddish (1946)
Med: SATB, cantor, org
Txt: liturgical Hebrew
Dur: 3'
Pub: unpubl.
Mss: LC

982   Jacobi, Frederick
May the words (1952)
Med: SATB, opt. org
Txt: not indicated
Dur: 2'
Pub: Transcontinental Music Publishers
Mss: LC (listed under "O may the words")

983   Jacobi, Frederick
Ode to Zion (c.1948)
Med: SATB, 2 hp
Txt: trad. Hebrew
Dur: 3'
Pub: unpubl.
Mss: LC

984   Jacobi, Frederick
The poet in the desert (1925)
Med: SATB div, orch

Txt: C.E.S. Wood
Dur: 20'
Pub: privately publ.; copy in NYPL
Mss: LC and NYPL

985   Jacobi, Frederick
Psalmody (1918)
Med: SATB, SSBar soli, orch
Txt: Book of Psalms
Dur: 15'
Pub: unpubl.
Mss: LC

986   Jacobi, Frederick
Saadia (1942)
Med: male vv
Src: Grove

987   Jacobi, Frederick
Sabbath evening service (1931)
Med: SATB, TBar soli, org
Txt: liturgical Hebrew
Dur: 13'
Pub: NY: Bloch Publishing; copy in NYPL

988   Jacobi, Frederick
Two pieces for women's chorus (n.d.)
Med: SSAA, pno
Txt: French, no author indicated
Dur: 6'
Pub: unpubl.
Mss: LC
       Grisélidis
       Les tricoteuses

989   James, Philip
Anthem for a church anniversary (1970)
Med: SATB, opt junior choir, cong, org
Txt: biblical
Dur: 12'
Pub: unpubl.
Src: James

990 James, Philip
As now the sun's declining rays, Op. 2, No. 1 (1912, rev. 1941)
Med: SATB
Txt: Charles Coffin
Dur: 4'
Pub: HW Gray

991 James, Philip
Away in a manger (1941, rev. 1948)
Med: SATB
Txt: Martin Luther
Dur: 4'
Pub: HW Gray

992 James, Philip
A ballad of trees and the master, Op. 22, No. 1 (1919)
Med: SATB
Txt: Sidney Lanier
Dur: 4'
Pub: Ditson

993 James, Philip
Behold, God is our salvation (1968?)
Med: SATB, S solo, org
Txt: Isaiah 12:2-4
Dur: 3'
Pub: unpubl.
Mss: LC

994 James, Philip
Beloved land (1947)
Med: SATB, pno
Txt: Brychan B. Powell
Dur: 3'
Pub: Leeds Music

995 James, Philip
Benedictus es Domine (1922)
Med: SATB, org
Txt: LU
Dur: 5'
Pub: HW Gray

996 James, Philip
Blessed are ye that hunger (1944)
Med: SATB, org
Txt: Luke 6
Dur: 5'
Pub: HW Gray

997 James, Philip
Blessed be the king (1922, rev. 1951)
Med: SATB, org
Txt: Luke, John, Isaiah
Dur: 4'30"
Pub: HW Gray

998 James, Philip
By the waters of Babylon (1920)
Med: SATB, pno
Txt: Ps. 137
Dur: 4'
Pub: HW Gray
N.B. Also arr. for SSAA, TTBB.

999 James, Philip
Child Jesus came to earth (1912)
Med: SATB
Txt: Hans Christian Andersen
Dur: 4'
Pub: Boston Music Co.

1000 James, Philip
The chimes of the Metropolitan tower (1912, rev. 1969)
Med: TTBB
Txt: Maria Sagari de Claire
Dur: 4'
Pub: unpubl.

1001 James, Philip
Chorus of shepherds and angels (1956)
Med: SSA, str quartet or str orch
Txt: W.H. Auden
Dur: 12'
Pub: Ricordi

1002   James, Philip
Christ is born (1912)
Med: SATB, org
Txt: J.M. Neale
Dur: 4'
Pub: Boston Music Co.

1003   James, Philip
Close thine eyes, and sleep secure
    (c.1949)
Med: SATB
Txt: King Charles I
Dur: 4'
Pub: Galaxy

1004   James, Philip
The cloud of witnesses (1958)
Med: SATB, org
Txt: Hebrews 11:35-12:2
Dur: 10'
Pub: unpubl.

1005   James, Philip
Come Holy Spirit (1964)
Med: SATB, SBar soli, org
Txt: Isaac Watts
Dur: 4'
Pub: HW Gray

1006   James, Philip
Creation's Lord, we give thee thanks
    (1956)
Med: SATB, org
Txt: William DeWitt Hyde
Dur: 1'
Pub: unpubl.

1007   James, Philip
The day is gently sinking to a close
    (1912)
Med: SATB, Bar solo, org
Txt: C. Wordsworth
Dur: 5'
Pub: G Schirmer

1008   James, Philip
Devouring time (1926)
Med: TTBB
Txt: William Shakespeare
Dur: 4'
Pub: Ditson
Mss: LC

1009   James, Philip
Eruditus in verbo reperiet bona (1939)
Med: TTBB
Txt: Proverbs 16:20-23
Dur: 3'30"
Pub: G Schirmer

1010   James, Philip
Founded for freedom (1940)
Med: SATB, orch
Txt: Francis Hartman Markoe
Dur: 48'30"
Pub: unpubl.
Mss: LC

1011   James, Philip
General William Booth enters into
    heaven (1932)
Med: TTBB, tpt, tbn, tamb, bass drum,
        tam-tam, 2 pnos
Txt: Vachel Lindsay
Dur: 14'
Pub: M Witmark

1012   James, Philip
God be in my head (1924)
Med: TTBB
Txt: anon 16th cent.
Dur: 4'
Pub: HW Gray

1013   James, Philip
God, creation's secret force (1939)
Med: SATB div
Txt: St. Ambrose, trans. J.M. Neale
Dur: 4'
Pub: Galaxy

1014   James, Philip
God grant us the serenity (1965)
Med: SATB, org
Txt: Reinhold Niebuhr
Dur: 2'30"
Pub: HW Gray

1015   James, Philip
Gwilym Gwent (1948)
Med: TTBB
Txt: Brychan B. Powell
Dur: 4'
Pub: HW Gray

1016   James, Philip
Hail, dear conqueror! (1916)
Med: SATB, org
Txt: Isaiah 48:20
Dur: 10'
Pub: G Schirmer

1017   James, Philip
Hail, glorious Lord (1938)
Med: SATB
Txt: anon.
Dur: 4'
Pub: HW Gray

1018   James, Philip
Hark! a thrilling voice is sounding (1958)
Med: SATB or SAB, S solo, org
Txt: 6th cent. Latin, trans. Ed. Caswall
Dur: 4'
Pub: HW Gray
Mss: LC

1019   James, Philip
Hear, O my people (1925)
Med: SATB, org
Txt: James G. Chesterman
Dur: 15'
Pub: HW Gray

1020   James, Philip
Home over the hill (1942)
Med: SSA, pno
Txt: Robert Nathan
Dur: 3'30"
Pub: Presser
N.B. Originally for solo voice, titled *A hush song.*

1021   James, Philip
I am the vine, ye are the branches (1916)
Med: SATB or SAB, S solo, org
Txt: John 25:4-5, 7, 12
Dur: 5'
Pub: NY: R.L. Huntzinger; copy in LC

1022   James, Philip
I have considered the days of old (1916, rev. 1944)
Med: SATB, org
Txt: Ps. 77
Dur: 3'30"
Pub: Ditson

1023   James, Philip
I know a maiden fair to see (1967)
Med: SATB, str
Txt: Henry W. Longfellow
Dur: 4'
Pub: unpubl.

1024   James, Philip
I must, and I will get married (1953)
Med: SATB
Txt: trad.
Dur: 2'30"
Pub: Presser

1025   James, Philip
Let us now praise famous men (1965)
Med: SATB, org, opt. chimes
Txt: Ecclesiastes 44:1-4
Dur: 4'
Pub: unpubl.
Src: James

1026 James, Philip
The light of God, Op. 27 (1920)
Med: SATB, TBar soli, orch
Txt: Frederick H. Martens
Dur: 25'
Pub: HW Gray
Mss: LC

1027 James, Philip
Little room o'dreams (1916)
Med: SSA, pno
Txt: Gertrude Brooke Hamilton
Dur: 2'
Pub: unpubl.
Mss: LC
N.B. Originally for solo voice.

1028 James, Philip
The Lord is my shepherd (1926)
Med: SATB, S solo, org
Txt: Ps. 23
Dur: 5'
Pub: HW Gray

1029 James, Philip
Love's springtide (1924)
Med: TTBB
Txt: Frank Dempster Sherman
Dur: 3'
Pub: HW Gray

1030 James, Philip
Lullaby (1912)
Med: SSAA, kybd
Txt: anon.
Dur: 3'
Pub: G Schirmer; Galaxy (with alter-
        nate title: *Tender vigil*)

1031 James, Philip
Magnificat (1910)
Med: SATB, STBar soli, org
Txt: LU
Dur: 15'
Pub: G Schirmer

1032 James, Philip
The marsh of Rhuddlan (1941)
Med: TTBB, pno
Txt: trad. Welsh
Dur: 4'
Pub: Galaxy
N.B. Also arr. for SATB, SSA.

1033 James, Philip
Mass in honor of St. Francis of Assisi
  (1965)
Med: unison vv, cong, org
Txt: LU
Dur: 10'
Pub: unpubl.
Src: James

1034 James, Philip
A May song (1917)
Med: SATB, pno
Txt: Alice Britton Nichols
Dur: 2'
Pub: unpubl.
Mss: LC

1035 James, Philip
A million little diamonds (1916?)
Med: SSA, pno
Txt: Mary Francis Butts
Dur: 3'
Pub: unpubl.

1036 James, Philip
Missa brevis (1963)
Med: SATB, org
Txt: LU
Dur: 12'
Pub: J Fischer
N.B. Later revised as the *Mass in honor
        of St. Mark* (1966).

1037 James, Philip
Missa imaginum (1929)
Med: SATB, org or orch

Txt: LU
Dur: 17'
Pub: HW Gray
N.B. Later revised as *Mass of the pictures*
(1966).

1038   James, Philip
My little pretty one (1918)
Med: SSA, pno
Txt: anon., 17th century
Dur: 3'30"
Pub: G Schirmer

1039   James, Philip
The mystic borderland (1941, rev.
1956)
Med: TTBB, opt. gong
Txt: Helen Field Fischer
Dur: 3'30"
Pub: unpubl.

1040   James, Philip
*The nightingale of Bethlehem: a legend
of the Nativity, Op. 24* (1920,
rev. 1923)
Med: SATB, SAB soli, org, opt. fl and
ob, or 2 vln
Txt: Frederick H. Martens
Dur: 30'
Pub: HW Gray
Mss: LC

1041   James, Philip
The nun, Op. 30 (1922)
Med: SSAA, A solo, pno
Txt: Ludwig Uhland, trans. Martha
Martin
Dur: 9'
Pub: HW Gray
N.B. Arr. for orchestra, 1923.

1042   James, Philip
O be joyful in the Lord (1915)
Med: SATB, kybd
Txt: Ps. 100

Dur: 2'30"
Pub: Ditson

1043   James, Philip
O blest is he that cometh (1922)
Med: SATB, S solo, org
Txt: Luke 19, John 12, Isaiah 61-63
Dur: 4'
Pub: HW Gray

1044   James, Philip
O saving victim (1935)
Med: SATB
Txt: LU
Dur: 4'
Pub: HW Gray

1045   James, Philip
Pat works on the railway (1953)
Med: SATB, pno
Txt: trad.
Dur: 4'
Pub: Presser

1046   James, Philip
Phillis (1912)
Med: SSAA, pno
Txt: Sir Charles Sedley
Dur: 2'
Pub: G Schirmer

1047   James, Philip
The pride of May (1913)
Med: SATB
Txt: Thomas Weelkes
Dur: 3'
Pub: HW Gray

1048   James, Philip
Psalm 117 (1944, rev. 1956)
Med: SATB, org or orch
Txt: Ps. 117
Dur: 4'30"
Pub: G Schirmer
Mss: LC

1049 James, Philip
Psalm 149, "Cantate Domino"
(1959)
Med: SATB, S solo, org, opt. 3 tpt, 2
tbn
Txt: Ps. 149
Dur: 5'
Pub: HW Gray
Mss: LC

1050 James, Philip
Psalm 150 (1940, rev. 1956)
Med: SATB, orch
Txt: Ps. 150
Dur: 7'
Pub: HW Gray

1051 James, Philip
Shirat ha-yam (1920, rev. 1958)
Med: SATB, SATB soli, orch
Txt: Frederick H. Martens
Dur: 40'
Pub: unpubl.
Mss: LC
　　Song of the sea
　　The triumph of Israel

1052 James, Philip
Skyscraper romance: the typist and the
mailman (c.1949)
Med: SSA, SBar soli, pno
Txt: Amy Bonner
Dur: 15'
Pub: Leeds Music

1053 James, Philip
A song of the future (1922)
Med: SATBB dbl choir
Txt: Sidney Lanier
Dur: 8'
Pub: HW Gray
Mss: LC

1054 James, Philip
The song of the miners (1947)
Med: TTBB, pno
Txt: Brychan B. Powell
Dur: 4'
Pub: HW Gray

1055 James, Philip
Spring in Mentone (1916)
Med: SSA, A solo, ch. orch
Txt: Frederick H. Martens
Dur: 20'
Pub: copy in NYPL
N.B. Original title: *Spring in Vienna.*

1056 James, Philip
A spring song (1916)
Med: SSA, pno
Txt: Thomas Nash
Dur: 1'
Pub: HW Gray

1057 James, Philip
Stabat mater speciosa, Op. 21 (1921,
　　rev. 1930)
Med: SATB, SBar soli, orch
Txt: LU, trans. J.M. Neale
Dur: 20'
Pub: HW Gray

1058 James, Philip
Te Deum (1910)
Med: SATB, org
Txt: LU
Dur: 10'
Pub: G Schirmer

1059 James, Philip
To an antique stiletto, Op. 111,
　　No. 2 (1922)
Med: TTBB, pno
Txt: Berton Braley
Dur: 3'
Pub: HW Gray

1060   James, Philip
To Cecilia (1966)
Med: SATB, S solo, ch. orch
Txt: W.H. Auden
Dur: 12'
Pub: unpubl.

1061   James, Philip
Tuku, Tuku, Tuku I'm calling (1937)
Med: SATB, pno
Txt: trad. Finnish
Dur: 4'
Pub: Galaxy

1062   James, Philip
The victors (1915, rev. 1955)
Med: TTBB
Txt: Charles Hanson Towne
Dur: 5'
Pub: Ditson

1063   James, Philip
The victory riders, Op. 25, No. 2
(1921, rev. 1930)
Med: TTBB, orch
Txt: Theodosia Garrison
Dur: 14'
Pub: HW Gray
Mss: LC
N.B. Originally for solo voice.

1064   James, Philip
The wait's carol (1941)
Med: SATB, org
Txt: Barbara Young
Dur: 3'
Pub: HW Gray
N.B. Also arr. for SA, kybd.

1065   James, Philip
We pray thee, gracious Lord (1914)
Med: SATB
Txt: Lillian C. Pitcher
Dur: 2'30"
Pub: G Schirmer

1066   James, Philip
Wisdom crieth without (1939)
Med: unison, pno
Txt: Proverbs 1:20-22; 3:13-15
Dur: 3'30"
Pub: HW Gray

1067   James, Philip
The wonder song (1944)
Med: SATB, ob, and 2 bsn or org
Txt: St. Germanus, trans. J.M. Neale
Dur: 2'30"
Pub: HW Gray

1068   James, Philip
The world of tomorrow (1938, rev.
1944)
Med: SATB, orch
Txt: Velma Hitchcock
Dur: 16'
Pub: HW Gray
Mss: LC

K

1069   Kay, Ulysses
The birds (1968)
Med: SSA, pno
Txt: see below
Dur: 12'
Pub: NY: Duchess Music
        The great black crow (P.J. Bailey)
        The skylark (J. Hogg)
        The peacock (William Cowper)
        The throstle (Alfred Lord Tennyson)
        Answer to a child's questions (Samuel
        T. Coleridge)

1070   Kay, Ulysses
Choral triptych (1962)
Med: SATB, kybd, opt. str
Txt: Ps. 5:1-7; Ps. 13
Dur: 13'
Pub: AMP
Mss: LC

Bib: B98
  Give ear to my words, O Lord
  How long wilt thou forget me, O
    Lord
  Alleluia

1071 Kay, Ulysses
Christmas carol (1943)
Med: SSA
Txt: Sara Teasdale
Dur: 2'30"
Pub: Peer Intl.

1072 Kay, Ulysses
Come away, come away death (1944)
Med: TBB
Txt: William Shakespeare
Dur: 3'
Pub: Peer Intl.
Rev: MLA *Notes* 13 (Mar, 1956) p348

1073 Kay, Ulysses
Dedication (1946)
Med: SATB, pno
Src: Grove
N.B. Later withdrawn by the composer.

1074 Kay, Ulysses
Emily Dickinson set (1964)
Med: SSA, pno
Txt: Emily Dickinson
Dur: 6'
Pub: unpubl.?
Mss: LC
  Elysium is as far
  Indian summer
  Ample make this bed

1075 Kay, Ulysses
Epigrams and hymns (c.1975)
Med: SATB, org
Txt: John Greenleaf Whittier, John
    Murray, Samuel Longfellow
Dur: 7'

Pub: C Fischer
Rev: *BMI* (Jan, 1977) p44

1076 Kay, Ulysses
Festival psalms (1983)
Med: SATB, Bar solo, pno
Src: Grove

1077 Kay, Ulysses
Flowers in the valley (1961)
Med: SATB
Txt: anon.
Dur: 5'
Pub: CF Peters
Mss: copy in LC

1078 Kay, Ulysses
Four hymn-anthems (1965)
Med: SATB, org
Txt: J. Kelbe, Henry W. Longfellow,
    Charles Wesley, S. Longfellow
Src: Grove

1079 Kay, Ulysses
Grace to you, and peace (1955)
Med: SATB, org
Txt: St. Paul
Dur: 7'
Pub: HW Gray
Mss: LC

1080 Kay, Ulysses
Hymn-anthem on the tune "Hanover"
    (1959)
Med: unison, pno
Txt: R. Grant
Dur: 5'
Pub: CF Peters

1081 Kay, Ulysses
Inscriptions from Whitman (1963)
Med: SATB, orch
Txt: Walt Whitman
Dur: 25'

Pub: unpubl.
Mss: copy in LC

1082 Kay, Ulysses
A Lincoln Letter (1953)
Med: SATB, B solo
Txt: Abraham Lincoln
Dur: 4'30"
Pub: CF Peters

1083 Kay, Ulysses
Once there was a man (1969)
Med: SATB, orch
Txt: Randall Caudill
Dur: 18'
Pub: C Fischer
Rev: *American Choral Review* 12/3
(1970) p118; *BMI* (Dec, 1969)
p13; *Music Journal* 28 (Jan, 1970),
p14

1084 Kay, Ulysses
Parables (1970)
Med: SATB, ch. orch
Txt: anon.
Dur: 10'
Pub: NY: Duchess Music
Rev: *BMI* (June, 1971) p16
The old armchair
The hellbound train

1085 Kay, Ulysses
Pentagraph (1972)
Med: women's vv, pno
Txt: see below
Dur: 10'
Pub: Pembroke Music Co.
The miller's song (Isaac Bickerstaffe)
King Arthur (anon.)
To be or not to be (anon.)
The flamingo (Lewis Gaylord Clark)
The monkey's glue (Goldwin Gold-
smith)

1086 Kay, Ulysses
Phoebus, arise (1959)
Med: SATB, SBar soli, orch
Txt: see below
Dur: 30'
Pub: Belwin-Mills
Rev: New York *Herald Tribune*, May
18, 1959; New York *Times*, May
18, 1959.
Prelude (composer)
No! (Thomas Hood)
Tears, flow no more (Lord Herbert of
Cherbury)
Phoebus, arise (William Drummond)
Song (Thomas Middleton and William
Rowley)
The Epicure (Abraham Cowley)
Epilogue (composer)

1087 Kay, Ulysses
Stephen Crane set (1967)
Med: SATB, 13 inst.
Txt: Stephen Crane
Dur: 16'
Pub: NY: Duchess Music
Rev: *BMI* (Apr, 1968) p20; *Music
Journal* 26 (Feb, 1968) p18
Black riders
Mystic shadows
A spirit
War is kind

1088 Kay, Ulysses
Song of Jeremiah (1945, rev. 1947)
Med: SATB, Bar solo, orch
Txt: Book of Jeremiah, arr. J. Moffatt
Dur: 20'
Pub: C Fischer
Rev: Nashville *Banner*, April 24, 1954.
N.B. Originally for SSA.

1089 Kay, Ulysses
To light that shines (1962)
Med: SATB, org

Txt: Samuel Johnson
Src: Grove

1090 Kay, Ulysses
Triple set (1971)
Med: 2 or 3-part men's vv
Txt: see below
Dur: 9'
Pub: NY: Duchess Music
  Ode: to the cuckoo (M. Bruce)
  Had I a heart (R.B. Sheridan)
  A toast (Sheridan)

1091 Kay, Ulysses
Triumvirate (1953)
Med: TTBB
Txt: Ralph W. Emerson, et al.
Dur: 13'
Pub: Peer Intl.
  Music
  The children's hour
  The nightmarch

1092 Kay, Ulysses
Two Dunbar lyrics (1965)
Med: SATB
Txt: Paul Laurence Dunbar
Dur: 10'
Pub: MCA Music
  A starry night
  A madrigal

1093 Kay, Ulysses
Two folksong settings (1975)
Med: SATB
Src: Grove

1094 Kay, Ulysses
Two madrigals (c.1956)
Med: SSATB
Txt: James Wolfe
Dur: 12'
Pub: Leeds Music (No. 1); AMP (No. 2)
  What's in a name?
  How stands the glass around?

1095 Kay, Ulysses
A wreath for waits (1954)
Med: SATB
Txt: trad. Christmas
Dur: 12'
Pub: AMP
Mss: LC
  Lully, lullay
  Noel
  Welcome yule

1096 Kubik, Gail
Abigail Adams (c.1949)
Med: SATB, pno
Txt: Rosemary Benét
Dur: 4'
Pub: G Schirmer

1097 Kubik, Gail
Adam in the garden pinnin' leaves (c.1960)
Med: SATB div, Bar solo
Txt: trad.
Dur: 8'
Pub: Ricordi

1098 Kubik, Gail
As I went a-walking one fine summer's evening (c.1949)
Med: SATB div
Txt: trad.
Dur: 4'
Pub: Southern

1099 Kubik, Gail
Black Jack Davy (c.1949)
Med: SATB div, pno
Txt: trad., arr. composer
Dur: 5'
Pub: Southern

1100 Kubik, Gail
Choral profiles. See individual titles:
  Abigail Adams
  George Washington

Miles Standish
Nancy Hanks
Oliver DeLancey
P.T. Barnum
Peregrine White and Virginia Dare
Pioneer women
Southern ships and settlers
Theodore Roosevelt
Woodrow Wilson

1101 Kubik, Gail
Choral sketches. See individual titles:
Listen to the mocking bird
Oh dear, what can the matter be?
Polly wolly doodle
Wee Cooper O'Fife

1102 Kubik, Gail
A Christmas offering (c.1968)
Med: SATB
Txt: trad.
Dur: 12'
Pub: BH

1103 Kubik, Gail
Christopher Columbus (c.1960)
Med: SATB, pno
Txt: Stephen Vincent Benét
Dur: 9'
Pub: Ricordi

1104 Kubik, Gail
Creep along, Moses (c.1949)
Med: SATB div
Txt: trad., arr. composer
Dur: 4'
Pub: Southern

1105 Kubik, Gail
Daniel Drew, Op. 10, No. 1
(c.1940)
Med: SATB, cello, bass or pno
Txt: Rosemary and Stephen Vincent
      Benét

Dur: 6'30"
Pub: Arrow Music Press

1106 Kubik, Gail
George Washington (c.1960)
Med: SATB, pno
Txt: Stephen Vincent Benét
Dur: 9'
Pub: Ricordi

1107 Kubik, Gail
He's goin' away (c.1949)
Med: SATB, SABar soli
Txt: trad.
Dur: 5'
Pub: G Schirmer

1108 Kubik, Gail
Hop up, my ladies (1948)
Med: TTBB, vln solo
Txt: trad., with additional text by
      composer
Dur: 4'30"
Pub: Southern

1109 Kubik, Gail
How lovely thy place (c.1953)
Med: SATB
Txt: Ps. 84
Dur: 3'
Pub: HW Gray

1110 Kubik, Gail
I ride an old paint (c.1960)
Med: SATB, SBar soli
Txt: trad.
Dur: 4'30"
Pub: Ricordi

1111 Kubik, Gail
In praise of Johnny Appleseed (c.1962)
Med: SATB, Bar solo, orch
Txt: Vachel Lindsay
Dur: 50'
Pub: Franco Colombo

1112   Kubik, Gail
John Henry (c.1960)
Med: TTBB, BarB soli, pno
Txt: trad.
Dur: 8'
Pub: Ricordi

1113   Kubik, Gail
Johnny Stiles (c.1950)
Med: TTBB, pno
Txt: trad.
Dur: 4'
Pub: Southern

1114   Kubik, Gail
Listen to the mocking bird (c.1949)
Med: SATB div
Txt: trad.
Dur: 4'
Pub: Southern

1115   Kubik, Gail
Litany and prayer (c.1953)
Med: TTBB, brass, perc
Txt: Book of Common Prayer
Dur: 18'
Pub: Southern
Rev: *Choral Guide* 7 (Apr, 1954) p33;
       MLA *Notes* 11 (June, 1954) p438
       and 14 (Sept, 1957) p18-19;
       Musical America 75 (Feb 1, 1955)
       p26
    Intercession for the war
    Deliverance from sin and guidance in
       the ways of peace

1116   Kubik, Gail
Little bird, little bird (c.1949)
Med: SATB dbl choir, pno
Txt: trad.
Dur: 4'
Pub: Southern
N.B. Also arr. for SSAA dbl choir.

1117   Kubik, Gail
Loch Lomond (c.1949)
Med: SATB
Txt: trad.
Dur: 5'
Pub: G Schirmer

1118   Kubik, Gail
Lolly too-dum (c.1960)
Med: SATB div, SA soli, pno
Txt: trad., with additional text by
       composer
Dur: 4'30"
Pub: Ricordi

1119   Kubik, Gail
Magic, magic, magic! (c.1977)
Med: SATB, AT solo, nar, pno or
       orch
Txt: J. Allred and E. Walter
Dur: 12'
Pub: Lawson-Gould
    Invocation
    Spell to bring the longed for letter
    E-xu-zi-nho

1120   Kubik, Gail
March of the men of Harlech (c.1950)
Med: SATB div, pno
Txt: William Duthie
Dur: 4'
Pub: Southern

1121   Kubik, Gail
Miles Standish (c.1950)
Med: SATB dbl choir, pno
Txt: Stephen Vincent Benét
Dur: 4'30"
Pub: Southern
Rev: *Music Clubs Magazine* (Feb, 1951)
       p19

1122   Kubik, Gail
A mirror for the sky (c.1958)
Med: SATB, T solo, orch

Txt: Jessamyn West
Dur: 60'
Pub: Ricordi
Rev: MLA *Notes* 15 (Mar, 1958) p254–5
N.B. A choral suite from the folk opera
    of the same title.
    Introduction
    My Lord's a forefended place
    Spendin' ain't a sin
    The little red fox
    Along about cockcrow
    Birthday song
    Freedom is a hard-bought thing

1123   Kubik, Gail
The monotony song (c.1960)
Med: TTBB, Bar solo, pno
Txt: Theodore Roethke
Dur: 8'
Pub: Ricordi

1124   Kubik, Gail
Nancy Hanks (c.1949)
Med: SATB, ABar soli, pno
Txt: Rosemary Benét
Dur: 4'30"
Pub: G Schirmer

1125   Kubik, Gail
Oh dear, what can the matter be?
   (c.1951)
Med: SSAA
Txt: trad.
Dur: 5'
Pub: G Schirmer

1126   Kubik, Gail
Oh, my liver and my lungs (c.1949)
Med: SATTBB
Txt: trad.
Dur: 6'
Pub: Southern

1127   Kubik, Gail
Oliver DeLancey (c.1949)
Med: TTBB, pno
Txt: Stephen Vincent Benét
Dur: 5'
Pub: G Schirmer

1128   Kubik, Gail
P.T. Barnum (c.1960)
Med: SATB dbl choir, SATB soli, pno
Txt: Stephen Vincent Benét
Dur: 14'
Pub: Ricordi

1129   Kubik, Gail
Peregrine White and Virginia Dare
   (c.1950)
Med: SAA
Txt: Stephen Vincent Benét
Dur: 4'30"
Pub: Southern

1130   Kubik, Gail
Pioneer women (c.1950)
Med: SATB div, pno
Txt: not indicated
Dur: 5'
Pub: Southern

1131   Kubik, Gail
Polly-wolly-doodle (c.1949)
Med: SATB, ST soli
Txt: trad.
Dur: 4'
Pub: G Schirmer
N.B. Also arr. for TTBB.

1132   Kubik, Gail
A record of our time (c.1975)
Med: SATB, ST soli, nar, orch
Txt: Mark Twain, Bible, W.B. Yeats,
    Zygelbojm Vanzetti, C. Badiali,
    J. J. Chapman; compiled by com-
    poser and Harvey Swados
Dur: 40'

Pub: MCA Music
Rev: *ASCAP* 5/1 (1971) p41; *Choral Journal* (March, 1977); *Instrumentalist* 25 (Feb, 1971) p26-7; *Music Educators Journal* 35 (Feb, 1977) p94; *Music Journal* 35 (Jan, 1977) p34-5; *World of Music* 13/2 (1971) p74

1133   Kubik, Gail
Scholastica: a medieval set (c.1972)
Med: SATB, TBar soli
Txt: anon. Latin, trans. Quincy Howe
Dur: 20'
Pub: Lawson-Gould
   Semester's end
   Alas, this world
   Questions trinitarian
   A nun at springtime
   Gaudeamus igitur

1134   Kubik, Gail
Southern ships and settlers (c.1950)
Med: SATB div
Txt: Stephen Vincent Benét
Dur: 5'30"
Pub: Southern

1135   Kubik, Gail
Tee-roo (c.1949)
Med: SATB, pno (incidental soli)
Txt: trad., arr. composer
Dur: 5'
Pub: G Schirmer
N.B. Also arr. for TTBB.

1136   Kubik, Gail
Theodore Roosevelt (c.1950)
Med: SATB div, pno
Txt: Stephen Vincent Benét
Dur: 5'30"
Pub: Southern
Rev: *Music Clubs Magazine* 30 (Feb, 1951) p19

1137   Kubik, Gail
Wee Cooper O'Fife (c.1950)
Med: SATB div
Txt: trad.
Dur: 10'
Pub: Southern

1138   Kubik, Gail
When I was but a maiden (c.1960)
Med: SATB div, SBar soli
Txt: trad.
Dur: 12'
Pub: Ricordi

1139   Kubik, Gail
Woodrow Wilson (c.1950)
Med: SATB div
Txt: Stephen Vincent Benét
Dur: 5'
Pub: Southern
Rev: *Music Clubs Magazine* (Feb, 1951) p19

L

1140   Larsen, Libby
...and sparrows everywhere (c.1985)
Med: SATB
Txt: Keith Gunderson
Dur: 4'
Pub: EC Schirmer
   Chameleon wedding
   Snail
   Hawks and sparrows

1141   Larsen, Libby
A Creely collection (c.1983)
Med: SATB, T solo, fl, pno, perc
Txt: Richard Creely
Dur: 9'
Pub: AMC

1142 Larsen, Libby
Dance set (1980)
Med: SATB, clar, cello, drum set, pno
Txt: nonsense text
Dur: 9'
Pub: AMC

1143 Larsen, Libby
Double joy (c.1982)
Med: SATB div, handbells, org
Txt: Michael Thwaites
Dur: 5'30"
Pub: EC Schirmer

1144 Larsen, Libby
A garden wall (c.1987)
Med: unison, nar, Orff inst., bells
Txt: composer
Dur: 8'
Pub: EC Schirmer

1145 Larsen, Libby
In a winter garden (1982)
Med: SATB, ST soli, orch
Txt: Patricia Hampl
Dur: 40'
Pub: AMC

1146 Larsen, Libby
Lacrimosa Christe (1974)
Med: SATB, soli, orch
Src: Grove

1147 Larsen, Libby
Peace, perfect peace (c.1986)
Med: SATB
Txt: Isaiah 26:3, adapt. Edward
    Bickersteth
Dur: 3'
Pub: EC Schirmer

1148 Larsen, Libby
Refuge (c.1988)
Med: SSAA
Txt: Sara Teasdale

Dur: 4'30"
Pub: EC Schirmer

1149 Larsen, Libby
Ringeltanze (c.1983)
Med: SATB, handbells, str
Txt: not indicated
Dur: 15'
Pub: EC Schirmer
    Welcome yule
    O hark the bell's glad song
    Beautiful star
    Le petit nouveau né
    At Christmas be merry
    The shepherds all are waking

1150 Larsen, Libby
She's like a swallow (c.1988)
Med: SATB, flute or S solo, pno
Txt: trad.
Dur: 4'
Pub: EC Schirmer

1151 Larsen, Libby
Songs of youth and pleasure (c.1986)
Med: SATB
Txt: not indicated
Dur: 13'
Pub: EC Schirmer
    Song for a dance
    Pluck the fruit and taste the pleasure
    Kisses
    Hey nonny no!

1152 Larsen, Libby
Who cannot weep, come learn of me
    (c.1986)
Med: SSAA
Txt: medieval English
Dur: 4'30"
Pub: EC Schirmer
N.B. Other title: *Virgin's lament over her
    dead son.*

1153 Levy, Marvin David
Alice in Wonderland (c.1966)
Med: SSA, bsn or cello or pno
Txt: Lewis Carroll
Dur: 8'
Pub: BH
    Turtle soup
    The little crocodile
    The little fishes
    The lobster quadrille

1154 Levy, Marvin David
Christmas oratorio (1959)
Src: Grove

1155 Levy, Marvin David
During wind and rain (c.1965)
Med: SATB, pno
Txt: Thomas Hardy
Dur: 11'
Pub: BH

1156 Levy, Marvin David
For the time being (c.1959)
Med: SATB, soli, nar, orch
Txt: W.H. Auden
Dur: 1 hr, 45'
Pub: Ricordi
Rev: MLA *Notes* 19 (Dec, 1961) p151;
    New York *Times*, Dec. 8, 1959.
    Advent
    The annunciation
    The temptation of Joseph
    The summons
    The vision of the shepherds
    At the manger
    Massacre of the innocents
    Flight into Egypt

1157 Levy, Marvin David
Masada (1973)
Med: SATB, T solo, nar, orch, org, tape
Txt: composer, from Bible, Isaac Lam-
    don, Emma Lazarus, *The Chron-*
    icles of Josephus

Dur: 75'
Pub: unpubl.
Mss: composer
Src: Dox
Rev: *ACA Bulletin* 6/4 (1957); Cin-
    cinnati *Enquirer*, Feb. 2, 1957,
    p20.

1158 Levy, Marvin David
Sacred service (1964)
Src: Grove

M

1159 Mechem, Kirke
American madrigals, Op. 46 (c.1976)
Med: SATB, orch or pno
Txt: American folk songs, adapt.
    composer
Dur: 17'
Pub: C Fischer
    Kind miss
    He's gone away
    Kansas boys
    Adam's bride
    New York girls

1160 Mechem, Kirke
Las Americas unidas (1986)
Med: SATB, S solo, opt. children, org,
    2 tpt, glockenspiel, bass
Txt: from a publication of the Beyond
    War Foundation, in Spanish and
    English
Dur: 6'
Pub: G Schirmer

1161 Mechem, Kirke
The ballad of Befana, Op. 35a,
    No. 2 (1972)
Med: SATB, amplified gtr
Txt: Phyllis McGinley
Dur: 5'
Pub: EC Schirmer

1162   Mechem, Kirke
Canon law for newlyweds, Op. 28
   (1965)
Med: SATB
Txt: Proverbs 4:1-2
Dur: 9'
Pub: EC Schirmer

1163   Mechem, Kirke
Catch 22 (and 21 other catches and
   canons), Op. 50 (c.1985)
Med: 2-9 part choir, opt. pno, cello,
   bells
Txt: composer and others
Dur: various short works
Pub: G. Schirmer

1164   Mechem, Kirke
The children of David, Op. 37 (1974)
Med: SATB, M solo, org
Txt: see below
Dur: 26'
Pub: BH
Rev: San Francisco *Chronicle*, Feb. 2,
   1972.
Bib: B142, 154
   Psalm (C. Dinkage)
   Joy (R. Jeffers)
   The song of David (C. Smart)
   Man of my own people (F.K. Frank)
   Pied beauty (Gerard Manley Hopkins)

1165   Mechem, Kirke
A choral tribute (c.1985)
Med: SATB, opt. pno
Txt: composer
Dur: 11'
Pub: G Schirmer

1166   Mechem, Kirke
Christmas carol, Op. 35a, No. 1
   (1972)
Med: SSAA, gtr
Txt: trad.

Dur: 3'30"
Pub: EC Schirmer

1167   Mechem, Kirke
English girls (c.1973)
Med: TBB, pno
Txt: see below
Dur: 8'
Pub: BH
   Jenny kissed me (Leigh Hunt)
   On Julia's voice (Robert Herrick)
   To Celia (Ben Jonson)

1168   Mechem, Kirke
Epigrams and epitaphs: 21 catches
   and canons, Op. 13 (1963)
Med: SATB
Txt: various, mostly anon.
Dur: various very short pieces
Pub: EC Schirmer

1169   Mechem, Kirke
Five centuries of spring, Op. 24
   (c.1968)
Med: SATB
Txt: see below
Dur: 13'
Pub: Presser
   Spring (Thomas Nash)
   From you have I been absent (Wm.
   Shakespeare)
   Laughing song (Wm. Blake)
   Loveliest of trees (A.E. Housman)
   Spring (Edna St. Vincent Millay)

1170   Mechem, Kirke
Forsake me not, O Lord, Op. 23
   (1964)
Med: SATB
Txt: Ps. 38; Eccl. 12
Dur: 6'
Pub: EC Schirmer

1171 Mechem, Kirke
*Give thanks unto the Lord, Op. 2,
No. 3* (1959)
Med: SSATTB
Txt: Ps. 136:1-5
Dur: 4'
Pub: CF Peters

1172 Mechem, Kirke
I will sing alleluia, Op. 40, No. 2
(1972)
Med: SATB, kybd
Txt: Ps. 92, 104
Dur: 6'
Pub: EC Schirmer
Bib: B142

1173 Mechem, Kirke
In the land of Morgenstern, Op. 21
(1963)
Med: SATB
Txt: Christian Morgenstern
Dur: 10'
Pub: AMP
   The questionnaire
   The odor-organ
   The lattice fence

1174 Mechem, Kirke
*Island in space: dona nobis pacem,
Op. 54* (1991)
Med: SATB
Txt: composer, after Russell
   Schweickart and Archibald Mac-
   Leish
Dur: 7'
Pub: G Schirmer

1175 Mechem, Kirke
*It is good to give thanks, Op.41,
No. 2* (1974)
Med: SATB, kybd
Txt: Ps. 92
Dur: 4'

Pub: C Fischer
Bib: B142, 154

1176 Mechem, Kirke
The king's contest, Op. 42 (1974)
Med: SATB, MTBar soli, ch. orch
Txt: Apocrypha (Esdras I:3-4)
Dur: 27'
Pub: C Fischer
Rev: San Francisco *Examiner,* June 17,
   1974.

1177 Mechem, Kirke
Lament for a choral conductor (c.1972)
Med: any chorus, inst.
Txt: Samuel T. Coleridge and Sir J.C.
   Squire
Dur: 2'
Pub: National Music Publishers

1178 Mechem, Kirke
*Let all mortal flesh keep silence,
Op. 26* (n.d.)
Med: SATB
Txt: LU
Dur: 4'
Pub: EC Schirmer

1179 Mechem, Kirke
The lighthearted lovers, Op. 47a
(c.1983)
Med: SATB, pno
Txt: John Dryden
Dur: 3'30"
Pub: G Schirmer

1180 Mechem, Kirke
*The Lord is in his holy temple
(Introit), Op. 7, No. 1* (1953)
Med: SATB, org
Txt: Habakkuk 2:20; Ps. 25:1, 4
Dur: 1'30"
Pub: EC Schirmer
Bib: B142

1181   Mechem, Kirke
Make a joyful noise unto the Lord,
Op. 2, No. 1 (1951)
Med: SATB
Txt: Ps. 100
Dur: 3'
Pub: EC Schirmer

1182   Mechem, Kirke
O Oriens, Op. 3 (1951)
Med: SATB
Txt: LU
Dur: 4'
Pub: EC Schirmer

1183   Mechem, Kirke
Praise him!, Op. 34 (1969)
Med: SATB, winds or pno
Txt: see below
Dur: 12'
Pub: EC Schirmer
    Greet him with joy (Carol Dinkage)
    Glory be to God (Gerard Manley
    Hopkins)

1184   Mechem, Kirke
Psalm 23, Op. 41, No. 1 (1974)
Med: SATB, kybd, cello
Txt: Ps. 23
Dur: 4'
Pub: C Fischer
Bib: B154

1185   Mechem, Kirke
Rules for behavior, Op. 7, No. 3
    (1954)
Med: SATB, pno
Txt: 18th. century church rules from
    Virginia
Dur: 4'
Pub: Lawson–Gould

1186   Mechem, Kirke
Seven joys of Christmas, Op. 25a
    (1964)

Med: SATB, S solo, opt. kybd or orch
Txt: trad., except (*)
Dur: 13'
Pub: EC Schirmer
    This is the truth
    Ding dong merrily on high
    Joseph dearest, Joseph mine
    Patapan
    New Year song
    Fum! fum! fum!
    *God bless this house (George R.
    Woodward)

1187   Mechem, Kirke
The shepherd and his love, Op. 30
    (1967)
Med: SATB, picc, vla, pno
Txt: Christopher Marlowe, Sir Walter
    Raleigh
Dur: 8'
Pub: EC Schirmer

1188   Mechem, Kirke
Sigh no more ladies, Op. 7, No. 2
    (1957)
Med: SSA, pno
Txt: William Shakespeare
Dur: 3'
Pub: EC Schirmer

1189   Mechem, Kirke
Sing unto the Lord a new song,
    Op. 27 (c.1965)
Med: ST/SAB dbl choir, tpt solo
Txt: Ps. 98:1, 4–6
Dur: 4'
Pub: Mark Foster

1190   Mechem, Kirke
Singing is so good a thing: an
    Elizabethan recreation (c.1967)
Med: SATB, ch. orch
Txt: William Byrd

Dur: 27'
Pub: CF Peters
Rev: MLA *Notes*, March, 1974.

1191 Mechem, Kirke
Songs of wisdom, Op. 14 (1959)
Med: SSATB, SATB soli
Txt: composer, from Old Testament
Dur: 33'
Pub: EC Schirmer
Rev: Palo Alto (Calif.) *Times*, Feb. 16, 1976.
Bib: B154
The song of Moses
A love song
The protest of Job
A song of comfort
A song of praise

1192 Mechem, Kirke
Speech to a crowd, Op. 44 (1974)
Med: SATB, Bar solo, orch
Txt: Archibald MacLeish
Dur: 15'
Pub: National Music Publishers

1193 Mechem, Kirke
Three American folk songs, Op. 6 (1954)
Med: TTBB, pno
Txt: trad.
Dur: 10'
Pub: EC Schirmer
Aunt Rhody
The wayfaring stranger
The blue-tail fly

1194 Mechem, Kirke
Three madrigals, Op. 1 (1953)
Med: SATB
Txt: Kirke F. Mechem (composer's father)
Dur: 7'30"
Pub: AMP
Impromptu

Deny it as she will
Moral precept

1195 Mechem, Kirke
Tourist time, Op. 11 (1957)
Med: SATB, pno
Txt: see below
Dur: 9'
Pub: EC Schirmer
Tourist time (F.R. Scott)
Boston (anon.)
Cologne (S.T. Coleridge)
Texas (composer)
Rome (Edward Lear)

1196 Mechem, Kirke
The tune (c.1965)
Med: SATB
Txt: not indicated
Dur: 1'30"
Pub: EC Schirmer

1197 Mechem, Kirke
Why art thou cast down? (1974)
Med: SAB, kybd
Txt: Book of Psalms
Dur: 4'30"
Pub: C Fischer
Bib: B142

1198 Mechem, Kirke
The winds of May, Op. 17 (c.1965)
Med: SATB div
Txt: Sara Teasdale
Dur: 13'
Pub: EC Schirmer
The tune
Let it be forgotten
Over the roofs
I shall not cease
Song (Love me with your whole heart)

1199 Mechem, Kirke
The winged joy, Op. 22 (1964)
Med: SSAA, S solo, pno

Txt: see below
Dur: 18'
Pub: EC Schirmer
  Love is a terrible thing (G.F. Norton)
  The message (Margaret Vita Sackville-
    West)
  The cynic (Theodosia Garrison)
  A farewell (Harriet Monroe)
  Love came back at fall of dew (Lizette
    Woodworth Reese)
  Red May (A.M.F. Robinson)
  You say there is no love (G.F. Norton)

1200   Mechem, Kirke
Zorobabel, Op. 19 (1962)
Med: SATB, STBarB soli, str quintet,
    wind quintet, pno
Txt: biblical
Dur: 27'
Pub: EC Schirmer
N.B.   Original title: *The victory of
    Zorobabel.*

1201   Mennin, Peter
Alleluia (1941)
Med: SATB
Src: Grove

1202   Mennin, Peter
Bought locks (1948)
Med: SSA, pno
Txt: Martial (Latin), trans. Sir John
    Harington
Dur: 4'
Pub: C Fischer
Mss: LC
Rev: MLA *Notes* 6 (Sept, 1949) p639–
    40

1203   Mennin, Peter
Cantata de virtue (c.1969)
Med: SATB, children, TBar soli, nar,
    orch
Txt: Robert Browning; Ps. 117; anon.
    13th cent.

Dur: 40'
Pub: C Fischer
Bib: B8

1204   Mennin, Peter
The Christmas story (c.1950)
Med: SATB, ST solo, brass quartet,
    timp, str
Txt: biblical
Dur: 25'
Pub: C Fischer
Rev: MLA *Notes* 8 (1951) p747; *Music
    Clubs Magazine* 30 (Feb, 1951)
    p19
Bib: B8

1205   Mennin, Peter
Crossing the Han river (1948)
Med: SATB
Txt: Kiang Kang-Hu, trans. Witter
    Bynner
Dur: 4'
Pub: C Fischer
Mss: LC

1206   Mennin, Peter
The cycle (Symphony No. 4) (c.1949)
Med: SATB, orch
Txt: composer
Dur: 25'
Pub: C Fischer
Bib: B8, 97
  The dark sea
  Come back to earth
  Time passing, waters flowing
Rev: Cincinnati *Enquirer*, May 20,
    1963; *Hi-Fidelity/Musical America*
    21 (Nov, 1971) p19ff; *Music Edu-
    cators Journal* 58 (Nov, 1971) p16;
    Musical Times 112 (Sept, 1961),
    p88–9
Bib: B85

1207 Mennin, Peter
The gold threaded robe (1948)
Med: SATB
Txt: Kiang Kang-Hu, trans. Witter
     Bynner
Dur: 5'
Pub: C Fischer
Mss: LC

1208 Mennin, Peter
In the quiet night (1948)
Med: SATB
Txt: Kiang Kang-Hu, trans. Witter
     Bynner
Dur: 3'
Pub: C Fischer
Mss: LC

1209 Mennin, Peter
The pied piper of Hamelin (1969)
Med: SATB div, children's chorus, TB
     soli, nar, orch
Txt: Robert Browning, liturgical
Src: Grove

1210 Mennin, Peter
Reflections of Emily (c.1979)
Med: SSA, hp, pno, perc
Txt: Emily Dickinson
Dur: 25'
Pub: G Schirmer
Rev: *American Harp Journal* 7 (Jan,
     1979) p19
Bib: B8
N.B. The composer prefers that boys'
    voices sing this work.
    This is my letter to the world
    'Tis so much joy
    That I did always love
    Cadenza capricciosa
    Read, sweet, how others strove
    Interlude
    Musicians wrestle everywhere

1211 Mennin, Peter
A song of the palace (1948)
Med: SATB
Txt: Kiang Kang-Hu, trans. Witter
     Bynner
Dur: 7'
Pub: C Fischer
Mss: LC

1212 Mennin, Peter
Tumbling hair (1948)
Med: SSA, pno
Txt: e.e. cummings
Dur: 4'
Pub: C Fischer
Mss: LC
Rev: MLA *Notes* 6 (Sept, 1949) p639–
     40

1213 Menotti, Gian Carlo
The death of the Bishop of Brindisi
    (1963)
Med: SATB, SB soli, children, orch
Txt: composer
Dur: 30'
Pub: G Schirmer
Mss: partial copy of holograph in LC
Rev: Cincinnati *Enquirer*, May 20,
     1963; *Hi-Fidelity/Musical America*
     21 (Nov, 1971) p19ff; *Music Edu-*
     cators Journal 58 (Nov, 1971) p16;
     Musical Times 112 (Sept, 1961),
     p88-9
Bib: B85

1214 Menotti, Gian Carlo
For the death of Orpheus (1990)
Med: SATB, soli
Txt: composer
Dur: 11'
Pub: G Schirmer

1215 Menotti, Gian Carlo
Landscapes and remembrances (1975)
Med: SATB, SATBar soli, orch
Txt: composer
Dur: 45'
Pub: G Schirmer

1216 Menotti, Gian Carlo
Llama de amor viva (1991)
Med: SATB, Bar solo
Txt: composer, after St. John of the
Cross
Dur: 10'
Pub: G Schirmer

1217 Menotti, Gian Carlo
*Mass: for the contemporary English
liturgy* (1985)
Med: SATB (opt.), cong, org
Txt: LU
Dur: 9'
Pub: G Schirmer

1218 Menotti, Gian Carlo
Miracles (1979)
Med: SSAA (or boy choir)
Txt: not indicated
Dur: 17'
Pub: G Schirmer
Rev: *Music Clubs Magazine* 58/4 (1979)
p22; *Music Educators Journal* 66
(Mar, 1980) p106; *Symphony
News* 30/6 (1979) p49

1219 Menotti, Gian Carlo
Missa "O pulchritudo" (1979)
Med: SATB, SATB soli, orch
Txt: LU
Dur: 45'
Pub: G Schirmer
Rev: *Hi-Fidelity/Musical America* 31
(Sept, 1981) pMA32-3; *Variety*
303 (June 10, 1981) p58.
Bib: B51, 183

1220 Menotti, Gian Carlo
Moans, groans, cries and sighs
(c.1978)
Med: SATBBB (or male vv, ATTBBB)
Txt: composer?
Dur: 6'
Pub: G Schirmer

1221 Menotti, Gian Carlo
Muero porque no muero (1982)
Med: SATB, S solo, ch. orch
Txt: composer, after St. Teresa of
Avila
Dur: 15'
Pub: G Schirmer

1222 Menotti, Gian Carlo
My Christmas (1987)
Med: TTBB, fl, ob, clar, hn, hp, bass
Txt: composer
Dur: 15'
Pub: G Schirmer

1223 Menotti, Gian Carlo
A song of hope (1980)
Med: SATB, Bar solo, orch
Txt: composer
Dur: 10'
Pub: G Schirmer

1224 Menotti, Gian Carlo
The trial of the gypsy (1978)
Med: boys' vv, 3 soli, pno, drums
Txt: composer
Dur: 22'
Pub: G Schirmer

1225 Menotti, Gian Carlo
*The unicorn, the gorgon, and the
manticore (or, Three Sundays of
a poet)* (1956)
Med: SATB div, ten dancers, nine inst.
Txt: composer

Dur: 45'
Pub: Belwin-Mills
Mss: LC
Rev: MLA *Notes* 15 (Dec, 1957) p144–
5; *Saturday Review* 55 (May, 1972)
p62
Bib: B19, 85, 104
N.B. A choral ballet.

1226 Mills, Charles
The ascension (1954)
Med: SATB, T solo
Txt: Luke 24:27-53
Dur: 10'
Pub: HW Gray

1227 Mills, Charles
Ballad of trees and the master (1958)
Med: SATB
Txt: Sidney Lanier
Dur: 1'30"
Pub: ACA

1228 Mills, Charles
The constant lover (1952)
Med: TTBB
Txt: J. Suckling
Src: Grove

1229 Mills, Charles
The dark night (1946)
Med: SSAA, str
Txt: biblical
Src: Grove

1230 Mills, Charles
The first Thanksgiving (1958)
Med: SATB, B solo, org
Txt: Governor William Bradford
Dur: 5'
Pub: ACA

1231 Mills, Charles
O Christ Redeemer (1958)
Med: SATB

Txt: composer
Src: Grove

1232 Mills, Charles
Why so pale and wan, fond lover?
(1952)
Med: TTBB
Txt: J. Suckling
Src: Grove

1233 Moevs, Robert
Alleluia for Michaelmas (1967)
Med: cong, org
Txt: LU
Dur: 4'
Mss: composer
Src: composer

1234 Moevs, Robert
Attis (Pt. 1: 1958; Pt. 2: 1963)
Med: SSAT, T solo, orch
Txt: Catullus
Dur: 46'
Pub: AMC
Bib: B23
N.B. Some selections from this work
also published by EB Marks.

1235 Moevs, Robert
The aulos player (1975)
Med: 2 choirs, S solo, 2 org
Txt: D'Annunzio
Dur: 9'
Mss: composer
Src: composer

1236 Moevs, Robert
Ave Maria (1966)
Med: SSATTB
Txt: LU
Dur: 8'
Pub: copy at Harvard
N.B. An unusual score, utilizing graphic
notation, unmetered rhythm, and
unusual vocal techniques.

1237 Moevs, Robert
The bacchantes (1948)
Med: SATB
Txt: Euripides
Dur: 12'
Mss: composer
Src: composer

1238 Moevs, Robert
A brief Mass (1968)
Med: SATB, org, vibraphone, gtr, bass
Txt: LU
Dur: 7'
Pub: Piedmont Music; EB Marks
Rev: *Current Musicology* 9 (1969)
p12-13
Bib: B4

1239 Moevs, Robert
Cantata sacra (1952)
Med: TTBB, B solo, fl, 4 tbn, timp
Txt: LU
Dur: 15'
Pub: unpubl.
Mss: composer
Src: Dox
Rev: Boston *Globe*, March 25, 1953;
New York *Herald Tribune* and
New York *Times*, April 16, 1955.

1240 Moevs, Robert
Et nunc reges (1963)
Med: SSA, fl, clar, bass clar
Txt: Ps. 2:10-13
Dur: 8'
Pub: EC Schirmer
Bib: B23

1241 Moevs, Robert
Et occidentem illustra (1965)
Med: SSATB, orch
Txt: *The Commission of Th. Freling-huysen*; Dante
Dur: 19'

Pub: Piedmont Music
Rev: *American Choral Review* 9/3 (1967)
p32-3
Bib: B4

1242 Moevs, Robert
Great nations of this earth (1942)
Med: SSAA
Txt: composer
Dur: 12'30"
Mss: composer
Src: composer

1243 Moevs, Robert
Itaque ut (1959)
Med: SSAT
Txt: Catullus
Dur: 3'30"
Pub: EB Marks
Bib: B23

1244 Moore, Douglas
The birds' counting song (c.1955)
Med: SATB, T solo, pno
Txt: trad., with additional text by
composer
Dur: 2'
Pub: Presser
Mss: LC

1245 Moore, Douglas
Dedication (c.1938)
Med: SATB div
Txt: Archibald MacLeish
Dur: 4'
Pub: Arrow Music Press
Mss: LC

1246 Moore, Douglas
The Greenfield Christmas tree (c.1963)
Med: SATB, soli, pno
Txt: Arnold Sundgaard
Dur: 20'
Pub: G Schirmer

1247 Moore, Douglas
In a glass of water before retiring
(1937)
Med: SSA
Txt: Stephen Vincent Benét
Dur: 3'30"
Pub: C Fischer
Mss: LC
N.B. Published as *Perhaps to dream.*

1248 Moore, Douglas
Mary's wedding prayer (n.d.)
Med: SSA, S solo
Txt: Stephen Vincent Benét
Dur: 1'30"
Pub: BH
Src: Locke
N.B. From the opera *The devil and Daniel Webster.*

1249 Moore, Douglas
The mysterious cat (1960)
Med: 3 equal vv
Txt: Vachel Lindsay
Dur: 2'30"
Pub: unpubl.?
Mss: LC

1250 (not used)

1251 Moore, Douglas
Poor wayfaring stranger (c.1955)
Med: SATB, pno
Txt: trad.
Dur: 2'
Pub: Presser
Mss: LC

1252 Moore, Douglas
A prayer for England (1940)
Med: TTBB, pno
Txt: William Rose Benét
Dur: 4'
Pub: unpubl.?
Mss: LC

1253 Moore, Douglas
Prayer for the United Nations (c.1943)
Med: SATB, A or Bar solo, orch
Txt: Stephen Vincent Benét and composer
Dur: 8'
Pub: HW Gray
Mss: LC

1254 Moore, Douglas
Simon Legree (1937)
Med: TTBB, pno
Txt: Vachel Lindsay
Dur: 7'
Pub: C Fischer
Mss: LC

1255 Moore, Douglas
Vayechulu (1948)
Med: SATB div, cantor, org
Txt: Genesis 2:1-3 (in Hebrew)
Dur: 2'
Pub: unpubl.?
Mss: LC

1256 Moore, Douglas
Western wind (1946?)
Med: 2 vv
Src: Grove

1257 Moore, Douglas
Youth gets a break (1940)
Med: SATB, orch
Txt: not indicated
Pub: unpubl.
Mss: LC
N.B. Part of a film score for the National Youth Administration.

1258 Musgrave, Thea
Black tambourine (1986)
Med: SSA, pno
Txt: Hart Crane
Dur: 17'
Src: B184

1259   Musgrave, Thea
Cantata for a summer's day (1954)
Med: SATB, fl, clar, str quartet, nar
Txt: Alexander Hume and Maurice
     Lindsay
Dur: 33'
Pub: Belwin-Mills

1260   Musgrave, Thea
The five ages of man (1963)
Med: SATB, pno
Txt: Hesiod, trans. Richmond Latti-
     more
Dur: 27'
Pub: JW Chester
Bib: B161

1261   Musgrave, Thea
*For the time being (A Christmas
oratorio)* (1988?)
Med: SATB
Txt: W.H. Auden
Dur: 50'
Pub: Novello
Src: B184

1262   Musgrave, Thea
Four madrigals (c.1958)
Med: SATB
Txt: Thomas Wyatt
Dur: 12'
Pub: JW Chester
Rev: *Composer* (London) 76-77 (1982)
     p49
     With serving still
     Tanglid I was in love's snare
     At most mischief
     Hate whom ye list

1263   Musgrave, Thea
John Cook (c.1963)
Med: SATB
Txt: anon.
Dur: 1'
Pub: Novello

1264   Musgrave, Thea
The last twilight (1980)
Med: SATB, brass ensemble, perc,
     vibraphone
Txt: D.H. Lawrence
Dur: 13'
Pub: Novello
Src: B184

1265   Musgrave, Thea
The Lord's prayer (1983)
Med: SATB, org
Txt: Gospel of Matthew
Dur: 5'
Pub: Novello
Rev: *Diapason* 75 (Oct, 1984) p6

1266   Musgrave, Thea
Make ye merry for him that is to come
(c.1963)
Med: SA, unison children, opt. org
Txt: anon., 15th cent.
Dur: 4'
Pub: JW Chester

1267   Musgrave, Thea
Memento creatoris (c.1967)
Med: SATB, SAT soli, opt. org
Txt: John Donne
Dur: 4'
Pub: JW Chester

1268   Musgrave, Thea
O caro m'è il sonno (1978)
Med: SATB div
Txt: Michelangelo
Dur: 1'30"
Pub: Novello

1269   Musgrave, Thea
The phoenix and the turtle (1962)
Med: SATB, orch
Txt: William Shakespeare
Dur: 18'
Pub: JW Chester

1270 Musgrave, Thea
Rorate coeli (1973)
Med: SATB div, SSATB soli
Txt: William Dunbar
Dur: 11'
Pub: Novello
Rev: *Composer* (London) 92 (Winter, 1987) p40
Bib: B161

1271 Musgrave, Thea
Two Christmas carols in traditional style (c.1968)
Med: SA or SATB, S solo; opt. ob and clar, or vln and str quartet
Txt: Norman Nicholson
Dur: 5'
Pub: JW Chester

P

1272 Parker, Alice
Ambivalence (1962)
Med: unison vv, pno
Txt: F. Pratt Green
Dur: 1'
Pub: *The Hymn*, 33/4 (Oct, 1982) p220

1273 Parker, Alice
Angels supposedly (1975)
Med: 2-part choir, pno, opt. perc
Txt: Molly Pyle
Dur: 2'
Pub: Hinshaw

1274 Parker, Alice
Away, melancholy (1973)
Med: SSAA, tamb
Txt: Stevie Smith
Dur: 7'
Pub: EC Schirmer

1275 Parker, Alice
Blessings (1965)
Med: SATB
Txt: Ps. 134
Dur: 4'
Pub: Lawson-Gould

1276 Parker, Alice
Brotherly love (1972)
Med: 2-5 vv, preferably children
Txt: composer
Dur: 3'
Pub: EC Schirmer

1277 Parker, Alice
Carols to play and sing (1971)
Med: SATB, perc, org
Txt: trad.
Dur: 9'
Pub: EC Schirmer
  In Bethlehem
  I saw a stable
  Shrill chanticleer

1278 Parker, Alice
Children, saints, and charming sounds (c.1980)
Med: SATB, children (SSA), wind trio, brass quartet
Txt: *American Mountain Hymns*
Dur: 14'
Pub: Hinshaw

1279 Parker, Alice
Christopher Dock (c.1967)
Med: SATB, soli, pno
Txt: John Ruth
Dur: 35'
Pub: unpubl.
Mss: copy of holograph in LC

1280 Parker, Alice
Commentaries (c.1977)
Med: SSA/SSA dbl choir, SA soli, orch

Txt: Emily Dickinson; Southern folk-
songs, hymns, and spirituals.
Dur: 35'
Pub: Hinshaw

1281 Parker, Alice
The day-spring (1979)
Med: SATB, SA (children), opt. ABar
soli; org, fl
Txt: *American Mountain Hymns*
Dur: 10'
Pub: Hinshaw

1282 Parker, Alice
Earth now is green (1972)
Med: SATB
Txt: Sir J. Davies
Dur: 3'
Pub: EC Schirmer

1283 Parker, Alice
An Easter rejoicing (1968)
Med: SATB, perc, hp or pno, org
Txt: composer
Dur: 25'
Pub: EC Schirmer
   Christ the Lord is risen!
   Earth now is green
   Gabriel's message
   We are a garden
   I got me flowers
   Seasons and times
   Like flowers
   Drop, drop slow tears
   Most glorious Lord
   O for a shout
   Christ, my beloved
   Jesus, whom every saint adores
   Christ the Lord is risen!

1284 Parker, Alice
An English Mass (c.1975)
Med: 2-part chorus, any vv
Txt: Book of Common Prayer
Dur: 4'
Pub: Hinshaw

1285 Parker, Alice
The feast of ingathering (1970)
Med: SATB, A solo, org
Txt: composer, from various Old Tes-
tament texts
Dur: 20'
Pub: C Fischer
N.B. In Dox, the title is given as *The
time of ingathering*.

1286 Parker, Alice
Gaudete (c.1977)
Med: SATB, pno or orch
Txt: Prudentius, Wade, et al.
Dur: 18'
Pub: EC Schirmer
Bib: B131
   Corde natus ex parentis
   Puer nobis nascitur
   Dormi, Jesu
   Personent hodie
   Resonent in laudibus
   Adeste, fideles

1287 Parker, Alice
Gabriel's message (1972)
Med: SSA, S solo, tamb, hp or pno
Txt: *Piæ cantiones*, trans. J.M. Neale
Dur: 3'
Pub: EC Schirmer

1288 Parker, Alice
The good shepherd (c.1988)
Med: TBB div
Txt: not indicated
Dur: 2'
Pub: Galaxy

1289 Parker, Alice
Grace and glory (1979)
Med: SATB, perc
Txt: Isaac Watts
Dur: 4'30"
Pub: EC Schirmer

1290   Parker, Alice
I will sing and give praise (1978)
Med: SATB, kybd
Txt: Book of Psalms
Dur: 5'
Pub: Hinshaw

1291   Parker, Alice
In praise of singing (1982?)
Med: SATB, str orch
Txt: Isaac Watts
Dur: 14'
Pub: Hinshaw

1292   Parker, Alice
Invocation: peace (c.1988)
Med: SA
Txt: not indicated
Dur: 1'30"
Pub: Galaxy

1293   Parker, Alice
It is a good thing to give thanks (1984)
Med: SATB, kybd
Txt: Ps. 92:1-4
Dur: 4'30"
Pub: Hinshaw

1294   Parker, Alice
Jesus, whom every saint adores (1972)
Med: SATB, perc
Txt: Isaac Watts
Dur: 1'
Pub: EC Schirmer

1295   Parker, Alice
Journeys: pilgrims and strangers (1976)
Med: SATB, SBar soli, orch
Txt: composer
Dur: 50'
Pub: Hinshaw
Rev: *Choral Journal* 16/9 (1976)
         p10-11

1296   Parker, Alice
Kentucky psalms (c.1987)
Med: SATB, fl, 2 vln, vla, cello, bass
Txt: trad., arr. by composer
Dur: 14'
Pub: Augsburg

1297   Parker, Alice
Love songs (c.1979)
Med: SATB, pno
Txt: see below
Dur: 8'30"
Pub: Hinshaw
         Sing heigh ho! (Charles Kingsley)
         Passions (Sir Walter Raleigh)
         Love is a sickness (Samuel Daniel)

1298   Parker, Alice
Meet and right it is to sing (1981)
Med: SATB, kybd
Txt: Charles Wesley
Dur: 4'
Pub: Hinshaw

1299   Parker, Alice
Melodious accord: a concert of praise
(c.1977)
Med: SATB, SATB soli, brass quartet, hp
Txt: *Harmonia sacra*
Dur: 70'
Pub: EC Schirmer

1300   Parker, Alice
Millay madrigals (1985)
Med: SATB div
Txt: Edna St. Vincent Millay
Dur: 12'
Pub: unpubl.

1301   Parker, Alice
Most glorious Lord of life (1972)
Med: SATB
Txt: Edmund Spenser
Dur: 1'30"
Pub: EC Schirmer

1302 Parker, Alice
Mountain hymns (c.1987)
Med: unison vv, pno
Txt: see below
Dur: 7'
Pub: Galaxy
    I will arise (Robert Robinson)
    O thou, in whose presence (Joseph
    Swain)
    Mansions in the skies (Isaac Watts)

1303 Parker, Alice
Now glad of heart (1960)
Med: SATB, B solo, orch or org
Txt: anon. 16th cent. German, trans.
    A.H. Fox-Strangways
Dur: 6'
Pub: Lawson-Gould

1304 Parker, Alice
Phonophobia (1977)
Med: SATB, pno or gtr
Txt: composer?
Dur: 8'
Pub: Hinshaw
    Tim's sisters
    She
    Betty Botter
    Hiawatha

1305 Parker, Alice
A play on numbers (1971)
Med: SA, pno
Txt: Stevie Smith
Dur: 10'
Pub: EC Schirmer

1306 Parker, Alice
Pray for peace (1985)
Med: SATB div
Txt: Ps. 122:6-9
Dur: 4'
Pub: AMP

1307 Parker, Alice
Prayer (1973)
Med: SATB dbl choir, inst.
Txt: Isaac Watts, after Ps. 119
Dur: 2'
Pub: Lawson-Gould

1308 Parker, Alice
A prayer for choirs (c.1979)
Med: unison or 2-part, electric bass,
    opt. melodic inst.
Txt: Henry M. Bartlett
Dur: 2'30"
Pub: EC Schirmer

1309 Parker, Alice
Psalm 136 (1966)
Med: SATB
Txt: Ps. 136
Dur: 3'30"
Pub: Lawson-Gould

1310 Parker, Alice
Psalms of praise (1968)
Med: TB, perc
Txt: Ps. 150; 147:1; 138:7-8; 145:10-
    11, 21; 148
Dur: 5'
Pub: Lawson-Gould

1311 Parker, Alice
Seasons and times (1972)
Med: STB, hp or pno, perc
Txt: Isaac Watts
Dur: 2'
Pub: EC Schirmer

1312 Parker, Alice
A sermon from the mountain (1969)
Med: SATB, Bar soli, gtr, drum, str
Txt: Martin Luther King
Dur: 35'
Pub: EC Schirmer
Rev: *American Choral Review* 11/2
    (1969) p17.

Bib: B131
  Invitation
  Blessings
  Exhortation
  The rule
  The promise
  The reward
Dur: 35'
Pub: EC Schirmer
Rev: *American Choral Review* 11/2 (1969) p17.
Bib: B131
  Invitation
  Blessings
  Exhortation
  The rule
  The promise
  The reward

1313 Parker, Alice
Seven carols (c.1972)
Med: SATB, orch
Txt: trad.
Dur: 2'-4' each
Pub: C Fischer
Bib: B131

1314 Parker, Alice
Six hymns to Dr. Watts (c.1977)
Med: SATB, opt. kybd
Txt: Isaac Watts; Ps. 95, 119, 122, 147, 151; Ascriptions 7, 8
Dur: 6'
Pub: EC Schirmer

1315 Parker, Alice
The song of Simeon (1979)
Med: SATB, brass quartet or kybd
Txt: Luke 2:29-32
Dur: 5'
Pub: Hinshaw

1316 Parker, Alice
The song of Solomon (c.1979)
Med: SATB, kybd

Txt: biblical
Dur: 7'
Pub: Hinshaw

1317 Parker, Alice
Songs for Sunday (c.1964)
Med: 2-part equal vv, kybd
Txt: trad.
Dur: 17'
Pub: Lawson-Gould

1318 Parker, Alice
Songstreams (c.1986)
Med: SATB, pno four hands
Txt: Edna St. Vincent Millay
Dur: 20'
Pub: Galaxy
  To Kathleen
  Mariposa
  The philosopher
  The spring and the fall
  Nuit blanche
  The merry maid
  Thursday
  Passer mortuus est
  Lethe

1319 Parker, Alice
A sun, a shield (1979)
Med: S or SA, autoharp, bass, perc
Txt: Ps. 84:11
Dur: 2'
Pub: EC Schirmer

1320 Parker, Alice
There and back again (1978)
Med: SATB, woodwind quartet or pno
Txt: Katherine Pyle
Dur: 11'
Pub: Hinshaw
  Colored looking glass
  The room
  Questions
  Fire thoughts
  Antecedents

1321   Parker, Alice
Three circles (1972)
Med: SATB, perc
Txt: Congo folk text, Jonathan Swift
Dur: 7'
Pub: C Fischer
    Choral suite
    The moon always follows the sun
    Sleep, as the world turns

1322   Parker, Alice
Three sacred symphonies (1984)
Med: SATB, fl, vln, cello, org
Txt: see below
Dur: 20'
Pub: AMP
    The wine (John 2:1-10)
    The daughter (Matthew 15:22-28)
    The anointing (John 12:3-8)

1323   Parker, Alice
The true use of music (1977)
Med: SATB, kybd
Txt: Charles Wesley
Dur: 5'
Pub: Hinshaw

1324   Parker, Alice
Universal praise (c.1983)
Med: SATB, kybd or brass quartet
Txt: Isaac Watts
Dur: 4'
Pub: Hinshaw

1325   Parker, Alice
The west wind (c.1945)
Med: SATB div, S solo
Txt: Archibald MacLeish
Dur: 3'30"
Pub: privately published? in Winchester, Mass.; copy in LC
Mss: copy of holograph in LC

1326   Parker, Alice
You called me father (1982)
Med: SAB, cong, kybd
Txt: Fred Kaan
Dur: 2'
Pub: Hinshaw

1327   Pasatieri, Thomas
Mass (1983)
Med: SATB, SATB soli, orch
Txt: LU
Dur: 90'
Pub: G Schirmer
Rev: *Hi-Fidelity/Musical America* 34 (Aug, 1984) pMA27; *Symphony Magazine* 34/5 (1983) p32
Bib: B51

1328   Pasatieri, Thomas
Permit me voyage (1976)
Med: SATB, S solo, orch
Txt: James Agee
Dur: 16'
Pub: Belwin-Mills

1329   Paulus, Stephen
Carol of the hill (c.1976)
Med: SATB
Txt: Michael Dennis Browne
Dur: 3'
Pub: Art Masters Studio

1330   Paulus, Stephen
Christmas tidings (1989)
Med: SATB, str
Txt: trad.
Dur: 12'
Pub: unpubl.; copy in Ohio State Univ. choral library
    Good King Wenceslas
    What child is this?
    On Christmas night
    Lo, how a rose e'er blooming
    Hark! the herald angels sing

1331 Paulus, Stephen
The first nowell (c.1981)
Med: SATB
Txt: trad.
Dur: 2'
Pub: European-American

1332 Paulus, Stephen
Jesu carols (c.1985)
Med: SATB, hp
Txt: see below
Dur: 11'
Pub: European-American
  Jesu's lyfelyne (Juliana Berners)
  The ship carol (anon., 16th cent.)
  Waye not his cribb (Robert Southwell)
  The neighbors of Bethlehem (13th.
  cent. French)

1333 Paulus, Stephen
Letters for the times (c.1980)
Med: SATB, STBar soli, ch. orch
Txt: newspaper letters from 17th-
  century America
Dur: 20'
Pub: European-American
Mss: copy in LC

1334 Paulus, Stephen
Madrigali de Michelangelo (1987)
Med: SATB div
Txt: Michelangelo
Dur: 9'
Pub: unpubl.; copy in Ohio State
  Univ. choral library

1335 Paulus, Stephen
Marginalia (1977)
Med: SATB div, fl, gtr, perc
Txt: anon. 13th cent.
Dur: 7'30"
Pub: AMC

1336 Paulus, Stephen
North shore (1977)
Med: SATB, MB soli, orch
Txt: Michael Dennis Browne
Dur: 40'
Pub: European-American
Rev: St. Paul *Dispatch*, Oct. 17, 1977.

1337 Paulus, Stephen
Now is the gentle season (c.1978)
Med: SATB
Txt: anon. English
Dur: 3'30"
Pub: European-American

1338 Paulus, Stephen
Personals (1975)
Med: SATB, fl, perc
Txt: anon. (from personal ads in
  newspapers)
Dur: 6'30"
Pub: AMC
Mss: copy in NYPL
  30, weird
  Seeking Mr. Right
  Good looking male
  Dancing

1339 Paulus, Stephen
Pium paum (c.1976)
Med: SATB, A solo, finger cymbals,
  hp or pno
Txt: Melva Rorem
Dur: 2'
Pub: European-American

1340 Paulus, Stephen
Shall we gather at the river (c.1982)
Med: SATB, S solo
Txt: trad.
Dur: 2'30"
Pub: European-American

1341 Paulus, Stephen
Silver the river (c.1976)
Med: SA, kybd
Txt: Michael Dennis Browne
Dur: 2'
Pub: European-American

1342 Paulus, Stephen
So hallowed is the time (1980)
Med: SATB, STBar and boy soprano
      soli, orch
Txt: Wm. Shakespeare, Wm. Dunbar,
      John Milton, Christopher Smart,
      Wm. Drummond, John Donne,
      Robert Herrick, Robert South-
      well
Dur: 38'
Pub: European-American
Rev: Greenwich (Conn.) *Times*, Dec.
      10, 1980.

1343 Paulus, Stephen
*Songs and rituals for Easter and the
      May* (1978)
Med: SATB, SM soli, nar, ch. orch
Txt: Michael Dennis Browne
Dur: 40'
Pub: European-American
N.B. Also known as *Canticles* (Ph.D.
      dissertation, University of Min-
      nesota, 1978).

1344 Paulus, Stephen
Three Chinese poems (1973)
Med: SATB
Src: Grove

1345 Paulus, Stephen
We give thee but thine own (c.1977)
Med: SAB, pno
Txt: William Walsham How
Dur: 4'
Pub: European-American

1346 Persichetti, Vincent
Canons, Op. 31 (1947)
Med: 3-part chorus, any vv
Txt: not indicated
Dur: 3'15"
Pub: Elkan-Vogel
      Should fancy cease
      Preface to canons
      Hallelujah, bum again

1347 Persichetti, Vincent
*Celebrations (Cantata No. 3), Op.
      103* (1966)
Med: SATB, wind ensemble
Txt: Walt Whitman
Dur: 23'
Pub: Elkan-Vogel
Mss: copy of holograph in LC
Bib: B7
      Stranger
      I celebrate myself
      You who celebrate bygones
      There is that in me
      Sing me the universal
      Flaunt out O sea
      I sing the body electric
      A clear midnight
      Voyage

1348 Persichetti, Vincent
The creation, Op. 111 (1969)
Med: SATB, SATB soli, orch
Txt: composer, from mythological,
      scientific, poetic, and biblical
      sources
Dur: 65'
Pub: Elkan-Vogel
Rev: *ASCAP* 4/2 (1970) p34; New
      York *Times*, April 18, 1970
Bib: B7, 12, 13, 192

1349 Persichetti, Vincent
Flower songs (Cantata No. 6) (1983)
Med: SATB, str orch
Txt: e.e. cummings

Dur: 21'
Pub: Elkan-Vogel
Rev: *American Organist* 18 (July, 1984)
       p29; *ASCAP* (Fall, 1984) p60
       Flowers of stone
       Sprouting violets
       Early flowers
       Is there a flower
       A yellow flower
       The rose is dying
       Lily has a rose

1350   Persichetti, Vincent
Four cummings choruses, Op. 98
       (1964)
Med: SA, TB, SB, or SATB, pno
Txt: e.e. cummings
Dur: 12'
Pub: Elkan-Vogel

1351   Persichetti, Vincent
Glad and very: five cummings choruses
       (1974)
Med: SA or TB, pno
Txt: e.e. cummings
Dur: 11'
Pub: Elkan-Vogel
       Little man
       I am so very glad
       Maybe God
       Jake hates all the girls
       A politician

1352   Persichetti, Vincent
Hist whist, Op. 46, No. 2 (c.1952)
Med: SA
Txt: e.e. cummings
Dur: 2'
Pub: C Fischer
Mss: LC

1353   Persichetti, Vincent
Hymns and responses for the church
       year, Op. 68 (1955)
Med: SATB

Txt: W.H. Auden, W. Romanis,
       Emily Dickinson, et al.
Dur: various short works
Pub: Elkan-Vogel
Bib: B7

1354   Persichetti, Vincent
Jimmie's got a goil, Op. 33, No. 2
       (c.1949)
Med: SA, SB, or TB, pno
Txt: e.e. cummings
Dur: 3'
Pub: G Schirmer
Bib: B12
N.B.   Published separately from Op.
       33, No. 1, *Sam was a man* (see
       No. 1360).

1355   Persichetti, Vincent
Love, Op. 116 (1971)
Med: SSA
Txt: Corinthians
Dur: 3'
Pub: Elkan-Vogel

1356   Persichetti, Vincent
Magnificat and nunc dimittis, Op. 8
       (1940)
Med: SATB, org or pno
Txt: Luke 1:46-55
Dur: 9'
Pub: Elkan-Vogel

1357   Persichetti, Vincent
Mass, Op. 84 (1960)
Med: SATB
Txt: LU
Dur: 18'
Pub: Elkan-Vogel
Rev: *Musical America* 81 (June, 1961)
       p55; *Musical Courier* 163 (June,
       1961) p19; *Musical Quarterly* 47/
       4 (1961) p526-27.
Bib: B14, 51, 218, 219

1358 Persichetti, Vincent
The pleiades, Op. 107 (1967)
Med: SATB div, tpt, str orch
Txt: Walt Whitman
Dur: 23'
Pub: Elkan-Vogel
Rev: *ASCAP* 2/3 (1968) p9

1359 Persichetti, Vincent
Proverb, Op. 34 (1948)
Med: SATB
Txt: American folklore
Dur: 2'
Pub: Elkan-Vogel
Rev: MLA *Notes* 13 (Sept, 1956) p703

1360 Persichetti, Vincent
Sam was a man, Op. 33, No. 1
(c.1948)
Med: 2-part chorus, any vv
Txt: e.e. cummings
Dur: 4'
Pub: G Schirmer
Bib: B12
N.B. Published separately from Op. 33, No. 2, *Jimmie's got a goil* (see No. 1354).

1361 Persichetti, Vincent
Seek the highest, Op. 78 (1957)
Med: SAB, pno
Txt: not indicated
Dur: 4'
Pub: Elkan-Vogel

1362 Persichetti, Vincent
Song of peace, Op. 82 (1959)
Med: TTBB, pno or org
Txt: anon.
Dur: 4'
Pub: Elkan-Vogel
Bib: B12

1363 Persichetti, Vincent
Spring cantata (Cantata No. 1), Op. 94 (1963)
Med: SSA, pno
Txt: e.e. cummings
Dur: 7'
Pub: Elkan-Vogel
Bib: B223
  Trees
  If the green
  Spring is like a perhaps hand
  In just-spring

1364 Persichetti, Vincent
Stabat mater, Op. 92 (1963)
Med: SATB, orch
Txt: LU
Dur: 28'
Pub: Elkan-Vogel
Mss: copy of holograph in LC
Bib: B7

1365 Persichetti, Vincent
Te Deum, Op. 93 (1963)
Med: SATB, orch
Txt: LU
Dur: 11'
Pub: Elkan-Vogel
Mss: copy of holograph in LC

1366 Persichetti, Vincent
This is the garden, Op. 46, No. 1
(c.1952)
Med: SSA
Txt: e.e. cummings
Dur: 2'15"
Pub: C Fischer
Mss: LC

1367 Persichetti, Vincent
Winter cantata (Cantata No. 2), Op. 97 (1965)
Med: SSA, fl, marimba

Txt: haiku poems by Kikaku, Bashô,
Hô-ô, Buson, Yaha, Rankô,
Ryôkan, Izembô
Dur: 19'
Pub: Elkan-Vogel
Mss: LC
Bib: B12, 14, 223
    A copper pheasant
    Winter's first drizzle
    Winter seclusion
    The wood cutter
    Gentlest fall of snow
    One umbrella
    Of crimson ice
    The branch is black
    Fallen leaves
    So deep
    The wind's whetstone
    Epilogue

1368 Pinkham, Daniel
Alleluia (1984)
Med: SSA or TTB, pno
Txt: "Alleluia"
Dur: 3'
Pub: EC Schirmer

1369 Pinkham, Daniel
Alleluia, acclamation and carol
(c.1975)
Med: SATB, 4-8 women's vv, timp,
    tape
Txt: biblical
Dur: indeterminate
Pub: EC Schirmer
N.B. An aleatoric composition; also
    known as *An Easter set.*

1370 Pinkham, Daniel
Amens (1975)
Med: SATB, tape
Txt: "Amen"
Dur: 3'
Pub: EC Schirmer

1371 Pinkham, Daniel
And peace attend thee (1983)
Med: SATB
Txt: Norma Farber
Dur: 2'
Pub: EC Schirmer

1372 Pinkham, Daniel
Angelus ad pastores ait (1959)
Med: SATB, brass choir
Txt: LU
Dur: 4'
Pub: Robert King Music
N.B. Also arr. for SSAA

1373 Pinkham, Daniel
Ascension cantata (1972)
Med: SATB, wind ensemble, opt. org
Txt: Psalms; Mark 6:14-19; LU
Dur: 13'
Pub: EC Schirmer
Bib: B205

1374 Pinkhan, Daniel
Ave Maria (1960)
Med: SA
Txt: LU
Dur: 2'
Pub: AMP

1375 Pinkham, Daniel
Ave verum corpus (1973)
Med: SATB, opt org
Txt: LU
Dur: 3'
Pub: EC Schirmer

1376 Pinkham, Daniel
Baptism canon (1974)
Med: SSA, org
Txt: Matthew 28:19
Dur: 2'
Pub: CF Peters

1377   Pinkham, Daniel
Before the cock crows (1984)
Med: SATB, SMATB soli, fl, clar, hp,
   str quintet
Txt: biblical
Dur: 12'
Pub: EC Schirmer

1378   Pinkham, Daniel
Before the dust returns (1981)
Med: SATB, 2 hn, bass, org
Txt: biblical
Dur: 9'
Pub: EC Schirmer

1379   Pinkham, Daniel
Behold, how good and how pleasant
   (1966)
Med: SATB
Txt: biblical
Dur: 1'30"
Pub: CF Peters

1380   Pinkham, Daniel
A biblical book of beasts (1985)
Med: SA, str quartet
Txt: biblical
Dur: 10'
Pub: EC Schirmer

1381   Pinkham, Daniel
Burning bright (1976)
Med: SATB
Txt: Howard Holtzman
Dur: 2'
Pub: EC Schirmer

1382   Pinkham, Daniel
The call of Isaiah (1971)
Med: any chorus, tape, opt. perc
Txt: Isaiah 6:1-9
Dur: 3'
Pub: EC Schirmer
Rev: *BMI* (Oct, 1971) p11

1383   Pinkham, Daniel
Canticle of praise (1965)
Med: SATB, S solo, brass, perc
Txt: biblical, Apocrypha
Dur: 13'
Pub: EC Schirmer
Mss: copy of holograph in LC

1384   Pinkham, Daniel
A carol for New Year's Day (1973)
Med: SATB
Txt: anon. medieval Latin
Dur: 2'
Pub: EC Schirmer

1385   Pinkham, Daniel
Christmas cantata (Sinfonia sacra)
   (1957)
Med: SATB div, dbl brass choir, opt. org
Txt: Luke, Ch. 1 and 2
Dur: 9'30"
Pub: Robert King Music

1386   Pinkham, Daniel
A Christmas carol (1948)
Med: SATB
Txt: Robert Hillyer
Dur: 2'
Pub: EC Schirmer

1387   Pinkham, Daniel
Clear mirrors (1980)
Med: SA, 2 hn, hp
Txt: Ben Jonson
Dur: 7'
Pub: EC Schirmer

1388   Pinkham, Daniel
Come, love we God (1970)
Med: SATB, gtr, pno or hp
Txt: Sir Richard Shanne
Dur: 2'
Pub: EC Schirmer

1389 Pinkham, Daniel
Communion service (1957)
Med: SATB, org
Txt: Book of Common Prayer
Dur: 4'
Pub: ACA

1390 Pinkham, Daniel
Company at the crèche (1977)
Med: SSA; handbells or glockenspiel;
    pno, org, or hp
Txt: Norma Farber
Dur: 8'30"
Pub: EC Schirmer
  Stork
  Dove
  Caterpillar
  Rooster
  Porcupine
  Spider
  Lion

1391 Pinkham, Daniel
The conversion of St. Paul (1961)
Med: SATB, TBar soli, tpt, org
Txt: biblical
Dur: 10'
Pub: EC Schirmer
N.B. Sometimes called *The conversion of Saul.*

1392 Pinkham, Daniel
A curse, a lament, and a vision
  (c.1984)
Med: SATB, opt. pno
Txt: biblical
Dur: 12'
Pub: EC Schirmer

1393 Pinkham, Daniel
The Dallas anthem book (1984)
Med: unison, 2, 3, and 4-part mixed
  vv, org
Txt: biblical
Dur: 3'-5' each

Pub: EC Schirmer
Rev: *American Organist* 19 (Aug, 1985)
  p32
Be alert, be wakeful
Hosanna to the son of David
Now at last
We have seen his star
O steadfast cross
Alleluia, tell the tidings
God has gone up
O God, the king of glory
Peace is my parting gift
Amen! Praise and glory

1394 Pinkham, Daniel
Daniel in the lion's den (1972)
Med: SATB, TBB soli, nar, 2 pno,
  perc, tape
Txt: biblical, arr. composer
Dur: 13'
Pub: EC Schirmer
Bib: B205
N.B. "...lends itself to a variety of
  multi-media production possibil-
  ities."

1395 Pinkham, Daniel
De profundis (1986)
Med: SATB, vla, opt. org
Txt: LU
Dur: 20'
Pub: EC Schirmer

1396 Pinkham, Daniel
The descent into hell (1979)
Med: SATB, soli, brass, perc, org, tape
Txt: biblical
Dur: 25'
Pub: EC Schirmer
Rev: MLA *Notes* 45 (Mar, 1989) p639–40

1397 Pinkham, Daniel
Draw near with faith and benediction
  (n.d.)
Med: SATB

Txt: not indicated
Dur: 2'
Pub: ACA

1398 Pinkham, Daniel
Easter cantata (1961)
Med: SATB, brass, perc
Txt: John 20:13; Matthew 28:5-7; Ps.
118:24; Ps. 68:10, 32-34
Dur: 11'30"
Pub: CF Peters

1399 Pinkham, Daniel
Elegy (1947)
Med: SATB
Txt: Robert Hillyer
Dur: 2'
Pub: EC Schirmer

1400 Pinkham, Daniel
An Emily Dickinson mosaic (1962)
Med: SSAA, pno or orch
Txt: Emily Dickinson
Dur: 10'
Pub: CF Peters
Bib: B223
The rain is wider than the sky
The heart is the capital of the mind
The mind lives on the heart
To be alive
Exhilaration is the breeze
Each life converges to some centre

1401 Pinkham, Daniel
Eternal are thy mercies, Lord (1956)
Med: SATB, org
Txt: biblical
Dur: 3'
Pub: ACA

1402 Pinkham, Daniel
Evergreen (c.1974)
Med: unison vv, org, tape
Txt: Robert Hillyer
Dur: 4'
Pub: EC Schirmer

1403 Pinkham, Daniel
Fanfares (1975)
Med: SATB, T solo, brass, perc, org,
opt. cong
Txt: Isaiah 11:1, 2, 6; 60:1; 62:10-11,
and Ps. 150
Dur: 12'
Pub: EC Schirmer
Bib: B205
Prophecy
Proclamation
Alleluia
Psalm

1404 Pinkham, Daniel
Farewell, vain world (1959)
Med: SATB
Txt: tombstone in Granary Burying
Ground, Boston
Dur: 2'
Pub: EC Schirmer

1405 Pinkham, Daniel
Festival magnificat and Nunc dimittis
(1962)
Med: SATB div, brass, org
Txt: Gospel of Luke; LU
Dur: 5'
Pub: CF Peters

1406 Pinkham, Daniel
Five canzonets (1958)
Med: SA
Txt: nursery rhymes (nos. 1, 4),
William Blake (nos. 2, 5), John
Donne (no. 3)
Dur: 5'30"
Pub: AMP
The nut tree
The blossom
Daybreak
Calico pie
Spring

1407 Pinkham, Daniel
For thee have I waited (1983)
Med: SATB, opt. org or pno
Txt: Ps. 23:5-6
Dur: 1'
Pub: CF Peters

1408 Pinkham, Daniel
Four elegies (1975)
Med: SATB, T solo, pno or ch. orch
Txt: see below
Dur: 20'
Pub: EC Schirmer
     To his dying brother (Robert Herrick)
     Upon the death of a friend (Richard
        Crashaw)
     Silence, and stealth of dayes (Henry
        Vaughan)
     At the round earth's imagined corners
        (John Donne)

1409 Pinkham, Daniel
Four poems of Norma Farber (1974)
Med: SATB, S solo
Txt: Norma Farber
Dur: 4'
Pub: EC Schirmer
     The hatch
     Dancer, how do you dare
     Fawn bridge
     Star and pulsar discovered dancing

1410 Pinkham, Daniel
*The garden of Artemis, or Apollo's
     revels* (c.1952)
Med: SSA, SABar soli, fl, clar, vln, vla,
     cello
Txt: Robert Hillyer
Dur: 5'30"
Pub: copy in LC

1411 Pinkham, Daniel
The gate of heaven (1986)
Med: SATB, brass, org
Txt: not indicated

Dur: 1'30"
Pub: EC Schirmer

1412 Pinkham, Daniel
Getting to heaven (1987)
Med: SATB, S solo, brass quintet, hp
Txt: Emily Dickinson
Dur: 15'
Pub: EC Schirmer

1413 Pinkham, Daniel
Glory be to God (c.1966)
Med: SATB dbl choir, opt. org
Txt: LU
Dur: 10'
Pub: EC Schirmer

1414 Pinkham, Daniel
God is a spirit (1961)
Med: SATB, org
Txt: biblical
Dur: 6'30"
Pub: EC Schirmer

1415 Pinkham, Daniel
Going and staying (1975)
Med: women's vv, electric gtr, offstage
     bells, opt. pno
Txt: Norma Farber
Dur: 4'
Pub: EC Schirmer

1416 Pinkham, Daniel
Grace is poured abroad (1970)
Med: SATB, opt kybd
Txt: Ps. 45:2, 4, 6
Dur: 2'
Pub: CF Peters

1417 Pinkham, Daniel
The heavens tell out the glory of God
     (1984)
Med: SATB, opt. kybd
Txt: Ps. 19

Dur: 2'
Pub: CF Peters

1418 Pinkham, Daniel
Here repose, O broken body (1956)
Med: SATB, opt. str
Txt: biblical
Dur: 4'30"
Pub: Highgate Music Press

1419 Pinkham, Daniel
Hezekiah (1979)
Med: SATB, STB soli, tpt, org
Txt: biblical
Dur: 10'
Pub: EC Schirmer

1420 Pinkham, Daniel
How precious is thy loving kindness (1967)
Med: SATB, opt. kybd
Txt: Ps. 36: 7–9
Dur: 2'
Pub: CF Peters

1421 Pinkham, Daniel
I have preached righteousness (1967)
Med: SATB, kybd
Txt: Ps. 104:9–10
Dur: 1'
Pub: CF Peters

1422 Pinkham, Daniel
I saw an angel (1974)
Med: SATB, tape
Txt: Book of Revelations
Dur: 4'
Pub: EC Schirmer

1423 Pinkham, Daniel
I was glad (1962)
Med: SATB, opt. kybd
Txt: Ps. 122
Dur: 1'30"
Pub: AMP

1424 Pinkham, Daniel
If ye love me (1963)
Med: SSA, org
Txt: John 14:15–16, 18, 21
Dur: 3'
Pub: EC Schirmer

1425 Pinkham, Daniel
In heaven soaring up (1986)
Med: SATB, AT soli, ob, hp, opt. pno
Txt: Edward Taylor
Dur: 15'
Pub: CF Peters

1426 Pinkham, Daniel
In the beginning of creation (1970)
Med: SATB, tape
Txt: Genesis 1:1–3
Dur: 3'08"
Pub: EC Schirmer
Rev: *BMI* (Oct, 1971) p11
Bib: B129
N.B. Score calls for some unusual vocal techniques.

1427 Pinkham, Daniel
In youth is pleasure (1953, rev. 1968)
Med: unison vv, gtr or pno
Txt: Robert Hillyer
Dur: 2'
Pub: EC Schirmer

1428 Pinkham, Daniel
Introit for Thanksgiving (1958)
Med: unison choir, org
Txt: biblical
Dur: 2'
Pub: ACA

1429 Pinkham, Daniel
Jonah (1966)
Med: SATB, MTB soli, orch
Txt: biblical, arr. composer
Dur: 28'

Pub: EC Schirmer
Mss: copy of holograph in LC
Rev: *Christian Science Monitor*, May 26, 1976.

1430 Pinkham, Daniel
Jubilate Deo (1964)
Med: SATB, org
Txt: Book of Psalms
Dur: 14'
Pub: EC Schirmer

1431 Pinkham, Daniel
The king and the shepherds (1974)
Med: SATB, opt. kybd
Txt: Robert Hillyer
Dur: 3'
Pub: EC Schirmer

1432 Pinkham, Daniel
The lament of David (1972)
Med: SATB, tape
Txt: 2 Samuel 1:19-28
Dur: 5'30"
Pub: EC Schirmer

1433 Pinkham, Daniel
Lamentations of Jeremiah (1966)
Med: SATB div, 10 players (2 tpt, 2 hn, 2 tbn, bass, timp, perc)
Txt: Lamentations 1:1-5
Dur: 12'
Pub: CF Peters
Rev: *Choral Journal* 6/5 (1966) p9ff

1434 Pinkham, Daniel
Lauds (1983)
Med: SA, TB, or ST/AB, 2 hn, bass, perc, org
Txt: Ps. 104:10-25, 42-43
Dur: 20'
Pub: EC Schirmer

1435 Pinkham, Daniel
Let us now praise famous men (1966)
Med: SA, opt. inst.
Txt: Apocrypha; Eccl. 45, 47-48
Dur: 8'
Pub: EC Schirmer
    The Lord brought forth Moses
    The Lord exalted Aaron
    David played with lions
    Solomon reigned in the days of peace
    The prophet Elijah rose

1436 Pinkham, Daniel
Listen to me: five motets (1965)
Med: SA, opt. inst.
Txt: Apocrypha, Eccl. 1, 18, 32, 39, 43
Dur: 5'
Pub: EC Schirmer
    Listen to me
    Hinder not music
    The number of man's days
    He scatters the snow
    The fear of the Lord

1437 Pinkham, Daniel
A litany (1961)
Med: 2-part chorus, kybd
Txt: Phineas Fletcher
Dur: 1'45"
Pub: AMP

1438 Pinkham, Daniel
Lord God, to whom vengeance belongeth (Motet 1) (c.1947)
Med: SSA, unfigured bass
Txt: Book of Psalms
Dur: 4'
Pub: copy in LC

1439 Pinkham, Daniel
The Lord has established his throne (1974)
Med: SATB, opt. org
Txt: Ps. 103

Dur: 1'
Pub: CF Peters
Rev: *Music Journal* 32 (Sept, 1974) p19

1440   Pinkham, Daniel
The Lord my shepherd is (1986)
Med: SATB, ob, org
Txt: Ps. 23
Dur: 3'30"
Pub: EC Schirmer

1441   Pinkham, Daniel
Love came down at Christmas (1972)
Med: SATB, opt. org
Txt: Christina Rossetti
Dur: 2'
Pub: EC Schirmer

1442   Pinkham, Daniel
Love can be still (1975)
Med: SSATB, opt. pno
Txt: Norma Farber
Dur: 11'
Pub: EC Schirmer
    Take me walking in your mind
    After the storm a star
    Da capo
    Love, bone-quiet, said

1443   Pinkham, Daniel
Love's yoke (1979)
Med: SA, 2 hn
Txt: Old English
Dur: 7'
Pub: EC Schirmer

1444   Pinkham, Daniel
Magnificat (1968)
Med: SSAA, S solo, 2 ob, 2 bsn, hp or
    opt. pno
Txt: biblical, arr. Jean Lunn
Dur: 9'
Pub: CF Peters

Rev: *BMI* (Oct, 1968) p25
Bib: B223

1445   Pinkham, Daniel
Manger scenes (1980)
Med: 2-part chorus, pno
Txt: Norma Farber
Dur: 6'
Pub: EC Schirmer
    A lamp in the manger
    The foundling
    The queens came late, but the queens
    were there

1446   Pinkham, Daniel
The martyrdom of St. Stephen (1967)
Med: SATB, gtr or pno
Txt: Acts 7: 55-60
Dur: 5'
Pub: EC Schirmer

1447   Pinkham, Daniel
Mass of the good shepherd (1966)
Med: unison, cong, org
Txt: LU
Dur: 13'
Pub: EC Schirmer
Rev: MLA *Notes* (Sept, 1967) p155.
Bib: B51

1448   Pinkham, Daniel
Mass of the Holy Eucharist (1966)
Med: unison vv, cong, org
Txt: LU
Dur: 10'
Pub: EC Schirmer
Bib: B51

1449   Pinkham, Daniel
Mass of the word of God (1966)
Med: SATB, cong, org
Txt: LU
Dur: 15'
Pub: EC Schirmer

Rev: *BMI* (Oct, 1966), p14; *Music Educators Journal* 52/3 (Nov, 1966), p9
Bib: B51

1450 Pinkham, Daniel
Memory, hither come (1959)
Med: SA
Txt: William Blake
Dur: 4'
Pub: EC Schirmer

1451 Pinkham, Daniel
The message (1968)
Med: SATB, gtr or pno
Txt: Siegfried Sassoon
Dur: 2'30"
Pub: EC Schirmer

1452 Pinkham, Daniel
Mizma L'Asaph (1968)
Med: TTBB, fl, hn, gtr, bass, vibraphone, perc
Txt: liturgical Hebrew
Dur: 7'
Pub: EC Schirmer

1453 Pinkham, Daniel
Most glorious Lord of life (1968)
Med: SATB, gtr or pno
Txt: biblical
Dur: 1'30"
Pub: EC Schirmer

1454 Pinkham, Daniel
My heart is steadfast (1977)
Med: SATB, opt. kybd
Txt: Ps. 57:7–10
Dur: 1'30"
Pub: CF Peters

1455 Pinkham, Daniel
Nativity madrigals (1981)
Med: SATB, org or pno
Txt: Norma Farber

Dur: 14'
Pub: EC Schirmer
Guardian owls
Get up! said Mary
What did the baby give the kings?
How they brought the good news by sea
After
Dur: 1'45"
Pub: AMP

1456 Pinkham, Daniel
O beautiful! my country (1975)
Med: SATB, opt. pno
Txt: see below
Dur: 8'
Pub: EC Schirmer
Take warning, tyrants (P. Freneau)
The happy flood (A. Bradstreet)
The promised land (James Russell Lowell)

1457 Pinkham, Daniel
O depth of wealth (1973)
Med: SATB, org, tape
Txt: Romans 11:33–36
Dur: 3'
Pub: EC Schirmer

1458 Pinkham, Daniel
On secret errands (1981)
Med: SATB, fl, clar
Txt: Howard Holtzman
Dur: 5'
Pub: EC Schirmer

1459 Pinkham, Daniel
On the dispute about images (1969)
Med: SATB, SATB soli, gtr or pno
Txt: Maximus of Tyre
Dur: 6'
Pub: EC Schirmer

1460 Pinkham, Daniel
On that day (1975)
Med: SATB, brass, opt. org

Txt: Book of Isaiah
Dur: 5'
Pub: EC Schirmer

1461   Pinkham, Daniel
One shade (1982)
Med: SATB
Txt: Howard Holtzman
Dur: 2'
Pub: EC Schirmer

1462   Pinkham, Daniel
Open to me the gates of righteousness (1966)
Med: SATB, opt. kybd
Txt: Ps. 118:19
Dur: 1'
Pub: CF Peters

1463   Pinkham, Daniel
The passion of Judas (1976)
Med: SATB, SMTBarB soli, clar, vla, bass, hp, org
Txt: Ps. 1, 15, 51
Dur: 30'
Pub: EC Schirmer
Rev: *Music Educators Journal* 63 (Sept, 1976) p23

1464   Pinkham, Daniel
Pater noster (1969)
Med: SATB, ob, Eng. hn, 2 bsn, opt. org
Txt: Gospel of Matthew
Dur: 3'
Pub: EC Schirmer

1465   Pinkham, Daniel
Piping Anne and husky Paul (1955)
Med: SATB
Txt: Robert Hillyer
Dur: 2'
Pub: EC Schirmer

1466   Pinkham, Daniel
Pleasure it is (1973)
Med: unison treble vv, opt. melodic inst. and org
Txt: see below
Dur: 6'
Pub: EC Schirmer
 Pleasure it is (William Randolph Cornish)
 For Saturday (Christopher Smart)
 Christ was the word (Queen Elizabeth I)

1467   Pinkham, Daniel
Psalm 81 (1959)
Med: SATB dbl choir, brass or org
Txt: Ps. 81
Dur: 3'
Pub: ACA

1468   Pinkham, Daniel
Psalm 96 (1951)
Med: SATB
Txt: Ps. 96
Dur: 2'
Pub: ACA

1469   Pinkham, Daniel
Psalm set (1968)
Med: SATB, 2 tpt, 2 tbn; opt. org, tuba, timp
Txt: Ps. 134, 117, 47
Dur: 7'
Pub: CF Peters
 Fanfare
 Benediction
 Jubilation

1470   Pinkham, Daniel
The reproaches (1960)
Med: SATB div
Txt: LU, trans. Jean Lunn
Dur: 18'
Pub: AMP

1471   Pinkham, Daniel
Requiem (1963)
Med: SATB, AT soli, 2 hn, 2 tpt, 2
  tbn, bass, org
Txt: LU
Dur: 15'
Pub: CF Peters
Rev: Boston *Globe*, March 14, 1963;
  Christian Science Monitor, January
  26, 1963; *Musical America* 83
  (March, 1963) p88.
Bib: B51

1472   Pinkham, Daniel
Sacred service (1967)
Med: SATB, SATB soli, cantor, org
Txt: liturgical Hebrew
Dur: 15'
Pub: EC Schirmer

1473   Pinkham, Daniel
St. Mark Passion (1965)
Med: SATB, STBB soli, brass, perc,
  dbl bass
Txt: Gospel of Mark
Dur: 33'
Pub: CF Peters

1474   Pinkham, Daniel
*The seven last words of Christ on the
  cross* (1971)
Med: SATB, TBB soli, org, tape
Txt: biblical
Dur: 15'
Pub: EC Schirmer

1475   Pinkham, Daniel
The sheepheards' song (1971)
Med: SATB, S solo, opt. tape
Txt: *England's Helicon*, 1600
Dur: 4'
Pub: EC Schirmer

1476   Pinkham, Daniel
The sick rose (1959)
Med: SA
Txt: William Blake
Dur: 2'
Pub: ACA

1477   Pinkham, Daniel
Signs will appear (1974)
Med: SATB, org, tape
Txt: not indicated
Dur: 4'
Pub: EC Schirmer

1478   Pinkham, Daniel
Slumber now (1982)
Med: SATB
Txt: Howard Holtzman
Dur: 2'
Pub: EC Schirmer

1479   Pinkham, Daniel
Sometimes the soul (1955)
Med: SATB, gtr or pno
Txt: Norma Farber
Dur: 3'
Pub: EC Schirmer

1480   Pinkham, Daniel
The song of Jeptha's daughter (c.1966)
Med: SSA, SBar soli, pno
Txt: Robert Hillyer
Dur: 13'
Pub: CF Peters
Rev: MLA *Notes* 24 (1975) p155.

1481   Pinkham, Daniel
Song of Simeon (1952)
Med: SATB, org
Txt: Luke 2:29-32
Dur: 5'
Pub: ACA

1482   Pinkham, Daniel
Songs of peaceful departure (1967)
Med: SATB, gtr or pno
Txt: Isaiah 40:6, 8; Ps. 103:16
Dur: 5'
Pub: EC Schirmer

1483   Pinkham, Daniel
Spring (c.1958)
Med: 2-part women's vv
Txt: William Blake
Dur: 2'
Pub: NY: Composer's Facsimile Editions

1484   Pinkham, Daniel
Stabat mater (1964)
Med: SATB, S solo, orch or org
Txt: LU
Dur: 16'
Pub: CF Peters
Bib: B226

1485   Pinkham, Daniel
Star-tree carol (1969)
Med: SATB
Txt: Robert Hillyer
Dur: 2'
Pub: C Fischer

1486   Pinkham, Daniel
Statement of faith (1961)
Med: SATB, SATB soli, org
Txt: from 1959 Statement of the United Church of Christ
Dur: 11'
Pub: copies in ACA, AMC

1487   Pinkham, Daniel
Take life (1978)
Med: SSAA
Txt: Norma Farber
Dur: 5'
Pub: EC Schirmer

1488   Pinkham, Daniel
Te Deum (1959)
Med: SATB, tpts, org
Txt: LU, trans. John Dryden
Dur: 5'
Pub: Robert King Music
N.B. Also arr. for SSAA, TTBB.

1489   Pinkham, Daniel
The temptation in the wilderness (1972)
Med: SATB, Bar solo, org, tape
Txt: Luke 4
Dur: 4'
Pub: EC Schirmer

1490   Pinkham, Daniel
Thou hast turned my laments into dancing (1973)
Med: SATB
Txt: Ps. 30:11-12
Dur: 1'
Pub: CF Peters

1491   Pinkham, Daniel
Thou hast loved righteousness (1963)
Med: SATB, opt. kybd
Txt: Ps. 45:7, 17
Dur: 3'
Pub: CF Peters

1492   Pinkham, Daniel
Three Campion poems (1981)
Med: SATB, handbells, xylophone
Txt: Thomas Campion
Dur: 7'
Pub: EC Schirmer

1493   Pinkham, Daniel
Three Lenten poems of Richard Crashaw (1963)
Med: SSA, handbells (or celesta or hp), str or kybd
Txt: Richard Crashaw

Dur: 5'
Pub: EC Schirmer
Bib: B223
N.B. Also arr. for SATB.
  On the still surviving marks of our
    Saviour's wounds
  Upon the body of our blessed Lord
  O save us then

1494 Pinkham, Daniel
Three motets (1947, rev. 1975)
Med: SSA, org or pno
Txt: Ps. 95:11-13; 115:1-3; 9:1-4
Dur: 7'
Pub: CF Peters
  Lætantur coeli
  Non nobis, Domine
  Celebrabro te, Domine

1495 Pinkham, Daniel
Three poems of William Blake
  (c.1959)
Med: SA
Txt: William Blake
Dur: 9'
Pub: ACA

1496 Pinkham, Daniel
Thy statutes have been my songs
  (1965)
Med: SATB, pno
Txt: Norma Farber
Dur: 8'
Pub: EC Schirmer

1497 Pinkham, Daniel
Time of times (1975-77)
Med: SATB, pno
Txt: Norma Farber
Dur: 8'30"
Pub: EC Schirmer
  Ongoing
  Long lullaby
  A quiet gospel
  A tree in the river

  A cage of half-light
  In the counting house
  Time of aster

1498 Pinkham, Daniel
To think of those absent (1969)
Med: SATB, gtr, hp or pno
Txt: Norma Farber
Dur: 3'
Pub: EC Schirmer

1499 Pinkham, Daniel
To troubled friends (1972)
Med: SATB, tape
Txt: James Wright
Dur: 14'
Pub: EC Schirmer
  To a troubled friend
  Father
  A fit against this country
  Evening

1500 Pinkham, Daniel
A tunnel in the leaves (1978)
Med: SATB, pno or str orch
Txt: Howard Holtzman
Dur: 8'
Pub: EC Schirmer

1501 Pinkham, Daniel
Twentieth century (1948)
Med: SATB
Txt: Robert Hillyer
Dur: 1'
Pub: ACA

1502 Pinkham, Daniel
Two poems of Howard Holtzman
  (1975)
Med: SSAA, tape
Txt: Howard Holtzman
Dur: 4'
Pub: EC Schirmer

1503 Pinkham, Daniel
Two secular choruses (1955)
Med: SATB
Txt: not indicated
Dur: 6'
Pub: EC Schirmer
 The leaf
 Henry was a worthy king

1504 Pinkham, Daniel
Versicle: call to prayer (1956)
Med: SATB, opt. org
Txt: liturgical
Dur: 1'
Pub: ACA

1505 Pinkham, Daniel
We have seen his star (1957)
Med: unison, org
Txt: Matthew 2:2
Dur: 1'
Pub: ACA

1506 Pinkham, Daniel
Wedding cantata (1956)
Med: SATB, ST soli, pno or org or 2
 hns, celesta, str
Txt: Solomon 2:10-12; 6:1-3; 8:7;
 4:16; 8:6
Dur: 10'
Pub: CF Peters

1507 Pinkham, Daniel
The Wellesley Hills psalm book
 (c.1986)
Med: unison, org
Txt: Book of Psalms
Dur: various short works
Pub: EC Schirmer

1508 Pinkham, Daniel
What do you want from me? (1987)
Med: SATB, ch. orch, tape
Txt: James Wright
Dur: 8'

Pub: unpubl.
 This morning my beloved rose before
  I did
 Beginning
 My grandfather's ghost
 Milkweed
 A breath of air

1509 Pinkham, Daniel
When God arose (1980)
Med: SATB, SSATBar soli, hpschd,
 org, perc
Txt: Ps. 76:9-10; Matthew 28:1-7;
 Colossians 3:1-4
Dur: 8'
Pub: EC Schirmer

1510 Pinkham, Daniel
Why art thou cast down? (1955)
Med: SATB, opt. kybd
Txt: Ps. 42:11
Dur: 2'
Pub: CF Peters

1511 Pinkham, Daniel
Witching hour (1975)
Med: SSA, electric gtr (or pno), tape
Txt: Norma Farber
Dur: 4'
Pub: EC Schirmer

1512 Pinkham, Daniel
Ye shall have a song (1986)
Med: SATB, orch
Txt: biblical
Dur: 4'
Pub: EC Schirmer
Bib: B176

1513 Pinkham, Daniel
Ye watchers and ye holy ones (1956)
Med: unison, 2 vln, vla, org
Txt: biblical
Dur: 4'
Pub: ACA

1514 Piston, Walter
Bow down thine ear, O Lord (1958)
Med: SATB, fl, clar, bsn, vn, vla, cello,
    bass
Txt: Ps. 86
Src: Grove

1515 Piston, Walter
Carnival song (c.1941)
Med: TBB, brass
Txt: Lorenzo de Medici
Dur: 8'
Pub: Arrow Music Press
Mss: LC
N.B. Accompaniment also arr. for two
    pianos.

1516 Piston, Walter
Psalm and prayer of David (1958)
Med: SATB, fl, clar, bsn, str quartet
Txt: Ps. 86, 96
Dur: 17'
Pub: AMP
Mss: BPL
    Bow down thine ear, O Lord
    Sing unto the Lord a new song

R

1517 Rochberg, George
*Behold, my servant (Everything that
is holy)* (1973)
Med: SATB
Txt: William Blake; Isaiah; Ps. 43
Dur: 7'
Pub: Presser
Mss: NYPL

1518 Rochberg, George
Five smooth stones (1949)
Med: SATB, S solo, orch
Txt: Stella Benson
Dur: 20'
Pub: unpubl.?
Mss: NYPL

1519 Rochberg, George
*Passions according to the twentieth
century* (1967)
Med: SATB, soli, jazz quintet, brass
    ensemble, perc, pno, tape
Src: Grove
N.B. Later withdrawn by the composer.

1520 Rochberg, George
Symphony No. 3 (1969)
Med: SATB, soli, orch
Txt: German text, author not indi-
    cated
Dur: 40'
Pub: Presser

1521 Rochberg, George
Tableaux (1968)
Med: TTBB, S solo, 2 actors' voices,
    12 players
Txt: Paul Rochberg
Dur: 25'
Pub: Presser
Mss: copy in LC

1522 Rochberg, George
Three psalms (1954)
Med: SATB div
Txt: Ps. 23, 43, 150
Dur: 14'
Pub: Presser
Rev: MLA *Notes* 14 (Sept, 1957) p18-
    19; *Musical Courier* 153 (May,
    1956) p37

1523 Rorem, Ned
All glorious God (1955)
Med: SATB
Txt: *Episcopal Hymnal* (1841)
Dur: 3'
Pub: CF Peters

1524 Rorem, Ned
An American oratorio (1984)
Med: SATB, T solo, orch

Txt: see below
Dur: 45'
Pub: BH
Rev: *Diapason* 76 (Sept, 1985) p3; *Hi-Fidelity/Musical America* 35 (Jan, 1985) pMA13 and 35 (May, 1985) pMA22-3; *New York Times*, Jan. 7, 1985; *Symphony Magazine* 35/5 (1984) p38; *Tempo* 151 (Dec, 1984) p55
Bib: B112
    The new Colossus (Emma Lazarus)
    To Helen (Edgar Allen Poe)
    Snowflakes (Henry W. Longfellow)
    Something lost (Mark Twain)
    Raven days (Sidney Lanier)
    Misgivings (Herman Melville)
    I saw a man pursuing (Stephen Crane)
    There was a crimson cloth (Crane)
    War is kind (Crane)
    A New York soldier (Walt Whitman)
    Here the frailest leaves (Whitman)
    To Ned (Melville)

1525 Rorem, Ned
Armenian love songs (1987)
Med: SATB
Txt: Nahapet Kuchak
Dur: 7'
Pub: unpubl.

1526 Rorem, Ned
The ascension (1963)
Med: SATB div, orch
Txt: Joseph Beaumont
Dur: 4'
Pub: BH
Mss: LC
N.B. Alternate title: *Lift up your heads.*

1527 Rorem, Ned
Breathe on me, breath of God (c.1989)
Med: SATB
Txt: Edwin Hatch

Dur: 1'40"
Pub: BH
Rev: *American Organist* 23 (Dec, 1989) p46-51

1528 Rorem, Ned
Canticle of the lamb (1972)
Med: SATB
Txt: composer
Dur: 2'
Pub: BH

1529 Rorem, Ned
Canticles (1971-2)
Med: SATB, in various combinations
Txt: LU, et al.
Dur: 12'
Pub: BH
Rev: *Diapason* 64 (Jan, 1973) p17; *Music* (AGO) 7 (Feb, 1973) p52-3; *Music Journal* 30 (Dec, 1972) p4ff
    Set 1
        Confitebor tibi
        Magnificat anima mea
        Nunc dimittis
    Set 2
        Benedictus es Domine
        Phos Hilarion
        Ecce Deus
        Canticle of the lamb

1530 Rorem, Ned
Christ the Lord is risen today (1955)
Med: SATB
Txt: Charles Wesley
Dur: 2'
Pub: CF Peters

1531 Rorem, Ned
The Corinthians (1953)
Med: SATB, org
Txt: 1 Corinthians 13
Dur: 9'
Pub: CF Peters

1532 Rorem, Ned
The death of Moses (c.1988)
Med: SATB, org
Txt: Deuteronomy 34:1-2
Dur: 7'
Pub: BH
Mss: copy in LC
Rev: *Tempo* 164 (Mar, 1988) p51

1533 Rorem, Ned
Fables: five very short operas (c.1974)
Med: SATB, pno
Txt: Jean de La Fontaine
Dur: 23'
Pub: BH
Rev: *Opera News* 49 (Jan 19, 1985) p39-40; *Opernwelt* 3 (Apr, 1989) p40; *Pan Pipes* 63/4 (1971) p11-13
N.B. "May be performed as lyric theatre, ballet, cantata, or in combination of these."
    The lion in love
    The sun and the frogs
    The bird wounded by an arrow
    The fox and the grapes
    The animals sick of the plague

1534 Rorem, Ned
A far island (1953)
Med: SSA
Txt: Kenward Elmslie
Dur: 4'
Pub: Presser

1535 Rorem, Ned
Five prayers for the young (1953)
Med: SSA
Txt: see below
Dur: 6'
Pub: Presser
    A nursery darling (Lewis Carroll)
    A dirge (Percy B. Shelley)
    Now I lay me down to sleep (Shelley)
    Fragment (Shelley)
    The virgin's cradle hymn (Samuel Taylor Coleridge)

1536 Rorem, Ned
Four hymns (1973)
Med: SATB
Txt: trad.
Dur: 8'
Pub: BH
    Come, pure hearts
    I heard a sound
    In Christ there is no east or west
    Jerusalem, my happy home

1537 Rorem, Ned
Four madrigals (1947)
Med: SATB
Txt: Sappho, trans. Cecil M. Bowra
Dur: 7'30"
Pub: Mercury Music
Rev: *Music and Letters* 30 (Jan, 1949) p93; *Music Review* 10 (Feb, 1949) p75-6
    Parting
    Flowers for the graces
    Love
    An absent friend

1538 Rorem, Ned
From an unknown past (1951)
Med: SATB
Txt: anon., John Donne, William Shakespeare
Dur: 8'
Pub: Southern
Rev: MLA *Notes* 11 (June, 1954) p438
    The lover in winter plaineth for the spring
    Hey nonny no!
    My blood is so red
    Suspira
    The miracle
    Tears
    Crabbed age and youth

1539 Rorem, Ned
Gentle visitations (1953)
Med: SSA
Txt: Percy Bysshe Shelley
Dur: 3'30"
Pub: Presser

1540 Rorem, Ned
Give all to love (1981)
Med: SA or TB, pno
Txt: Ralph Waldo Emerson
Dur: 6'
Pub: BH

1541 Rorem, Ned
Goodbye my fancy (1988)
Med: SATB, ABar soli, orch
Txt: Walt Whitman
Dur: 48'
Pub: BH

1542 Rorem, Ned
He shall rule from sea to sea (1967)
Med: SATB, org
Txt: Ps. 71
Dur: 5'
Pub: BH

1543 Rorem, Ned
Homer: three scenes from the Iliad
(c.1986)
Med: SATB, fl, ob, bsn, tpt, pno, vln,
vla, cello
Txt: Homer
Dur: 20'
Pub: BH
Mss: copy in LC

1544 Rorem, Ned
I feel death... (1953)
Med: TTB
Txt: John Dryden
Dur: 2'
Pub: BH

1545 Rorem, Ned
In time of pestilence: six short madrigals
(1973)
Med: SATB
Txt: Thomas Nashe [*sic*]
Dur: 5'
Pub: BH
Adieu, farewell earth's bliss
Beauty if but a flower
Haste therefore each degree
Rich men, trust not in wealth
Strength stoops unto the grave
With his wantoness

1546 Rorem, Ned
Laudemus tempus actum (1964)
Med: SATB, orch
Txt: composer
Dur: 3'
Pub: BH

1547 Rorem, Ned
Letters from Paris (1966)
Med: SATB, ch. orch
Txt: Genét (Janet Flanner)
Dur: 25'
Pub: BH
Mss: LC
Spring
The French telephone
Summer
Colette
Autumn
The sex of the automobile
Winter
Mistinguett
Spring again

1548 Rorem, Ned
Little lamb who made thee? (1982)
Med: SATB, org
Txt: William Blake
Dur: 3'
Pub: BH

1549 Rorem, Ned
Little prayers (1973)
Med: SATB, SBar soli, orch
Txt: Paul Goodman
Dur: 35'
Pub: BH
Rev: *Choral Journal* 14/7 (1974) p20;
    Hi-Fidelity/Musical America 24 (May,
    1974) pMA7; *International Musician*
    72 (Apr, 1974) p11; *Music Journal*
    32 (Sept, 1974) p19; *School Musician*
    45 (Apr, 1974) p41
    Rest well
    Creator of the worlds
    God, I prayed to me restore
    Creator spirit, please
    Novices of art understate
    O God of fire and the secret
    Father, guide and lead
    Long lines
    Creator spirit
    Rest well
    God bless my small home
    I waited in the parlor
    Rest well
    A prayer to St. Harmony

1550 Rorem, Ned
The long home (1946)
Med: SATB, orch
Txt: not indicated
Pub: unpubl.
Src: McDonald

1551 Rorem, Ned
Love alone (c.1989)
Med: TB, pno four hands
Txt: Paul Monette
Dur: 6'
Pub: BH

1552 Rorem, Ned
Love divine, all loves excelling (1966)
Med: SATB
Txt: Charles Wesley

Dur: 1'
Pub: BH

1553 Rorem, Ned
Mercy and truth are met (1983)
Med: SATB, kybd
Txt: Ps. 85:10-13
Dur: 3'30"
Pub: BH

1554 Rorem, Ned
The mild mother (1952)
Med: unison children's choirs, pno
Txt: anon. 15th century
Dur: 1'30"
Pub: EC Schirmer

1555 Rorem, Ned
Miracles of Christmas (1959)
Med: SATB, org
Txt: Ruth Apprich Jacob
Dur: 17'
Pub: EC Schirmer
    The cherry tree
    The rooster
    The wise men
    In the stable
    The white rose
    The spider and the fly
    The land

1556 Rorem, Ned
Missa brevis (1973)
Med: SATB, STBarB soli
Txt: LU
Dur: 16'
Pub: BH
Bib: B51, 175

1557 Rorem, Ned
O magnum mysterium (1978)
Med: SATB
Txt: LU
Dur: 3'
Pub: BH

1558   Rorem, Ned
The oxen (1978)
Med: SATB
Txt: Thomas Hardy
Dur: 4'
Pub: BH

1559   Rorem, Ned
Pilgrim strangers (1984)
Med: AATBBB (male vv)
Txt: Walt Whitman
Dur: 14'
Pub: BH
Mss: copy in LC
Rev: *Hi-Fidelity/Musical America* 35
       (Mar, 1985) pMA25-6; *Tempo*
       150 (Sept, 1984) p58

1560   Rorem, Ned
The poet's Requiem (1955)
Med: SATB, S solo, orch
Txt: Franz Kafka, Rainer Maria Rilke,
       Jean Cocteau, Stephen Mallarmé,
       Sigmund Freud, Paul Goodman,
       André Gide
Dur: 22'
Pub: BH
Rev: *American Organist* 40 (April, 1957)
       p26; *Musical America* 71 (July,
       1957), p30; *Musical Courier* 155/
       5 (March 15, 1957) p14; *Pan
       Pipes* 49 (1957), p67 and 50
       (1958) p70; MLA *Notes* 8 (Sept,
       1957) p753; *Time* 69 (Feb 25,
       1957) p60-1.
Bib: B175

1561   Rorem, Ned
Praise the Lord, O my soul (1982)
Med: SATB, org
Txt: Ps. 146
Dur: 3'
Pub: BH

1562   Rorem, Ned
Praises for the nativity (1970)
Med: SAATTB, SATB soli, org
Txt: Book of Common Prayer
Dur: 5'
Pub: BH

1563   Rorem, Ned
Prayer to Jesus (1973)
Med: SATB
Txt: Gerard Manley Hopkins
Dur: 2'
Pub: BH

1564   Rorem, Ned
Prayers and responses (1960)
Med: SATB, cong
Txt: Book of Common Prayer
Dur: 4'
Pub: BH

1565   Rorem, Ned
*Proper for the votive Mass of the Holy
       Spirit* (1966)
Med: unison, org
Txt: Book of Common Prayer
Dur: 10'
Pub: BH

1566   Rorem, Ned
A sermon on miracles (1947)
Med: unison, str
Txt: Paul Goodman
Dur: 5'30"
Pub: BH

1567   Rorem, Ned
Seven motets for the church year (1986)
Med: SATB, wind ensemble
Txt: liturgical
Dur: 19'
Pub: BH
       Christmas (While all things were in
       quiet silence)

Epiphany (Before the morning star
forgotten)
Ash Wednesday (Lay up for yourselves)
Easter (Praise him who was crucified)
Pentecost (Today the Holy Spirit ap-
peareth)
Ascension (God is gone up)
All Saints' Day (Rejoice we all in the
Lord)

1568   Rorem, Ned
The seventieth psalm (1943)
Med: SATB, wind ensemble
Txt: Ps. 70
Dur: 4'
Pub: BH

1569   Rorem, Ned
Shout the glad tidings (1978)
Med: SATB
Txt: Muhlenberg, from *The Hymnal*
Dur: 2'30"
Pub: BH

1570   Rorem, Ned
Sing my soul his wondrous love (1955)
Med: SATB
Txt: Episcopal Hymnal (1841)
Dur: 4'
Pub: CF Peters

1571   Rorem, Ned
Surge, illuminare (1979)
Med: SATB, org
Txt: Isaiah 3
Dur: 4'
Pub: BH
N.B. English title: *Arise, shine.*

1572   Rorem, Ned
Te Deum (1987)
Med: SATB, brass, org
Txt: LU
Dur: 10'
Pub: BH

1573   Rorem, Ned
Three choruses for Christmas (1978)
Med: SATB
Src: Grove

1574   Rorem, Ned
Three incantations (1948)
Med: unison vv, pno
Txt: Boulterhouse
Src: Grove

1575   Rorem, Ned
*Three motets on poems of Gerard
Manley Hopkins* (1973)
Med: SATB, org
Txt: Gerard Manley Hopkins
Dur: 6'
Pub: BH
O Deus, ego amo te
Oratorio patris condren: O Jesu vivens
in Maria
Thee, God

1576   Rorem, Ned
Three poems of Baudelaire (1986)
Med: SATB
Txt: Charles Pierre Baudelaire
Dur: 15'
Pub: BH
Invitation to the voyage
Cat
Satan's litanies

1577   Rorem, Ned
Three prayers (1974)
Med: SATB
Txt: Paul Goodman
Dur: 6'
Pub: BH
Creator spirit, who dost lightly hover
Father, guide and lead me
Creator spirit, please

1578 Rorem, Ned
Truth in the night season (1966)
Med: SATB, org
Txt: Ps. 92
Dur: 4'
Pub: BH

1579 Rorem, Ned
Two holy songs (1969)
Med: SATB, pno
Txt: Ps. 134, 150
Dur: 7'
Pub: Southern
N.B. Originally for solo voice.

1580 Rorem, Ned
Two psalms and a proverb (1962)
Med: SATB, str quartet
Txt: Ps. 133, 13; Proverbs 23
Dur: 13'
Pub: EC Schirmer
Behold how good and pleasant it is
Wounds without cause
How long wilt thou forget me, O God?

1581 Rorem, Ned
Virelai (1965)
Med: SATB
Txt: Chaucer
Dur: 2'
Pub: Novello; BH

1582 Rorem, Ned
A Whitman cantata (1983)
Med: TTBB, brass, timp
Txt: Walt Whitman
Dur: 21'
Pub: BH
Rev: *Tempo* 147 (Dec, 1983) p49
Some strange musician
That shadow, my likeness
All for love
The soul, reaching
Now thy sullen notes
Tears
All over joy!

S

1583 Schuman, William
At the crossroads (1939)
Med: SATB
Txt: Richard Hovey
Dur: 3'
Pub: unpubl.
Mss: LC
N.B. "...for the World's Fair, NYC, 1939."

1584 Schuman, William
Canonic choruses (c.1942)
Med: SATB
Txt: see below
Dur: 6'
Pub: G Schirmer
Mss: copy in LC
Epitaph (Edna St. Vincent Millay)
Epitaph for Joseph Conrad (Countee Cullen)
Night stuff (Carl Sandburg)
Come not (Alfred Lord Tennyson)

1585 Schuman, William
Carols of death (1958)
Med: SATB
Txt: Walt Whitman
Dur: 12'
Pub: Presser
Mss: LC
Bib: B82, 83
The last invocation
The unknown region
To all, to each

1586 Schuman, William
Casey at the bat (1976)
Med: SATB, S solo, orch
Txt: J. Gury
Src: Grove
N.B. A choral suite arranged from the composer's opera of the same title.

1587 Schuman, William
Choral etude (1937)
Med: SATB
Txt: no text
Dur: 3'
Pub: C Fischer
Mss: LC

1588 Schuman, William
Concerto on old English rounds (1974)
Med: SSA, solo vla, orch
Txt: trad. English
Src: Grove
Rev: *Hi-Fidelity/Musical America* 29
      (Mar, 1979) p29; *International
      Musician* 73 (Dec, 1974) p15;
      New Yorker 52 (May 3, 1976)
      p117; *Symphony Magazine* 25/6
      (1974) p27

1589 Schuman, William
Declaration chorale (c.1971)
Med: SATB
Txt: composer, after Walt Whitman
Dur: 5'
Pub: Presser
Rev: *Music Clubs Magazine* 51 (May,
      1972) p11

1590 Schuman, William
Deo ac veritati (1963)
Med: TBB
Txt: text is motto of Colgate Uni-
      versity
Dur: 3'30"
Pub: Presser
Mss: LC

1591 Schuman, William
*Esses: short suite for singers on words
      beginning with S* (1982)
Med: SATB
Pub: Presser
Src: Grove

1592 Schuman, William
Five rounds on famous words (1969)
Med: SATB or SSA
Txt: not specified
Dur: 7'
Pub: Presser
Mss: LC
N.B. *Haste* mss. at LC filed separately
      from others, which were origi-
      nally published as *Four rounds*....
      Health
      Thrift
      Caution
      Beauty
      Haste

1593 Schuman, William
A free song: secular cantata No. 2
      (1942)
Med: SATB, orch or 2 pnos
Txt: Walt Whitman
Dur: 13'
Pub: G Schirmer
Rev: Boston *Daily Globe*, March 27,
      1943.
Bib: B82
      Long, too long, America
      Look down, fair moon
      Song of the banner

1594 Schuman, William
Holiday song (1942)
Med: SATB, pno
Txt: Genevieve Taggard
Dur: 3'30"
Pub: G Schirmer
Mss: LC
N.B. Also arr. for TTBB, SAB.

1595 Schuman, William
The Lord has a child (1956)
Med: SATB or SSA, kybd
Txt: Langston Hughes
Dur: 3'30"
Pub: Presser

Mss: LC

N.B. Originally for solo voice.

1596   Schuman, William
Mail order madrigals (1971)
Med: see below
Txt: Sears, Roebuck catalog, 1897
Dur: 12'
Pub: Presser
Rev: *Hi-Fidelity/Musical America* 22
   (Aug, 1972) pMA21
   Attention, ladies (TBB)
   Superfluous hair (SSAA)
   Sweet refreshing sleep (SATB)
   Dr. Worden's pills (SATB)

1597   Schuman, William
On freedom's ground (1985)
Med: SATB, Bar solo, orch
Txt: Richard Wilbur
Dur: 40'
Pub: Merion Music
Rev: *American Organist* 20 (Nov, 1986)
   p47; *Instrumentalist* 41 (Dec, 1986)
   p85; *Musical America* 107/2 (1987)
   p49-50; *Ovation* 7 (June, 1986)
   p29ff; *Symphony Magazine* 36/6
   (1985) p14 and 37/5 (1986) p22
   Back then
   Our risen states
   Like a great statue
   Come dance
   Immigrants still

1598   Schuman, William
Orpheus with his lute (c.1970)
Med: SATB, pno
Txt: William Shakespeare
Dur: 2'
Pub: G Schirmer
N.B. Originally for solo voice.

1599   Schuman, William
Perceptions (1982)
Med: SATB

Txt: Walt Whitman
Dur: 4'
Pub: Presser

1600   Schuman, William
Pioneers! (1937)
Med: SATB div
Txt: Walt Whitman
Dur: 11'
Pub: EB Marks; JW Chester
Mss: LC (several versions)
Bib: B82

1601   Schuman, William
Prelude for [women's] voices (c.1940)
Med: SSAA, S solo
Txt: Thomas Wolfe
Dur: 6'
Pub: G Schirmer
Mss: LC (several versions)
N.B. Also arr. for SATB div.

1602   Schuman, William
Prologue (1939)
Med: SSATB, orch
Txt: Genevieve Taggard
Dur: 4'
Pub: G Schirmer
Mss: LC

1603   Schuman, William
Requiescat (1942)
Med: SSAA, pno
Txt: no text
Dur: 4'
Pub: G Schirmer
Mss: LC

1604   Schuman, William
Te Deum (c.1945)
Med: SATB
Txt: LU
Dur: 3'
Pub: G Schirmer
Mss: LC

N.B. Written as incidental music to the coronation scene in Shakespeare's *Henry VIII.*

1605 Schuman, William
This is our time (secular cantata No. 1) (1940)
Med: SATB, orch
Txt: Genevieve Taggard
Dur: 25'
Pub: BH
Mss: LC
Rev: New York *Times,* July 5, 1940.

1606 Schuman, William
To thy love: choral fantasy on Old English rounds (1973)
Med: SSA
Txt: anon.
Dur: 15'
Pub: Merion Music
N.B. Also titled, *To my love...* in some catalogs; orchestral version with viola solo, 1974? (See above, *Concerto on old English rounds,* No. 1588)

1607 Schuman, William
Truth shall deliver: ballade of good advice (c.1946)
Med: TTB
Txt: Chaucer, adapt. M. Farquhar
Dur: 4'30"
Pub: G Schirmer

1608 Sessions, Roger
Mass (1955)
Med: unison, org
Txt: LU
Dur: 15'
Pub: EB Marks
Mss: Princeton University, and LC
Rev: *Diapason* 60 (April, 1969) p18-19; MLA *Notes* 16 (Dec, 1958)

p151-2; *Musical Times* 97 (May, 1956) p268-9 and 102 (Nov, 1958), p696-7
Bib: B51, 136, 165, 218, 219

1609 Sessions, Roger
Three choruses on biblical texts (c.1976)
Med: SATB, ch. orch
Txt: Ps. 130; Isaiah 1, 2; Ps. 147, 148, 150
Dur: 15'
Pub: Presser
Rev: *Diapason* 66 (May, 1975) p8; *Hi-Fidelity/Musical America* 25 (June, 1975) pMA27; *Music* (AGO) 9 (June, 1975) p24; *Music Educators Journal* 62 (Sept, 1975) p96; *Symphony News* 26/2 (1975) p26
Bib: B166
Out of the depths
Ah, sinful nations
Praise ye the Lord

1610 Sessions, Roger
Turn, O libertad (1943)
Med: SATB, pno four hands
Txt: Walt Whitman
Dur: 4'
Pub: EB Marks
Rev: MLA *Notes* 10 (June, 1953) p494; *Musical America* 75 (Jan 1, 1955) p32; *Pan Pipes* 46 (Mar, 1954) p8
Bib: B166

1611 Sessions, Roger
When lilacs last in the dooryard bloomed (1970)
Med: SATB, SBar soli, orch
Txt: Walt Whitman
Dur: 40'
Pub: Merion Music
Mss: copy in LC

Rev: *BMI* (Oct, 1971) p12; *Hi-Fidelity/ Musical America* 26 (June, 1976) pMA22-3, and 28 (Feb, 1978) pMA70-1; *Musical Quarterly* 58/2 (1972) p297-307; *The Nation*, April 19, 1975; New York *Times*, Aug. 15, 1977; *New Yorker* 53 (May 16, 1977) p133-6ff; *Perspectives of New Music* 10/2 (1972) p175; *Tempo* 125 (June, 1978) p35-7; *Time*, June 26, 1978; *Village Voice*, Feb 16, 1976; *World of Music* 14/2 (1972) p79
Bib: B51, 75, 165, 178
    When lilacs last. . .
    Over the breast of the spring
    Now while I sat in the day

1612   Shapero, Harold
Hebrew cantata (1954)
Med: SATB, SATB soli, fl, tpt, vln, hp, org
Txt: Jehuda Halevi
Dur: 29'
Pub: Southern

1613   Shapero, Harold
A song of the mountains (1956)
Med: SATB, orch
Txt: F.E. Allen
Src: Grove

1614   Shapero, Harold
Two psalms (1952)
Med: SATB
Txt: Ps. 146, 117
Dur: 7'
Pub: Southern
Rev: *Choral Guide* 7 (May, 1954) p31; *MLA Notes* 11 (June, 1954) p439
    Lauda
    Jubilate

1615   Shepherd, Arthur
A ballad of trees and the master (1935)
Med: SATB div
Txt: Sidney Lanier
Dur: 4'
Pub: CC Birchard

1616   Shepherd, Arthur
Build thee more stately mansions (1938)
Med: SSAA
Txt: Oliver Wendell Holmes
Src: Newman (B164)

1617   Shepherd, Arthur
Carol (1944)
Med: SA, pno
Txt: anon. 15th-century
Dur: 1'
Pub: Presser

1618   Shepherd, Arthur
The city in the sea (1913)
Med: SATB dbl choir, Bar solo, orch
Txt: Bliss Carman
Dur: 20'
Pub: Boston Music Co.

1619   Shepherd, Arthur
Drive on! (1947)
Med: SATB, Bar solo
Txt: Gary Merit
Dur: 4'
Pub: CC Birchard

1620   Shepherd, Arthur
He came all so still (1915)
Med: SSAA, pno
Txt: anon.
Dur: 2'
Pub: AP Schmidt

1621   Shepherd, Arthur
Invitation to the dance (1937)
Med: SATB, orch
Txt: Sidonius Apollinaris
Dur: 7'
Pub: unpubl.?
Mss: copy in LC

1622   Shepherd, Arthur
Jolly wat, canticum nativitate Christi
(1944)
Med: 2 equal vv, pno
Txt: anon. 15th-century
Dur: 4'
Pub: Music Press

1623   Shepherd, Arthur
The Lord hath brought again Zion
(1907)
Med: SATB, Bar solo
Txt: biblical
Src: Newman (B164)

1624   Shepherd, Arthur
O Jesu who art gone before (1918)
Med: SATB
Src: Newman (B164)

1625   Shepherd, Arthur
Planting a tree (1942)
Med: SATB
Src: Newman (B164)

1626   Shepherd, Arthur
Psalm XLII (1944)
Med: SATB, SATB soli, org
Txt: Ps. 42
Dur: 6'
Pub: CC Birchard
Rev: *Music Clubs Magazine* 30 (Feb,
1951) p25; *Musical America* 70
(Dec, 1950) p28
Bib: B164

1627   Shepherd, Arthur
Slowly, silently now the moon (1942)
Med: SSAA
Txt: Walter de la Mare
Src: Newman (B164)

1628   Shepherd, Arthur
Song of the pilgrims (1934)
Med: SATB dbl choir, T solo, orch
Txt: Rupert Brooke
Dur: 13'
Pub: CC Birchard

1629   Shepherd, Arthur
Song of the sea wind (1915)
Med: SSA, pno
Txt: William Sharp
Dur: 5'
Pub: AP Schmidt

1630   Shepherd, Arthur
The word (c.1951)
Med: SATB, org
Txt: Eben Tourjeé
Dur: 4'
Pub: CC Birchard

1631   Shepherd, Arthur
Ye mariners of England (1941)
Med: TTBB, pno
Txt: Thomas Campbell
Dur: 8'
Pub: BH

1632   Skilton, Charles S.
The ballad of Carmilhan (n.d.)
Med: not indicated
Txt: Henry W. Longfellow
Dur: unfinished
Mss: University of Missouri-Kansas
City (incomplete)
Src: Dox

1633   Skilton, Charles S.
Communion service (1937)
Med: SATB, soli, org, orch
Txt: LU
Src: Grove

1634   Skilton, Charles S.
La corona (n.d.)
Med: SATB, orch
Txt: John Donne
Src: Grove

1635   Skilton, Charles S.
Electra (1918)
Med: SSA, orch
Txt: Sophocles
Dur: 30'
Pub: AP Schmidt
Rev: *Musical America* 30/13 (1919) p9
N.B. Incidental music to the play.

1636   Skilton, Charles S.
The fountain (c.1923)
Med: SATB
Txt: James Russell Lowell
Dur: 4'30"
Pub: AP Schmidt

1637   Skilton, Charles S.
From forest and stream (1930)
Med: SSA
Txt: Charles O. Roos
Dur: 15'
Pub: C Fischer
    Ghost pipes
    The south wind
    Hollow oak
    Chickadee
    Red bird
    Crane
    The night hawk
    Buck
    Pussy willow
    Cat tails
    Maple sugar
    Forest trail

1638   Skilton, Charles S.
The guardian angel (1925)
Med: SATB, children, SSSATB soli,
    orch
Txt: Abbie Farwell Brown
Dur: 90'
Pub: J Fischer
Mss: LC
    The meadow
    The forest
    The search

1639   Skilton, Charles S.
Lenore (1895)
Med: SATB, Bar solo, orch
Txt: Edgar Allen Poe
Dur: 6'
Pub: Phil.: WH Boner & Co.; copy
    in LC

1640   Skilton, Charles S.
Mass (1930)
Med: SATB
Txt: LU
Src: Grove

1641   Skilton, Charles S.
Midnight (c.1923)
Med: SSAA, pno
Txt: James Russell Lowell
Dur: 4'
Pub: AP Schmidt

1642   Skilton, Charles S.
Music-makers of Kansas (c.1937)
Med: unison and 2-part chorus, pno
Txt: not indicated
Dur: 6'
Pub: C Fischer

1643   Skilton, Charles S.
Pervigilium veneris (1916)
Med: SATB, orch
Txt: not indicated

Mss: University of Missouri-Kansas
City
Src: Dox

1644 Skilton, Charles S.
Ticonderoga (1932)
Med: TTBB, TBar soli, orch
Txt: Robert Louis Stevenson
Dur: 1 hr, 30'
Pub: unpubl.
Mss: University of Missouri-Kansas
City
Src: Dox

1645 Skilton, Charles S.
The witch's daughter (1918)
Med: SATB, SBar soli, orch
Txt: John Greenleaf Whittier
Dur: 35'
Pub: C Fischer
Mss: St. Louis Public Library
Rev: *Musical America* 30/13 (1919) p9

1646 Sowerby, Leo
Ad te levavi animam meam (1959)
Med: SATB
Txt: Ps. 24:1
Dur: 2'
Pub: Summy–Birchard

1647 Sowerby, Leo
Agnus Dei (c.1928)
Med: SATB, S solo
Txt: LU
Dur: 2'
Pub: G Schirmer

1648 Sowerby, Leo
All hail, adored Trinity (1958)
Med: SATB, org
Txt: anon. 11th cent., trans. J.D.
Chambers
Dur: 2'
Pub: Oxford
Mss: LC

1649 Sowerby, Leo
All my heart this night rejoices (1966)
Med: SATB, TBar soli, org
Txt: trad.
Dur: 3'
Pub: HT FitzSimons

1650 Sowerby, Leo
All they from Saba shall come (1934)
Med: SATB, T solo, org
Txt: biblical
Dur: 6'
Pub: HW Gray
Mss: LC

1651 Sowerby, Leo
All things are thine (1949)
Med: SATB, T solo, org
Txt: John Greenleaf Whittier
Dur: 3'
Pub: HW Gray
Rev: MLA *Notes* 7 (Sept, 1950) p635

1652 Sowerby, Leo
*Alleluia for the second Sunday after
Easter* (1966?)
Med: TBB, org
Txt: LU
Dur: 1'
Pub: unpubl.?
Mss: LC

1653 Sowerby, Leo
*Alleluia for the third Sunday after
Easter* (1966?)
Med: TBB, org
Txt: LU
Dur: 1'
Pub: unpubl.?
Mss: LC

1654 Sowerby, Leo
*Alleluia for the fourth Sunday after
Easter* (1966?)
Med: TBB, org

Txt: LU
Dur: 2'
Pub: unpubl.?
Mss: LC

1655   Sowerby, Leo
Alleluia for the fifth Sunday after Easter (1966?)
Med: TBB, org
Txt: LU
Dur: 1'
Pub: unpubl.?
Mss: LC

1656   Sowerby, Leo
Alleluia for the sixth Sunday after Easter (1966?)
Med: TBB, org
Txt: LU
Dur: 1'30"
Pub: unpubl.?
Mss: LC

1657   Sowerby, Leo
And they drew nigh (1960)
Med: SATB, org
Txt: Luke 24:28-31
Dur: 4'
Pub: HW Gray

1658   Sowerby, Leo
An angel stood by the altar of the temple (1955)
Med: SATB, org
Txt: Revelations, Psalms
Dur: 8'
Pub: HW Gray
Mss: LC

1659   Sowerby, Leo
The ark of the covenant (1960)
Med: SATB, TBar soli, nar, org
Txt: 2 Chronicles 5, 6
Dur: 18'
Pub: HW Gray
Mss: LC

1660   Sowerby, Leo
The armor of God (1953)
Med: SATB, org
Txt: Ephesians 6
Dur: 7'
Pub: HW Gray
Mss: LC

1661   Sowerby, Leo
Be ye followers of God (1962)
Med: SATB, org
Txt: Ephesians 5:1-2; 6:10, 13
Dur: 4'
Pub: HW Gray
Mss: LC

1662   Sowerby, Leo
Behold, God is my salvation (1961)
Med: 2-part children, org
Txt: Isaiah 12:2, 5-6
Dur: 3'30"
Pub: HW Gray
Mss: LC

1663   Sowerby, Leo
Behold, O God our defender (1966?)
Med: SATB
Txt: Ps. 84
Dur: 4'30"
Pub: HW Gray
Mss: LC

1664   Sowerby, Leo
Behold, what manner of love (1960)
Med: SSA, org
Txt: 1 John 3:1-3
Dur: 5'
Pub: HW Gray
Mss: LC

1665   Sowerby, Leo
Benedicite omnia opera in D minor (c.1929)
Med: SATB, org
Txt: LU

Dur: 6'
Pub: HW Gray

1666 Sowerby, Leo
Benedictus es Domine (c.1930)
Med: SATB, org
Txt: LU
Dur: 4'30"
Pub: HW Gray

1667 Sowerby, Leo
Benedictus es Domine in B-flat
(c.1930)
Med: SATB, org
Txt: LU
Dur: 4'30"
Pub: HW Gray

1668 Sowerby, Leo
Benedictus es, Domine in D minor
(c.1967)
Med: SA, org
Txt: LU
Dur: 4'
Pub: HW Gray
Mss: LC

1669 Sowerby, Leo
Benedictus es Domine in E major
(1967)
Med: SA, org
Txt: LU
Dur: 2'30"
Pub: HW Gray
Mss: LC

1670 Sowerby, Leo
Blessed are they that fear the Lord
(1939)
Med: SATB, org
Txt: Ps. 128
Dur: 4'
Pub: HW Gray

1671 Sowerby, Leo
Blessed are you, O Lord (1966)
Med: TBB, org
Txt: Daniel 3:55-56, 52
Dur: 3'
Pub: WLSM

1672 Sowerby, Leo
Bow down thine ear (1939)
Med: SATB, ST soli, org
Txt: biblical
Dur: 4'30"
Pub: HT FitzSimons

1673 Sowerby, Leo
Can you count the stars? (1957?)
Med: SAB or unison, kybd
Txt: trad.
Dur: 2'
Pub: HW Gray
Mss: LC (several versions)

1674 Sowerby, Leo
The canticle of the sun (1944)
Med: SATB, orch
Txt: St. Francis of Assisi, trans.
Matthew Arnold
Dur: 30'
Pub: HW Gray
N.B. Awarded the Pulitzer Prize in
music, 1946.

1675 Sowerby, Leo
Christ became obedient for us (1965)
Med: TBB
Txt: Philippians 2:8-9
Dur: 1'
Pub: WLSM

1676 Sowerby, Leo
Christ is risen (1966)
Med: TBB, org
Txt: John 16:28
Dur: 2'
Pub: WLSM

1677   Sowerby, Leo
Christ reborn (1951)
Med: SATB, STB soli, org
Txt: Edward William Borgers
Dur: 40'
Pub: HW Gray
Mss: LC (sketches)
Rev: *Repertoire* 1 (Jan, 1952) p180-2

1678   Sowerby, Leo
Christians, to the paschal victim
(1966?)
Med: SATB, org
Txt: LU
Dur: 4'
Pub: HW Gray
Mss: LC

1679   Sowerby, Leo
City of God (c.1965)
Med: SATB, org
Txt: Samuel Johnson
Dur: 5'30"
Pub: HW Gray
Mss: LC

1680   Sowerby, Leo
Come children, hear me (1966)
Med: SB, org
Txt: Ps. 33:12, 6
Dur: 1'
Pub: WLSM

1681   Sowerby, Leo
Come Holy Ghost: Veni creator
(c.1949)
Med: SATB, org
Txt: LU
Dur: 4'
Pub: HW Gray
Rev: *Musical Courier* 140 (July, 1949)
p15

1682   Sowerby, Leo
Come Holy Ghost, draw near us
(1958)
Med: SATB, org
Txt: anon. 11th cent., trans. George
R. Woodward
Dur: 4'
Pub: Oxford
Mss: LC

1683   Sowerby, Leo
Come ye, and let us go up (1952)
Med: SATB, org
Txt: biblical
Dur: 4'
Pub: HW Gray
Mss: LC

1684   Sowerby, Leo
Communion service in C (1963)
Med: SATB div
Txt: Book of Common Prayer
Dur: 12'
Pub: HW Gray
Mss: original published edition, with
composer's corrections, in LC

1685   Sowerby, Leo
Communion service in D (1959)
Med: SATB, org
Txt: Book of Common Prayer
Dur: 13'
Pub: HW Gray
Mss: LC

1686   Sowerby, Leo
Communion Service in E minor
(1964)
Med: SA, org
Txt: Book of Common Prayer
Dur: 12'
Pub: HW Gray
Mss: LC

1687   Sowerby, Leo
Communion service in F (1954)
Med: SATB, org
Txt: Book of Common Prayer
Dur: 13'
Pub: HW Gray
Mss: LC

1688   Sowerby, Leo
Communion service in G (1957)
Med: SATB, org
Txt: Book of Common Prayer
Dur: 12'
Pub: HW Gray
Mss: LC

1689   Sowerby, Leo
*Cradle hymn: hush, my dear, lie still
    and slumber* (1957?)
Med: SATB, org
Txt: Isaac Watts
Dur: 3'
Pub: HW Gray
Mss: LC

1690   Sowerby, Leo
De profundis (1942)
Med: TTBB
Txt: Ps. 130
Dur: 4'
Pub: unpubl.
Mss: LC

1691   Sowerby, Leo
The disciples recognized the Lord Jesus
    (1965)
Med: TBB, org
Txt: Luke 24:35, John 10:14
Dur: 1'30"
Pub: WLSM

1692   Sowerby, Leo
Double alleluia for Ascension Day
    (1966?)
Med: SATB, org

Txt: "Alleluia"
Dur: 2'
Pub: unpubl.?
Mss: LC

1693   Sowerby, Leo
*Easter Sunday: gradual, alleluia, and
    sequence* (1966)
Med: SSTBB, org
Txt: LU
Dur: 4'
Pub: WLSM
Mss: LC

1694   Sowerby, Leo
Eternal light: a choral grace (1958)
Med: SATB
Txt: Alcuin
Dur: 2'
Pub: HW Gray
Mss: LC

1695   Sowerby, Leo
Except the Lord build the house
    (c.1965)
Med: SATB, org
Txt: Ps. 127
Dur: 4'30"
Pub: HW Gray
Mss: LC

1696   Sowerby, Leo
*Feast of the Holy Family: gradual
    and alleluia* (1965)
Med: TBB, org
Txt: Ps. 105:47; Isaiah 63:16
Dur: 5'
Pub: WLSM
Mss: LC

1697   Sowerby, Leo
Fight the good fight of faith (1953)
Med: SATB
Txt: 1 Timothy 6
Dur: 3'

Pub: HW Gray
Mss: LC

1698   Sowerby, Leo
First-fourth Sunday of Advent: gradual and alleluia (1966)
Med: TBB, org
Txt: Book of Common Prayer
Dur: 4'30"
Pub: WLSM
Mss: LC

1699   Sowerby, Leo
First Mass of Christmas: gradual and alleluia (1966)
Med: SSTBB, org
Txt: Book of Common Prayer
Dur: 3'
Pub: WLSM
Mss: LC

1700   Sowerby, Leo
For we are laborers together with God (c.1965)
Med: SATB, Bar solo, org
Txt: 1 Corinthians 3:9, 16, 17; Genesis 28:17
Dur: 7'
Pub: HW Gray
Mss: LC

1701   Sowerby, Leo
Forsaken of man (1939)
Med: SATB, SATB soli, org
Txt: Gospels and Edward William Borgers
Dur: 35'
Pub: HW Gray
Mss: partial holograph in LC
Bib: B67.5, 206
    The hope of Jesus
    The traitor
    The deserters
    The death of Jesus

1702   Sowerby, Leo
From Sion, perfect in beauty (1965)
Med: TBB, org
Txt: Ps. 49:2-3, 5; 121:1
Dur: 2'
Pub: WLSM

1703   Sowerby, Leo
From your throne, O God (1965)
Med: TBB, org
Txt: Ps. 79:2-3
Dur: 2'
Pub: WLSM

1704   Sowerby, Leo
God mounts his throne (1965)
Med: SB, org
Txt: Ps. 46, 67
Dur: 2'30"
Pub: WLSM

1705   Sowerby, Leo
God who made the earth (1943)
Med: SSA, pno
Txt: Sarah Betts Rhoades
Dur: 2'
Pub: J Fischer

1706   Sowerby, Leo
Gradual for Holy Thursday (c.1966)
Med: TBB
Txt: Book of Common Prayer
Dur: 1'
Pub: unpubl.?
Mss: LC

1707   Sowerby, Leo
A great and mighty wonder (196-?)
Med: SATB
Txt: not indicated
Dur: 3'
Pub: HW Gray
Mss: LC

1708 Sowerby, Leo
Great is the Lord (1933)
Med: SATB, orch or org
Txt: Ps. 48
Dur: 9'
Pub: HW Gray
Mss: LC

1709 Sowerby, Leo
Happy the nation (1966)
Med: SB, org
Txt: Ps. 32, 101
Dur: 3'
Pub: WLSM

1710 Sowerby, Leo
He shall rule from sea to sea (1966)
Med: unison vv, org
Txt: Ps. 71, Daniel 7:14
Dur: 4'30"
Pub: WLSM

1711 Sowerby, Leo
I call with my whole heart (1956)
Med: SATB
Txt: Ps. 119:145, 147-8, 150-1
Dur: 3'
Pub: HW Gray
Mss: LC
Rev: *Musical Courier* 156 (July, 1957)
p28

1712 Sowerby, Leo
I sing a song of the saints of God
(1953)
Med: SATB, org
Txt: Lesbia Scott
Dur: 4'
Pub: HW Gray

1713 Sowerby, Leo
I was glad when they said unto me
(1941)
Med: SATB, org
Txt: Ps. 122

Dur: 4'
Pub: HW Gray

1714 Sowerby, Leo
I will lift up mine eyes (c.1920)
Med: SATB, org
Txt: Ps. 121
Dur: 3'
Pub: Boston Music
Rev: *American Organist* 32 (May, 1949)
p150

1715 Sowerby, Leo
I will love thee, O Lord (1955)
Med: SATB, org
Txt: Ps. 18:1-2, 6-7, 17, 29, 42
Dur: 11'
Pub: HW Gray
Mss: LC

1716 Sowerby, Leo
In God my heart trusts (1966)
Med: unison vv, org
Txt: Ps. 27, 80
Dur: 2'30"
Pub: WLSM

1717 Sowerby, Leo
Jesu, bright and morning star (1958)
Med: SAB, org
Txt: German hymn
Dur: 3'
Pub: Oxford
Mss: LC

1718 Sowerby, Leo
Jubilate Deo in B-flat (c.1928)
Med: SATB, org
Txt: Book of Psalms
Dur: 4'
Pub: HW Gray

1719 Sowerby, Leo
Let us now praise famous men (1959)
Med: SATB, org

Txt: Ecclesiastes 44:1-5, 10, 14
Dur: 4'
Pub: unpubl.

1720   Sowerby, Leo
Like the beams (c.1930)
Med: SATB, kybd
Txt: Book of Common Prayer
Dur: 4'
Pub: HW Gray
Mss: sketch in LC

1721   Sowerby, Leo
Little Jesus, sweetly sleep (1959)
Med: unison, org
Txt: trad. Czech. carol
Dur: 2'
Pub: HT FitzSimons
Mss: LC

1722   Sowerby, Leo
A liturgy of hope (c.1928)
Med: TTBB, S solo, org
Txt: not indicated (Book of Common
      Prayer?)
Dur: 12'
Pub: Boston Music Co.

1723   Sowerby, Leo
The Lord ascendeth up on high (1958)
Med: SA or TB, org
Txt: A.T. Russell
Dur: 3'
Pub: Oxford
Mss: LC

1724   Sowerby, Leo
The Lord bless thee (1916)
Med: SATB, org
Txt: Numbers 6:24–26
Dur: 2'
Pub: Boston Music Co.

1725   Sowerby, Leo
The Lord has sent deliverance (1966)
Med: TBB, org
Txt: Ps. 110, Luke 24:46
Dur: 1'30"
Pub: WLSM

1726   Sowerby, Leo
The Lord is king (1963)
Med: SATB, org
Txt: Ps. 93
Dur: 7'
Pub: HW Gray
Mss: LC

1727   Sowerby, Leo
*The Lord is near to all who call upon
      him* (1965)
Med: TBB, org
Txt: Ps. 121:1, 7; 124:1-2
Dur: 2'
Pub: WLSM

1728   Sowerby, Leo
The Lord reigneth (c.1920)
Med: SATB, org
Txt: Book of Psalms
Dur: 6'
Pub: Boston Music Co.

1729   Sowerby, Leo
The Lord reigns over all the nations
      (1966)
Med: TBB, org
Txt: Ps. 46, John 14:18
Dur: 3'
Pub: WLSM

1730   Sowerby, Leo
The Lord sent forth his word (1965)
Med: TBB, org
Txt: Ps. 96, 148
Dur: 3'30"
Pub: WLSM

1731 Sowerby, Leo
Love came down at Christmas
    (c.1935)
Med: SATB, org
Txt: Christina Rossetti
Dur: 2'30"
Pub: HT FitzSimons
N.B. Also arr. for SSA.

1732 Sowerby, Leo
Lovely infant (1963)
Med: SATB, org
Txt: not indicated
Dur: 2'
Pub: HW Gray
Mss: LC

1733 Sowerby, Leo
Lover of souls hide me within thy
    heart (1965)
Med: SATB
Txt: *St. Veronica Manual*
Dur: 2'
Pub: HW Gray
Mss: LC

1734 Sowerby, Leo
Magnificat and nunc dimittis in D
    (c.1930)
Med: SATB, org
Txt: Book of Common Prayer
Dur: 8'
Pub: HW Gray

1735 Sowerby, Leo
Magnificat and nunc dimittis in E
    minor (1957)
Med: SATB, org
Txt: Book of Common Prayer
Dur: 9'
Pub: HW Gray
Mss: LC

1736 Sowerby, Leo
Make a joyful noise (c.1924)
Med: SATB, org
Txt: Book of Psalms
Dur: 3'
Pub: Boston Music Co.

1737 Sowerby, Leo
Manger carol (1955)
Med: unison, org
Txt: 13th cent. French, trans. Winfred
    Douglas
Dur: 2'
Pub: HW Gray
Mss: LC

1738 Sowerby, Leo
Martyr of God (1958)
Med: SATB, org
Txt: anon.
Dur: 3'
Pub: Oxford
Mss: LC

1739 Sowerby, Leo
Mass in E (1966?)
Med: SATB, org
Txt: LU
Dur: 6'
Pub: WLSM
Mss: LC (both sketches and complete mss.)

1740 Sowerby, Leo
Mass in E-flat (1965)
Med: unison, org
Txt: LU
Dur: 9'
Pub: WLSM
Mss: LC (both sketches and complete mss.)

1741 Sowerby, Leo
Missa festiva (Office of Holy Commun-
    ion in B minor) (193-?)
Med: SSA, org
Txt: Book of Common Prayer

Dur: 10'
Pub: unpubl.?
Mss: LC
N.B. Also arr. (original version?) for SATB; sometimes identified as the *Jubilate Mass*.

1742 Sowerby, Leo
My heart is fixed, O God (c.1956)
Med: SATB, org
Txt: Ps. 57:8; Ps. 16:12, 11, 10
Dur: 5'
Pub: HW Gray
Mss: LC

1743 Sowerby, Leo
My master hath a garden (1958)
Med: SA or unison, org
Txt: anon.
Dur: 3'
Pub: HW Gray
Mss: LC

1744 Sowerby, Leo
My son, if thou wilt receive (1962)
Med: SATB, org
Txt: Proverbs 2:1-6, 8
Dur: 5'
Pub: HW Gray
Mss: LC

1745 Sowerby, Leo
The nations shall revere your name (1965)
Med: TBB, org
Txt: LU
Dur: 3'
Pub: WLSM

1746 Sowerby, Leo
Nicene Credo (1941)
Med: unison, priest, org
Txt: LU
Dur: 2'
Pub: HW Gray
Mss: LC

1747 Sowerby, Leo
No one who waits for you shall be put to shame (1965)
Med: TBB, org
Txt: Ps. 24:3-4; 121:1
Dur: 2'
Pub: WLSM

1748 Sowerby, Leo
Norse lullaby (c.1948)
Med: TBB
Txt: Eugene Field
Dur: 3'
Pub: CC Birchard

1749 Sowerby, Leo
Not unto us, O Lord (1949)
Med: SATB, T or Bar solo
Txt: Ps. 115
Dur: 4'
Pub: HW Gray

1750 Sowerby, Leo
Now there lightens upon us (1934)
Med: SATB, kybd
Txt: biblical
Dur: 6'
Pub: unpubl.?
Mss: LC

1751 Sowerby, Leo
O dearest Jesus (1926)
Med: SATB, org
Txt; Martin Luther
Dur: 6'
Pub: HT FitzSimons

1752 Sowerby, Leo
O give thanks unto the Lord (c.1965)
Med: SATB, org
Txt: Ps. 136:1-9, 23-26
Dur: 5'
Pub: HW Gray
Mss: LC

1753 Sowerby, Leo
O God, my heart is ready (1963)
Med: SATB
Txt: Ps. 108:1-6
Dur: 3'
Pub: unpubl.?
Mss: LC

1754 Sowerby, Leo
O God, our help in ages past (1967)
Med: SATB, org
Txt: Isaac Watts
Dur: 4'
Pub: WLSM

1755 Sowerby, Leo
O God, the protector of all (c.1968)
Med: SATB, S solo, org
Txt: Book of Common Prayer
Dur: 2'30"
Pub: HW Gray

1756 Sowerby, Leo
O holy city seen of John (1964)
Med: 2-part mixed vv, org
Txt: Walter Russell Bowie
Dur: 3'
Pub: HW Gray
Mss: LC

1757 Sowerby, Leo
O Jesu, thou the beauty art (c.1938)
Med: SSA
Txt: St. Bernard of Clairvaux, trans.
Edward Caswall
Dur: 3'
Pub: HW Gray
Mss: sketches in LC

1758 Sowerby, Leo
O light, from age to age (c.1937)
Med: SATB
Txt: F.L. Hosmer
Dur: 3'
Pub: HW Gray

1759 Sowerby, Leo
O Lord, you have been our refuge
(1966)
Med: SB, org
Txt: Ps. 89, 113
Dur: 2'20"
Pub: WLSM

1760 Sowerby, Leo
O praise the Lord, all ye nations
(1961)
Med: SATB, org
Txt: Ps. 117
Dur: 6'
Pub: HW Gray
Mss: LC

1761 Sowerby, Leo
O praise the Lord, for it is a good
thing (1965)
Med: SATB, org
Txt: Ps. 147:1-3, 7-9, 12-14
Dur: 5'
Pub: H Flammer

1762 Sowerby, Leo
O sing unto the Lord a new song (1962)
Med: SATB, org
Txt: Ps. 96
Dur: 10'
Pub: HW Gray
Mss: LC

1763 Sowerby, Leo
The office of Holy Communion in C
(c.1930)
Med: SATB
Txt: Book of Common Prayer
Dur: 7'30"
Pub: HW Gray

1764 Sowerby, Leo
The office of Holy Communion in E
(c.1937)
Med: unison, org

Txt: Book of Common Prayer
Dur: 4'30"
Pub: HW Gray

1765 Sowerby, Leo
Olaynu (1947)
Med: SATB, org
Txt: liturgical Hebrew
Dur: 3'
Pub: G Schirmer
Mss: LC

1766 Sowerby, Leo
On the day of my resurrection (1966)
Med: TBB, org
Txt: Matthew 28:7; John 20:26
Dur: 3'
Pub: WLSM

1767 Sowerby, Leo
One thing I ask of the Lord (1965)
Med: TBB, org
Txt: Ps. 26, 83; Isaiah 45:15
Dur: 3'30"
Pub: WLSM

1768 Sowerby, Leo
Only-begotten, word of God eternal (1966)
Med: SATB, org
Txt: *Mozarabic breviary,* trans. M.J. Blacker
Dur: 6'
Pub: HW Gray
Mss: LC
Rev: *Diapason* 58 (Jan, 1967) p22

1769 Sowerby, Leo
The pool of Bethesda (c.1964)
Med: SATB, org
Txt: anon.
Dur: 4'
Pub: HW Gray
Mss: LC

1770 Sowerby, Leo
Praise the Lord (1933)
Med: SATB, org
Txt: LU
Dur: 6'
Pub: HT FitzSimons

1771 Sowerby, Leo
A prayer for Christmas (1967)
Med: SATB, org
Txt: Robert Spencer
Dur: 4'15"
Pub: HW Gray

1772 Sowerby, Leo
Prayer of King Manasses of Juda (c.1964)
Med: SATB, org
Txt: Apocrypha
Dur: 8'
Pub: HW Gray
Mss: LC

1773 Sowerby, Leo
Psalm 70 (1966)
Med: TTBB, org
Txt: Ps. 70
Dur: 4'
Pub: HW Gray

1774 Sowerby, Leo
Psalm 96 (c.1963)
Med: SATB, org
Txt: Ps. 96
Dur: 11'
Pub: HW Gray

1775 Sowerby, Leo
Psalm 115 (c.1950)
Med: SATB, T or Bar solo
Txt: Ps. 115
Dur: 4'
Pub: HW Gray

1776   Sowerby, Leo
Psalm 124 (1966)
Med: TTBB, org
Txt: Ps. 124
Dur: 2'30"
Pub: HW Gray

1777   Sowerby, Leo
Psalm 125 (1949)
Med: SATB
Txt: Ps. 125
Dur: 3'
Pub: HW Gray
Mss: LC

1778   Sowerby, Leo
Psalm 133 (1966)
Med: TTBB, org
Txt: Ps. 133
Dur: 2'
Pub: HW Gray

1779   Sowerby, Leo
Psalm 134 (c.1923)
Med: SATB
Txt: Ps. 134
Dur: 3'30"
Pub: Boston Music Co.

1780   Sowerby, Leo
Put off the garment of thy mourning
   (1963)
Med: SATB, org
Txt: Baruch 5:1-5, 7, 9
Dur: 5'
Pub: HW Gray
Mss: LC

1781   Sowerby, Leo
Put on as the elect of God (1968)
Med: SATB, org
Txt: Colossians 3:12–16
Dur: 3'30"
Pub: unpubl.

1782   Sowerby, Leo
The right hand of the Lord (1966)
Med: TBB, org
Txt: Ps. 117:16; Romans 6:9
Dur: 1'30"
Pub: WLSM

1783   Sowerby, Leo
The righteous live evermore (1958)
Med: SATB, org
Txt: Wisdom 5:15-16
Dur: 3'30"
Pub: Oxford
Mss: LC

1784   Sowerby, Leo
The risen Lord (c.1920)
Med: SATB dbl choir, soli, org
Txt: J. Arnold, *Compleat Psalmodist*
Dur: 11'
Pub: Boston Music Co.

1785   Sowerby, Leo
Save us, O Lord, our God (1965)
Med: TBB, org
Txt: Ps. 105:47; Isaiah 63:16; Ps.
   144:21
Dur: 3'
Pub: WLSM

1786   Sowerby, Leo
Second Sunday after Epiphany: gradual
   and alleluia (c.1966)
Med: TBB, org
Txt: Book of Common Prayer
Dur: 4'
Pub: WLSM
Mss: copy of publication proof with
   composer's corrections in LC

1787   Sowerby, Leo
Seeing we also are compassed about
   (1957)
Med: SATB
Txt: not indicated

Dur: 4'30"
Pub: HT FitzSimons
Mss: LC

1788 Sowerby, Leo
Send forth your spirit (1966)
Med: TBB, org
Txt: Ps. 103:30, others
Dur: 3'30"
Pub: WLSM

1789 Sowerby, Leo
Solomon's garden (1964)
Med: SATB, T solo, ch. orch, org
Txt: Song of Solomon
Dur: 12'
Pub: HW Gray
Mss: LC
Rev: *Diapason* 58 (Jan, 1967) p28

1790 Sowerby, Leo
Song for America (1942)
Med: SATB, orch
Txt: Norman Rosten
Dur: 12'
Pub: HW Gray
Mss: LC

1791 Sowerby, Leo
Song of immortal hope (c.1921)
Med: SATB, S or T solo, org
Txt: not indicated
Dur: 3'30"
Pub: Boston Music Co.

1792 Sowerby, Leo
The snow lay on the ground (c.1964)
Med: SSA, kybd
Txt: trad.
Dur: 4'
Pub: HW Gray

1793 Sowerby, Leo
Te Deum laudamus (c.1930)
Med: SATB, org
Txt: Book of Common Prayer
Dur: 10'
Pub: HW Gray

1794 Sowerby, Leo
Te Deum laudamus (c.1936)
Med: SATB, org
Txt: Book of Common Prayer
Dur: 8'
Pub: HT FitzSimons

1795 Sowerby, Leo
Te Deum laudamus in B-flat (1962)
Med: unison, org
Txt: Book of Common Prayer
Dur: 7'
Pub: HW Gray
Mss: LC

1796 Sowerby, Leo
Te Deum laudamus in E-flat (1961)
Med: SATB, org
Txt: Book of Common Prayer
Dur: 9'
Pub: HW Gray
Mss: LC

1797 Sowerby, Leo
There comes a ship a sailing (Song of the ship) (1959)
Med: SATB, org
Txt: anon. German, 1608
Dur: 3'
Pub: HT FitzSimons
Mss: LC

1798 Sowerby, Leo
This is the day (1965)
Med: SSTBB, org
Txt: Ps. 117:24; I Corinthians 5:7
Dur: 2'
Pub: WLSM

1799 Sowerby, Leo
Third Mass of Christmas: gradual and alleluia (c.1965)
Med: STBB, org
Txt: Book of Common Prayer
Dur: 6'
Pub: WLSM
Mss: copy of publication proof in LC

1800 Sowerby, Leo
Third Sunday after Epiphany: gradual and alleluia (c.1966)
Med: TBB, org
Txt: Book of Common Prayer
Dur: 5'
Pub: WLSM

1801 Sowerby, Leo
Thou hallowed chosen morn of praise (1958)
Med: SATB, org
Txt: St. John Damascene, trans. J.M. Neale
Dur: 4'30"
Pub: HW Gray
Mss: LC

1802 Sowerby, Leo
Thou shalt love the Lord thy God (1966)
Med: SATB, org
Txt: Deuteronomy 6:5-9; Numbers 15:40
Dur: 3'
Pub: HW Gray
Mss: LC

1803 Sowerby, Leo
The throne of God (1956)
Med: SATB, orch
Txt: Book of Revelations
Dur: 33'
Pub: HW Gray
Mss: LC

1804 Sowerby, Leo
Thy word is a lantern unto my feet (1964)
Med: SATB
Txt: Ps. 119:105, 114, 120, 125, 135, 144
Dur: 3'
Pub: HW Gray
Mss: LC

1805 Sowerby, Leo
Tu es vas electionis (1940)
Med: SATB
Txt: biblical
Dur: 4'
Pub: HW Gray
N.B. English title: *Lord, to thee we lift up our voices.*

1806 Sowerby, Leo
Turn thou to thy God (1957)
Med: SATB, org
Txt: Hosea 12:6; 6:3; 10:12; Micah 7:7
Dur: 7'30'
Pub: HW Gray
Mss: LC

1807 Sowerby, Leo
Turn thou us, O God (1966)
Med: SATB, org
Txt: Book of Common Prayer
Dur: 3'30"
Pub: unpubl.

1808 Sowerby, Leo
Two anthems (1965)
Med: SATB, org
Txt: Ps. 97:3-4; Hebrews 1:1-2
Dur: 2'
Pub: WLSM
   God, who in diverse ways
   All the ends of the earth
Txt: biblical

1809 Sowerby, Leo
The vision of Sir Launfal (1925)
Med: SATB, children, ATB soli, pno
Txt: James Russell Lowell
Dur: 30'
Pub: HW Gray

1810 Sowerby, Leo
When the Lord turned again (c.1926)
Med: SATB, SSATB soli
Txt: Ps. 126
Dur: 7'30"
Pub: HW Gray

1811 Sowerby, Leo
Will God indeed dwell on the earth?
(1962)
Med: SATB, org
Txt: 1 Kings 8:27-30; 37-39; 9:3
Dur: 8'
Pub: HW Gray
Mss: LC

1812 Sowerby, Leo
Yours is princely power (1965)
Med: SSTBB, org
Txt: Ps. 109:3, 1; Ps. 2:7
Dur: 4'
Pub: WLSM

1813 Stevens, Halsey
The amphisbæna (1972)
Med: SATB, pno
Txt: A.E. Housman
Dur: 1'10"
Pub: Mark Foster

1814 Stevens, Halsey
The ballad of William Sycamore
(1955)
Med: SATB, orch
Txt: Stephen Vincent Benét
Dur: 18'30"
Pub: Galaxy
Bib: B18

1815 Stevens, Halsey
Blessed be thy glorious name (1963)
Med: SATB
Txt: biblical
Dur: 3'
Pub: Mark Foster

1816 Stevens, Halsey
Campion suite (1967)
Med: SATB
Txt: Thomas Campion
Dur: 7'
Pub: Cincinnati: Greenwood Press
There is a garden in her face
Thrice toss these oaken ashes
When to her lute Corinna sings
To music bent
Night as well as brightest day

1817 Stevens, Halsey
Chansons courtoises (1967)
Med: TBB
Txt: trad. French
Dur: 6'
Pub: Mark Foster

1818 Stevens, Halsey
An epitaph for Sara and Richard
Cotton (c.1972)
Med: SATB
Txt: John Cotton
Dur: 2'
Pub: Mark Foster

1819 Stevens, Halsey
Four carols (1952)
Med: TTB
Txt: see below
Dur: 12'
Pub: Peer Intl.
Rev: MLA *Notes* 13 (Dec, 1955) p137;
Musical America 75 (July, 1955) p28
All this night shrill chanticleer (William
Austin)
What sweeter music (Robert Herrick)

As I rode out this endless night (anon. English)

A virgin most pure (trad.)

1820   Stevens, Halsey
Go, lovely rose (1942)
Med: SATB
Txt: Edmund Waller
Dur: 1'30"
Pub: Helios Music Editions

1821   Stevens, Halsey
God is my strong salvation (1966)
Med: SATB
Txt: Ps. 24
Dur: 2'
Pub: Mark Foster

1822   Stevens, Halsey
Hungarian folksongs (c.1970)
Med: SATB
Txt: trad., trans. composer
Dur: 6'
Pub: Mark Foster
     Lovely is the forest
     In the dark earth
     In the blackbird's nest

1823   Stevens, Halsey
If luck and I should meet (1950)
Med: SATB
Src: Grove

1824   Stevens, Halsey
In te, Domine, speravi (1962)
Med: SATB div, kybd
Txt: Ps. 31
Dur: 3'
Pub: CF Peters
Mss: LC

1825   Stevens, Halsey
Lady, as thy fair swan (c.1972)
Med: SATB
Txt: Gerald Bullett
Dur: 1'20"
Pub: Mark Foster

1826   Stevens, Halsey
Like as the culver on the bared bough
     (1954)
Med: SSATB
Txt: Edmund Spenser
Dur: 3'
Pub: AMP

1827   Stevens, Halsey
Magnificat (1962)
Med: SATB, tpt, str orch or kybd
Txt: LU
Dur: 6'
Pub: Mark Foster
Bib: B18, 111

1828   Stevens, Halsey
Le mois de Mai (1960)
Med: SATB
Txt: trad.
Dur: 4'
Pub: Mark Foster
Bib: B18

1829   Stevens, Halsey
A new year carol (1960)
Med: SATB
Txt: trad.
Dur: 4'
Pub: copy in LC

1830   Stevens, Halsey
Nunc dimittis (1971)
Med: SATB
Txt: LU
Dur: 1'25"
Pub: Mark Foster

1831   Stevens, Halsey
O God, the refuge of our fears (c.1971)
Med: SATB
Txt: Stephen Vincent Benét
Dur: 2'
Pub: Mark Foster

1832 Stevens, Halsey
O sing unto the Lord a new song (1955)
Med: SSA, pno
Txt: Ps. 98
Dur: 4'
Pub: Peer Intl.

1833 Stevens, Halsey
O worship the king (1966)
Med: SATB
Txt: biblical
Dur: 4'
Pub: Mark Foster

1834 Stevens, Halsey
Of the heavenly bodies (1964)
Med: SATB
Txt: Roger Williams
Dur: 2'30"
Pub: Helios Music Editions

1835 Stevens, Halsey
Old rhymes (1954)
Med: SSA
Src: Grove

1836 Stevens, Halsey
Psalm VIII: O Lord, our governor (c.1971)
Med: SATB
Txt: Ps. 8
Dur: 2'15"
Pub: Mark Foster

1837 Stevens, Halsey
Psalm 148 (1953)
Med: SATB
Txt: Ps. 148
Dur: 6'
Pub: Helios Music Editions

1843 Stevens, Halsey
Three hymns (1955)
Med: SATB

Txt: John Greenleaf Whittier
Dur: 3'
Pub: ACA; copy in NYPL
Mss: copy in NYPL

1838 Stevens, Halsey
Remember me (c.1973)
Med: TBB
Txt: Christina Rossetti
Dur: 2'30"
Pub: Mark Foster

1839 Stevens, Halsey
A set of three (1951)
Med: TTBB
Txt: see below
Dur: 5'30"
Pub: Helios Music Editions
    Weeping cross (anon.)
    The waning man (anon.)
    She that denies me (Thomas Heywood)

1840 Stevens, Halsey
Songs from the Paiute (1976)
Med: SATB, 4 fl, timp
Txt: trans. Mary Austin and Bourke Lee
Dur: 14'
Pub: Mark Foster
    Winter
    The grass on the mountain
    The rattlesnake
    The river
    Heart's friend
    A song in depression
    Song for the passing of a beautiful woman
    Storm

1841 Stevens, Halsey
Te Deum (1967)
Med: SATB, brass ensemble, timp, org
Txt: LU
Dur: 10'

Pub: Mark Foster
Rev: *BMI* (Feb, 1968) p21; National
Music Council *Bulletin* 28/2
(1968) p22

1842 Stevens, Halsey
A testament of life (1959)
Med: SATB, orch
Txt: Ps. 129, 150
Dur: 23'
Pub: Mark Foster

1843 Stevens, Halsey
Three hymns (1955)
Med: SATB
Txt: John Greenleaf Whittier
Dur: 3'
Pub: ACA; copy in NYPL
Mss: copy in NYPL

1844 Stevens, Halsey
The way of Jehovah (1963)
Med: SATB, kybd
Txt: biblical
Dur: 3'
Pub: Mark Foster

1845 Stevens, Halsey
Weepe, O mine eyes (1959)
Med: SSATB
Txt: Thomas Weelkes
Dur: 3'30"
Pub: Mark Foster

1846 Stevens, Halsey
When I am dead, my dearest (1938)
Med: SATB
Txt: trad.
Dur: 3'30"
Pub: Arrow Music

1847 Still, William Grant
And they lynched him on a tree
(1940)
Med: SATB dbl choir, A solo, nar, orch

Txt: Katherine Garrison Chapin
Dur: 20'
Pub: J Fischer
Bib: B187, 201

1848 Still, William Grant
*Christmas in the Western World (Las
pascuas)* (1967)
Med: SATB; str orch and pno, or pno
quintet
Txt: trad., adapt. by Verna Arvey
Dur: 16'
Pub: Southern
A maiden was adoring God, the Lord
Ven, niño divino
Aguinaldo
Jesous ahatonhia
Tell me, shepherdess
De virgin Mary had a baby boy
Los reyes magos
La piñata
Glad Christmas bells
Sing, shout, tell the story

1849 Still, William Grant
From a lost continent (1948)
Med: SATB
Txt: composer
Src: Grove

1850 Still, William Grant
Here's one (c.1955)
Med: SATB, S solo, pno
Txt: trad.
Dur: 4'
Pub: J Church

1851 Still, William Grant
I feel like my time ain't long (c.1956)
Med: SATB
Txt: trad.
Dur: 3'
Pub: Presser

1852 Still, William Grant
Is there anybody here? (c.1956)
Med: SATB, pno
Txt: trad.
Dur: 3'
Pub: Presser

1853 Still, William Grant
Plain-chant for America (1941, rev.
1967)
Med: SATB, Bar solo, orch
Txt: Katherine Garrison Chapin
Dur: 10'
Pub: WGS Music

1854 Still, William Grant
A psalm for the living (1954)
Med: SATB, orch
Txt: Verna Arvey
Dur: 12'
Pub: Bourne

1855 Still, William Grant
Rising tide (1940)
Med: SSATBB
Txt: Albert Stillman
Dur: 2'30"
Pub: J Fischer
N.B. Originally for solo voice. Also,
with *Victory tide*, comprises sym-
phonic work called *Song of a city*.

1856 Still, William Grant
Sahdji (c.1961)
Med: SATB, B soli, pno
Txt: Richard Bruce and Alain Locke
Dur: 15'
Pub: C Fischer
Mss: copy in LC
N.B. A ballet with chorus.

1857 Still, William Grant
Those who wait (1942)
Med: SATB, soli, orch
Txt: Verna Arvey

Dur: 14'
Pub: "Los Angeles" (no publisher
indicated on LC score)
Mss: copy in LC

1858 Still, William Grant
Three rhythmic spirituals (c.1961)
Med: SATB
Txt: trad.
Dur: 9'
Pub: Bourne
Lord, I looked down the road
Hard trials
Holy spirit, don't you leave me

1859 Still, William Grant
Tomorrow's city (c.1938)
Med: SATB, nar, orch
Txt: not indicated
Dur: 8'
Pub: unpubl.?
Mss: copies of two versions in LC

1860 Still, William Grant
Victory tide (1940)
Med: SATB, pno
Txt: Albert Stillman
Dur: 2'30"
Pub: J Fischer
N.B. See note with *Rising tide* (1855),
above.

1861 Still, William Grant
The voice of the Lord (c.1946)
Med: SATB, T solo, org
Txt: Ps. 29
Dur: 3'
Pub: M Witmark

1862 Still, William Grant
Wailing woman (n.d.)
Med: SATB, S solo, orch
Txt: Verna Arvey
Dur: 10'
Pub: unpubl.
Src: Arvey

T

1863   Taylor, Deems
The banks o'Doon (c.1926)
Med: SSA, pno
Txt: Robert Burns
Dur: 4'
Pub: J Fischer
N.B. Originally for solo voice.

1864   Taylor, Deems
The chambered nautilus, Op. 7 (1914)
Med: SATB, pno, org, orch
Txt: Oliver Wendell Holmes
Dur: 15'
Pub: Ditson
Mss: LC and NYPL

1865   Taylor, Deems
Czech and Hungarian folksongs
(1921)
Med: SSA, pno
Txt: trad.
Dur: 18'
Pub: J Fischer

1866   Taylor, Deems
The highwayman, Op. 8 (1914)
Med: SSAA, Bar solo, orch
Txt: Alfred Noyes
Dur: 30'
Pub: Ditson

1867   Taylor, Deems
*Nineteen numbers in honor of Edna
St. Vincent Millay* (c.1977)
Med: SATB, pno, nar
Txt: Edna St. Vincent Millay
Dur: 20'
Pub: copy in LC

1868   Taylor, Deems
Que fais-tu, bergère (c.1919)
Med: SSAA, pno

Txt: anon., 18th cent.
Dur: 2'30"
Pub: J Church

1869   Taylor, Deems
Song to Bohemia (c.1932)
Med: TTBB, pno
Txt: trad. Czech
Dur: 7'
Pub: J Fischer

1870   Taylor, Deems
Southern melody (c.1924)
Med: SSAA, opt. pno
Txt: trad.
Dur: 5'
Pub: Ditson

1871   Taylor, Deems
Tricolor (c.1918)
Med: TTBB
Txt: Paul Scott Mowrer
Dur: 3'
Pub: J Fischer
Mss: LC
N.B. Also arr. SSAA.

1872   Taylor, Deems
Wake thee, now, dearest (c.1932)
Med: TTBB, pno
Txt: trad. Czech
Dur: 4'30"
Pub: J Fischer

1873   Taylor, Deems
Waters ripple and flow (c.1926)
Med: SATB
Txt: trad. Czech
Dur: 8'
Pub: J Fischer

1874   Thompson, Randall
Alleluia (1940)
Med: SATB
Txt: "Alleluia"

Dur: 6'30"
Pub: EC Schirmer
Bib: B213
N.B. Also arr. for SSAA, TTBB.

1875 Thompson, Randall
Americana (1932)
Med: SATB, pno or orch
Txt: *The American Mercury*
Dur: 22'
Pub: EC Schirmer
Mss: LC
   May every tongue
   The staff necromancer
   God's bottles
   The sublime process of law enforce-
     ment
   Lovli-lines

1876 Thompson, Randall
Antiphon (1970)
Med: SATB
Txt: George Herbert
Src: Grove

1877 Thompson, Randall
The best of rooms (1963)
Med: SATB
Txt: Robert Herrick
Dur: 4'
Pub: EC Schirmer

1878 Thompson, Randall
Bitter-sweet (1970)
Med: SATB
Txt: George Herbert
Dur: 3'
Pub: EC Schirmer

1879 Thompson, Randall
Canon (n.d.)
Med: 3 vv
Txt: Ps. 121
Src: Grove

1880 Thompson, Randall
A Concord cantata (1975)
Med: SATB, pno or orch
Txt: see below
Dur: 22'
Pub: EC Schirmer
   The ballad of the bridge (Edward E.
     Hale)
   Inscription (Allen French)
   The gift outright (Robert Frost)

1881 Thompson, Randall
The eternal dove (1968)
Med: SATB
Txt: Joseph Beaumont
Dur: 10'
Pub: EC Schirmer

1882 Thompson, Randall
Farewell (c.1973)
Med: SATB
Txt: Walter de la Mare
Dur: 3'30"
Pub: EC Schirmer
Mss: copy in LC

1883 Thompson, Randall
A feast of praise (1963)
Med: SATB, pno or brass and hp
Txt: Baruch 3:34; Ps. 81:3; Ps. 47:5-7
Dur: 14'
Pub: EC Schirmer

1884 Thompson, Randall
Frostiana (1959)
Med: various voicings (see below), with
     orch
Txt: Robert Frost
Dur: 25'
Pub: EC Schirmer
   The road not taken (SATB)
   The pasture (TBB)
   Come in (SAA)
   The telephone (SAA or TTBB)

A girl's garden (SAA)
Stopping by woods on a snowy evening (TBB)
Choose something like a star (SATB)

1885 Thompson, Randall
The gate of heaven (1959)
Med: SATB
Txt: Ps. 122:1; Habakkuk 2:20; Genesis 28:17
Dur: 8'
Pub: EC Schirmer
N.B. Also arr. SSAA, TTBB.

1886 Thompson, Randall
Glory to God in the highest (1958)
Med: SATB
Txt: Luke 2:14
Dur: 2'30"
Pub: EC Schirmer

1887 Thompson, Randall
A hymn for scholars and pupils (1973)
Med: SATB, brass and str, or pno and fl
Txt: George Wither
Dur: 5'30"
Pub: EC Schirmer
N.B. Originally for SSA, fl, 2 tpt, tbn, tuba, str, org.

1888 Thompson, Randall
Hymn: thy book falls open (1964)
Med: SATB, org or band
Txt: David McCord
Src: Grove

1889 Thompson, Randall
The lark in the morn (1940)
Med: SATB
Txt: trad.
Dur: 3'
Pub: EC Schirmer

1890 Thompson, Randall
The last invocation (c.1989)
Med: SSATTB
Txt: Walt Whitman
Dur: 6'
Pub: EC Schirmer

1891 Thompson, Randall
The last words of David (1949)
Med: TTBB, orch
Txt: 2 Samuel 23:3-4
Dur: 4'
Pub: EC Schirmer
Rev: *Diapason* 42 (June 1, 1951) p22
N.B. Also arr. for SATB.

1892 Thompson, Randall
The light of the stars (1976)
Med: SATB
Txt: Henry W. Longfellow
Dur: 4'
Pub: EC Schirmer

1893 Thompson, Randall
The Lord is my shepherd (1964)
Med: SATB, pno, org, or hp
Txt: Ps. 23
Dur: 9'
Pub: EC Schirmer
Mss: LC
N.B. Originally for women's voices.

1894 Thompson, Randall
Mass of the Holy Spirit (1956)
Med: SATB
Txt: LU
Dur: 34'
Pub: EC Schirmer
Mss: copy in LC
Rev: *American Organist* 44 (Sept, 1961) p24.
Bib: B51, 87, 218

1895   Thompson, Randall
The mirror of St. Anne (1972)
Med: SATB dbl choir
Txt: Isaac Watts
Dur: 6'30"
Pub: EC Schirmer
N.B. "An antiphonal setting in reverse
    contrary motion."

1896   Thompson, Randall
The nativity of St. Luke (c.1961)
Med: SATB, 12 soli, org, ch. orch
Txt: Gospel of Luke
Dur: 90'
Pub: EC Schirmer
Mss: copy in LC
Rev: Boston *Globe*, Dec. 13, 1961
Bib: B197

1897   Thompson, Randall
Noel (1947)
Med: SATB
Pub: unpubl.
Src: Grove

1898   Thompson, Randall
Now I lay me down to sleep (1947)
Med: SSA
Txt: The New England Primer
Dur: 4'
Pub: EC Schirmer

1899   Thompson, Randall
Odes of Horace (1953)
Med: SATB; ★TTBB (all unaccom-
    panied except No. 1, with kybd)
Txt: Horace
Dur: 11'30"
Pub: EC Schirmer
Bib: B222
    A Venus, regina Cnidi Paphique
    Vitas hinuleo me similis, Chloë
    Montium custos numorumque, virgo
    Quis multa gracilis★
    O fons Bandusiæ, splendidior vitro
    Felices ter (Thrice happy they)

1900   Thompson, Randall
Ode to the Virginian voyage (1957)
Med: SATB, orch
Txt: Michael Drayton
Dur: 20'
Pub: EC Schirmer
    Sinfonia
    Yon brave heroic minds
    Earth's only paradise
    In kenning of the shore
    And in regions far
    Thy voyages attend
    Finale

1901   Thompson, Randall
The passion according to St. Luke
    (1965)
Med: SATB, soli, orch
Txt: Luke 19, 22, 23
Dur: 1 hr, 32'
Pub: EC Schirmer
Mss: copy in LC
Rev: *Christian Science Monitor*, April 1,
    1965; MLA *Notes* 24/2 (Dec,
    1967)

1902   Thompson, Randall
The peaceable kingdom (1936)
Med: SATB dbl choir
Txt: Isaiah
Dur: 30'
Pub: EC Schirmer
Bib: B63
    Say ye to the righteous
    Woe unto them
    The noise of the multitude
    Howl ye
    The paper reeds by the brooks
    But these are they that forsake the
        Lord
    For ye shall go out with joy
    Have ye not known
    Ye shall have a song

1903 Thompson, Randall
The place of the blest (1969)
Med: SSAA, orch
Txt: Robert Herrick and Richard Wilbur
Dur: 25'
Pub: EC Schirmer
Mss: LC
Rev: *American Organist* 42 (May, 1969) p27; *Diapason* 60 (Apr, 1969) p1

1904 Thompson, Randall
Poscimur (1929)
Med: SATB, Bar solo, orch
Txt: LU
Pub: unpubl.
Src: B222
Bib: B222

1905 Thompson, Randall
A psalm of thanksgiving (1967)
Med: SATB, children, orch
Txt: Ps. 107; Johann Crüger
Dur: 25'
Pub: EC Schirmer
Rev: *American Choral Review* 10/2 (1968) p69-71; *Music Journal* 26 (Jan 14, 1968) p26
 Oh give thanks unto the Lord
 They wandered into the wilderness in a solitary way
 Such as sin and darkness and in the shadow of death
 Foolish men are plagued for their offense
 They that go down to the sea in ships
 He turneth the wilderness into a standing water
 Now thank we all our God

1906 Thompson, Randall
Pueri Hebræorum (1927)
Med: SSAA dbl choir, opt. inst. doubling
Txt: biblical

Dur: 8'
Pub: EC Schirmer
N.B. Also arr. for SATB.

1907 Thompson, Randall
Requiem (1958)
Med: SATB dbl choir
Txt: biblical
Dur: 80'
Pub: EC Schirmer
Rev: *Musical Quarterly* 44 (July, 1958) p370.
Bib: B26, 51, 123
 Lamentations
 The triumph of faith
 The call to song
 The garment of praise
 The leave-taking

1908 (not used)

1909 Thompson, Randall
Rosemary (1929)
Med: SSAA
Txt: Stephen Vincent Benét
Dur: 15'
Pub: EC Schirmer
 Chemical analysis
 A sad song
 A nonsense song
 To Rosemary on the methods by which she might become an angel

1910 Thompson, Randall
Tarantella (c.1937)
Med: TTBB, pno or orch
Txt: Hilaire Belloc
Dur: 11'
Pub: EC Schirmer

1911 Thompson, Randall
The testament of freedom (1943)
Med: TTBB, orch
Txt: Thomas Jefferson
Dur: 24'

Pub: EC Schirmer
N.B. Also arr. with band accompaniment (1960).
  The God who gave us life
  We have counted the cost
  We fight not for glory
  I shall not die without a hope

1912 Thompson, Randall
Two worlds (c.1978)
Med: SATB, pno
Txt: Edmund Waller
Dur: 4'
Pub: EC Schirmer

1913 Thompson, Randall
Velvet shoes (c.1960)
Med: SA
Txt: Elinor Wylie
Dur: 2'30"
Pub: EC Schirmer

1914 Thomson, Virgil
Agnus Dei (1924)
Med: 3 equal vv
Txt: LU
Dur: 2'
Pub: Reichenbach, ed. *Modern Canons*, Music Press Int., 1946
Rev: *Music News* 43 (April, 1951) p25.

1915 Thomson, Virgil
Agnus Dei (1925)
Med: TTBB
Txt: LU
Dur: 1'
Pub: copy in NYPL

1916 Thomson, Virgil
Benedictus (1926)
Med: TTBB
Txt: LU
Dur: 1'
Pub: unpubl.

1917 Thomson, Virgil
The bugle song (1941)
Med: unison children, pno
Txt: Alfred Lord Tennyson
Dur: 4'
Pub: unpubl.
Src: Grove
N.B. Later arr. for 2-part children's chorus.

1918 Thomson, Virgil
Cantata on poems of Edward Lear (1973, rev. 1974)
Med: SATB, SBar soli, orch
Txt: Edward Lear
Dur: 30'
Pub: G Schirmer
  The owl and the pussycat
  The jumblies
  The pelican chorus
  Half an alphabet
  The akond of swat

1919 Thomson, Virgil
Cantantes eamus (1982)
Med: TTBB, pno, brass
Txt: P.V. Maro
Src: Grove

1920 Thomson, Virgil
Capital capitals (1927, rev. 1968)
Med: TTBB, pno
Txt: Gertrude Stein
Src: Grove
Bib: B216

1921 Thomson, Virgil
Crossing Brooklyn ferry (1958)
Med: SATB, pno
Txt: Walt Whitman
Dur: 7'30"
Pub: BH

1922   Thomson, Virgil
Dance in praise: let us live, then, and
   be glad (1962)
Med: SATB, orch
Txt: anon. 12th cent.
Dur: 9'
Pub: BH

1923   Thomson, Virgil
De profundis (1920, rev. 1951)
Med: SATB
Txt: Ps. 130
Dur: 4'30"
Pub: Weintraub Music
Rev: MLA *Notes* 9 (June, 1952) p494

1924   Thomson, Virgil
Fanfare for peace (1980, rev. 1983)
Med: SATB, kybd
Txt: Jack Larson
Dur: 1'30"
Pub: Southern
N.B. Originally titled *The peace place.*

1925   Thomson, Virgil
Five Auvergnat folk songs (1962–4)
Med: SATB, pno or orch
Txt: trad. French
Src: Grove
     La pastoura als camp
     Ballero
     Pastourelle
     La fiolaire
     Pasap pel prat (arr. from a work by J.
     Canteloube)

1926   Thomson, Virgil
Four songs to poems of Thomas
   Campion (1955)
Med: SATB, pno
Txt: Thomas Campion
Dur: 6'
Pub: Southern
N.B. Originally for solo voice.
     Follow your saint

There is a garden in her face
Rose cheek'd Laura
Follow thy fair sun

1927   Thomson, Virgil
How will ye have your partridge today?
   (1967)
Med: 4 vv (round)
Txt: N. Brown
Src: Grove

1928   Thomson, Virgil
Hymn for Pratt Institute (1968)
Med: SATB
Txt: R. Fjelde
Dur: 3'30"
Pub: unpubl.

1929   Thomson, Virgil
Hymns from the Old South (1949)
Med: SATB
Txt: see below
Dur: 3'-4' each
Pub: HW Gray
Mss: LC (No. 1 only)
Rev: *Choir Guide* 2 (May-June, 1949)
     p39; MLA *Notes* 11 (June, 1954)
     p439
     My shepherd will supply my need
     (Ps. 23) (Also arr. for SSAA)
     The morning star (trad.)
     Green fields (John Newton)
     Death, 'tis a melancholy day (Isaac
     Watts)

1930   Thomson, Virgil
It seems that God bestowed somehow
   (1955)
Med: SATB
Txt: A.B. Hall
Src: Grove
N.B. Originally titled *Song for the stable.*

1931 Thomson, Virgil
Mass (1934)
Med: 2-part chorus, perc
Txt: LU
Dur: 14'
Pub: Leeds Music
Mss: Yale?
Bib: B2, 51, 103, 216, 218, 223, 228

1932 Thomson, Virgil
Mass (1960)
Med: for solo voice or unison chorus
Txt: LU
Dur: 9'
Pub: G Schirmer
Bib: B51

1933 Thomson, Virgil
Missa brevis (1924)
Med: SATB
Txt: LU
Dur: 14'
Pub: unpubl.
Mss: Yale?

1934 Thomson, Virgil
Missa pro defunctis (1960)
Med: men's chorus, women's chorus,
    orch
Txt: LU
Dur: 45'
Pub: HW Gray; Novello
Rev: *Musical America* 80 (June, 1960)
    p17; 80 (Nov, 1960) p63; 82
    (July, 1962) p24-5; *Musical Cour-
    ier* 162 (Dec, 1960), p34; *New
    Yorker* 38 (May 19, 1962) p183-
    4; *Saturday Review* 45 (May 26,
    1962) p39.

1935 Thomson, Virgil
My master hath a garden (1963)
Med: SATB, pno
Txt: anon.

Dur: 3'
Pub: G Schirmer
N.B. Originally for solo voice; also arr.
    for SSA.

1936 Thomson, Virgil
The nativity as sung by the shepherds
(1967)
Med: SATB, pno
Txt: Richard Crashaw
Dur: 9'
Pub: G Schirmer
Rev: *American Choral Review* 9/4 (1967)
    p53-4

1937 Thomson, Virgil
O my deir heart (1921, rev. 1978)
Med: SATB
Txt: Martin Luther
Dur: 2'30"
Pub: Heritage Music Press

1938 Thomson, Virgil
Praise him who makes us happy
(1955)
Med: SATB
Txt: M. Van Doren
Src: Grove
N.B. Originally titled *Never another.*

1939 Thomson, Virgil
A prayer to Venus (1981)
Med: SATB, pno
Txt: J. Fletcher
Src: Grove

1940 Thomson, Virgil
Saint's procession (1908)
Med: SATB, MB soli, pno
Txt: Gertrude Stein
Dur: 4'30"
Pub: G Schirmer
N.B. Taken from his opera *Four saints
    in three acts.*

1941   Thomson, Virgil
Sanctus (1921)
Med: TTBB
Txt: LU
Dur: 2'
Pub: unpubl.

1942   Thomson, Virgil
Sanctus (1926)
Med: TTBB, children
Txt: LU
Dur: 2'
Pub: unpubl.
Mss: Yale?

1943   Thomson, Virgil
Scenes from the holy infancy according to St. Matthew (1937)
Med: SATB, ATB soli
Txt: Gospel of Matthew
Dur: 9'30"
Pub: Mercury Music
 Joseph and the angel
 The wise men
 The flight into Egypt

1944   Thomson, Virgil
Seven choruses from Medea (1934)
Med: SSAA, opt. perc
Txt: Euripides, trans. Countee Cullen
Dur: 7'
Pub: G Schirmer; Weaner-Levant Publications
Bib: B223
 O gentle heart
 Love, like a leaf
 O, happy were our fathers
 Weep for the little lamb
 Go down, O sun
 Behold, O earth
 Immortal Zeus controls the fate of man

1945   Thomson, Virgil
Southern Hymns (1984)
Med: SATB, kybd

Txt: see below
Dur: various short works
Pub: Southern
 How bright is the day! (S.B. Sawyer)
 Mississippi (Kentucky Harmony)
 Death of General Washington (Stephen Jenks)
 Convention (Union Harmony)

1946   Thomson, Virgil
Surrey apple-howler's song (1941)
Med: children
Txt: trad. English
Src: Grove

1947   Thomson, Virgil
Three antiphonal psalms (c.1951)
Med: SA or TB
Txt: see below
Dur: 3'30"
Pub: Leeds Music
N.B. "reportedly permanently out of print" (note in Roberts).
 Unto thee I lift up mine eyes (Ps. 123)
 Behold how good and pleasant (Ps. 133)
 O give thanks unto the Lord (Ps. 136)

1948   Thomson, Virgil
Tiger! tiger! (c.1953)
Med: TTBB, orch
Txt: William Blake
Dur: 4'
Pub: Ricordi
N.B. Originally for solo voice.

1949   Thomson, Virgil
Tribulationes civitatum (1922)
Med: SATB
Txt: Latin (LU?)
Dur: 4'
Pub: Weintraub Music Co.
Rev: MLA *Notes* 9 (June, 1952) p494

1950   Thomson, Virgil
Welcome to the new year (1941)
Med: 2-part children, pno
Txt: Farjeon
Pub: unpubl.
Src: Grove

1951   Thomson, Virgil
When I survey the bright celestial sphere (1964)
Med: unison, kybd
Txt: W. Habbingdon
Dur: 6'
Pub: CF Peters

W

1952   Ward, Robert
Concord hymn (c.1979)
Med: SATB
Txt: Ralph W. Emerson
Dur: 4'30"
Pub: Highgate Press

1953   Ward, Robert
Earth shall be fair (1960)
Med: SATB dbl choir, children's chorus or S solo, orch or org
Txt: Book of Psalms, selected by John Dexter and Clifford Bax
Dur: 26'
Pub: Highgate Press

1954   Ward, Robert
Fifth symphony: canticles of America (1976)
Med: SATB, SBar soli, nar, orch
Txt: Walt Whitman, Henry W. Longfellow
Dur: 35'
Pub: Highgate Press

1955   Ward, Robert
Hush'd be the camps today (1941)
Med: SATB, pno
Txt: Walt Whitman
Dur: 4'
Pub: HW Gray

1956   Ward, Robert
Let the word go forth (1965)
Med: SATB, brass, hp, str or kybd
Txt: John F. Kennedy
Dur: 14'
Pub: Galaxy Music
Mss: copy in LC

1957   Ward, Robert
New Hampshire (1938)
Med: SSA div, str quartet
Txt: T.S. Eliot
Dur: 2'
Pub: unpubl.
Mss: Duke University
N.B. Later withdrawn by the composer.

1958   Ward, Robert
Promised land (c.1977)
Med: cong, org
Txt: trad. hymn
Dur: 3'
Pub: Highgate Press
N.B. Alternate title: *On Jordan's stormy banks.*

1959   Ward, Robert
Sweet freedom's song, a New England chronicle (1965)
Med: SATB, SBar soli, nar, orch
Txt: Mary and Robert Ward, after William Bradford; Ps. 88; et al.
Dur: 40'
Pub: Galaxy

1960 Ward, Robert
When Christ rode into Jerusalem
(1946)
Med: SATB, S solo, org
Txt: not indicated
Dur: 7'
Pub: Galaxy

1961 Ward, Robert
With rue my heart is laden (c.1970)
Med: SATB
Txt: A.E. Housman
Dur: 4'
Pub: Merrymount Music Press

1962 Wuorinen, Charles
An anthem for Epiphany (1974)
Med: SATB, tpt, org
Txt: biblical
Dur: 4'
Pub: CF Peters

1963 Wuorinen, Charles
A solus ortu (1988)
Med: SATB
Txt: LU
Dur: 2'
Pub: CF Peters

1964 Wuorinen, Charles
Be merry all that be present (1964)
Med: SATB, org
Txt: medieval English
Dur: 4'
Pub: CF Peters

1965 Wuorinen, Charles
The celestial sphere (1980)
Med: SATB, orch
Txt: see below
Dur: 60'
Pub: CF Peters
Rev: *Hi-Fidelity/Musical America* 31
(Oct, 1981) pMA20ff; *Symphony
Magazine* 32/3 (1981) p154;

Symphony about the empyrean: Lord,
what is man? (William Fuller)
Symphony about the ascension (Acts
of the Apostles)
Symphony about the Holy Ghost
(Acts)
Second symphony about the empyrean: Lord, what is man?

1966 Wuorinen, Charles
Genesis (1989)
Med: SATB, orch
Txt: biblical
Dur: 35'
Pub: CF Peters

1967 Wuorinen, Charles
*Madrigale spirituale sopra salmo
secondo* (1960)
Med: TB, 2 ob, 2 vln, cello, pno
Txt: Ps. 2
Dur: 4'30"
Pub: CF Peters

1968 Wuorinen, Charles
Manheim 87. 87. 87. (1973)
Med: unison vv, org
Txt: Episcopal hymn
Dur: 3'
Pub: CF Peters

1969 Wuorinen, Charles
*Mass for the restoration of St. Luke in
the Fields* (1982)
Med: SATB, vln, 3 tbn, org
Txt: LU
Dur: 30'
Pub: CF Peters
Rev: *Diapason* 75 (Jan, 1984) p14
N.B. Later revised as *Missa Renovata*
(1989?).

1970 Wuorinen, Charles
Missa brevis (1991)
Med: SATB, org

Txt: LU
Dur: 8'
Pub: CF Peters

1971 Wuorinen, Charles
The prayer of Jonah (1962)
Med: SATB, str quartet
Txt: biblical
Src: Grove

1972 Wuorinen, Charles
Super salutem (1964)
Med: TTBB, brass, pno, perc
Txt: not indicated
Dur: 7'
Pub: CF Peters
Mss: copies in LC, NYPL

Y

1973 Yardumian, Richard
Christmas chorales (c.1978)
Med: SATB
Txt: biblical
Dur: 5'
Pub: Elkan-Vogel
  High in heaven
  Magnificat
  Fear not, Mary
  Emptiness and void the earth
  The Lord came down
  Sing a new song

1974 Yardumian, Richard
Create in me a clean heart (1962)
Med: SATB, A or Bar solo
Txt: Isaiah 26:9; Ps. 51:1-3, 6-10, 12, 15, 17-18; Ezekiel 18:31; Zechariah 12:1
Dur: 6'
Pub: HW Gray

1975 Yardumian, Richard
Magnificat (1965)
Med: SSAA
Txt: Gospel of Luke
Dur: 6'
Pub: Elkan-Vogel
Mss: copies in LC, NYPL

1976 Yardumian, Richard
Mass "Veni Sancti Spiritu" (1966)
Med: SATB, SATB soli, orch
Txt: LU
Dur: 42'
Pub: Elkan-Vogel
Rev: *American Choral Review* 10/2 (1968) p74; *Music and Musicians* 21 (Sept, 1972) p86-7; *New Yorker* 43 (Apr 8, 1967) p160; *Saturday Review* 51 (Feb 24, 1968; *Variety* 246 (Apr 5, 1967) p69
Bib: B35

1977 Yardumian, Richard
The story of Abraham (1971, rev. 1973)
Med: SATB, SMTBar soli, orch
Txt: Genesis 12, 15
Dur: 75'
Pub: Elkan-Vogel
Rev: *ASCAP* 5/3 (1972) p33; *Hi-Fidelity/Musical America* 24 (Feb, 1974) pMA27 and 33 (Dec, 1983) pMA14-15; *Inter-American Music Review* 84 (July-Oct, 1972) p9-11; *Music* (AGO) 6 (Sept, 1972) p16ff; *Music Journal* 29 (Dec, 1971) p77; *Music and Musicians* 20 (Aug, 1972) p65; *Musical Opinion* 95 (June, 1962) p454-5
Bib: B35
N.B. Score calls for slide projections and optional staging.

Bibliography of Selected Writings

B1 Amman, Douglas D. "The choral music of Ross Lee Finney." Ph.D. dissertation, University of Cincinnati, 1972.
Divides the choral music into three periods, drawing conclusions about stylistic characteristics common to each. Among the works discussed are *Pilgrim psalms, Spherical madrigals, Edge of shadow, Still are new worlds,* and *The martyr's elegy.*

B2 Anagnost, Dean Z. "The choral music of Virgil Thomson." Ph.D. dissertation, Columbia University, 1977.
An overview of the choral works from 1920-1973, including stylistic analysis of the Masses and the Requiem. Includes a complete catalog of works and a series of transcripts from interviews with the composer.

B3 Andre, Don Alan. "Leonard Bernstein's Mass as social and political commentary on the sixties." Ph.D. dissertation, University of Washington, 1979.
Discusses the Mass as a theatre piece, not a liturgical work, dealing with it as a product of the 1960s. Its principal textual theme, says the author, is the loss of innocence through the acquisition of knowledge.

B4 Archibald, Bruce. "Composers of today: Robert Moevs." *Music News,* 1/2 (April, 1971), pp 19-21.
A brief summary of the composer's life and works, with a detailed discussion of several choral works, including *A brief Mass* and *Et occidentem illustra.*

Includes a discography and a list of published works.

B5 Arvey, Verna. *Choreographic music.* New York: E.P. Dutton & Co., 1941.
Pp. 286-300: a discussion of the ballet music of Still and Carpenter, including the latter's *Skyscrapers.*

B6 Arvey, Verna. *William Grant Still.* New York: J. Fischer, 1939.
A very short monograph, useful for its insights into the early years of this composer. Discusses many choral works.

B7 Ashizawa, Theodore Fumio. "The choral music of Vincent Persichetti." D.M.A. dissertation, University of Washington, 1977.
Includes an analysis of the Mass and a general survey and discussion of all of Persichetti's choral works, in particular, *Hymns and responses for the church year, Stabat mater, Dominic has a doll, Celebrations,* and *The creation.*

B8 Ayers, Mary J. "The major choral works of Peter Mennin." D.M.A. dissertation, University of Miami, 1982.
Discusses and analyzes *The cycle, The Christmas story, Cantata de virtue,* and *Reflections of Emily.*

B9 Bacon, Ernst. "The value of choral music." *Choral and Organ Guide,* 18 (May, 1965), pp. 21-3.
Laments the lack of opportunities for adult choral singing in this country, and pleads for new choral music from the nation's best composers.

B10 Bailey, Donald Lee. "A study of stylistic and compositional elements of *Anthem* (Stravinsky), *Fragments of Archilochos* (Foss) and *Creation prologue* (Ussachevsky)." D.A. dissertation, University of Northern Colorado, 1976.

The author suggests that the primary characteristic of *Fragments* is Foss's use of indeterminate techniques.

B11 Baker, David, Lida M. Belt, and Herman C. Hudson, ed. *The Black composer speaks*: a project of the Afro-American Arts Institute, Indiana University. Metuchen, NJ: Scarecrow Press, 1978.

B12 Barham, Terry J. "A macroanalytic view of the choral music of Vincent Persichetti." Ph.D. dissertation, University of Oklahoma, 1981.

A stylistic analysis of six major works: Mass, *Sam was a man, Jimmie's got a goil, Song of peace, Winter cantata,* and *The creation.* Focuses on principal unifying devices in the choral works, as well as form, harmonic practice, melody, meter, tempo, and texture.

B13 Barham, Terry J. "A macroanalytic view of Vincent Persichetti's *The Creation,* Op. 111." *Choral Journal,* 24/7 (1984), p. 5-9.

The article dissects this work through eight areas of inquiry: distribution of sonorities, nature of text, forms employed, types of sectional articulation, large-scale climaxes, contrast of tonal centers, unifying devices or tonal sonorities, and meters and tempi used.

B14 Barham, Terry J. "Unifying elements in the Mass and *Winter Cantata* by Vincent Persichetti." *Choral Journal,* 26/5 (December, 1985), pp. 5-10.

A thematic and motivic analysis of each work, and a comparison of the two works, using many musical examples.

B15 Barnard, Jack Richard. "The choral music of Vincent Persichetti: a descriptive analysis." Ph.D. dissertation, Florida State University, 1974.

Analyzes the melodic, rhythmic, harmonic, texture, formal, and textual elements of the twenty-two published choral works of Persichetti. Discusses the evolution of the composer's choral style, and offers much information on performance problems in these works, with suggestions on how to overcome them.

B16 Balough, Teresa. "Kipling and Grainger." *Studies in Music,* 11 (1977), pp. 71-110 and 15 (1981) pp. 121-31.

Two very thorough, in-depth articles trace the influence of poet on composer, although the men never became close friends. Many musical examples illustrate the text, and the Balough includes a number of quotes from Grainger's contemporaries.

B17 Bender, James F. "Three American composers from the Young Composers Project: style analysis of selected works by Emma Lou Diemer, Donald Martin Jenni, and Richard Lane." Ph.D. dissertation, New York University, 1988.

Bender's purpose was to analyze both early and later works by these composers, leading to a discussion of stylistic changes and musical growth in their works.

B18 Berry, Wallace. "The music of Halsey Stevens." *Musical Quarterly,* 54/3 (1968), pp. 287-308.

In this article, written on the occasion of Stevens's sixtieth birthday, Berry traces the influences on the composer's style, including those of Bartók and Baroque music. Berry discusses several choral works, but only a few in any detail: *Magnificat*, *The ballad of William Sycamore*, and *Le mois de mai*. Includes a list of works.

B19 Bilanchone, Victor, Jr. "*The unicorn, the gorgon, and the manticore* by Gian Carlo Menotti: a study of a twentieth-century madrigal fable." D.M.A. dissertation, University of Miami, 1977.

Studies the musical and dramatic elements of this work and influences on it, such as the 16th-century madrigal comedies. Also discusses performance problems of the work.

B20 Bird, John. *Percy Grainger*. London: Paul Elek, 1976.

A very thorough biography, particularly useful for understanding influences on the composer. Gives a great deal of background information on the choral music, set in a biographical context.

B21 Bloch, Suzanne, and Irene Heskes. *Ernest Bloch, creative spirit: a program source book*. New York: National Jewish Council, 1976.

Presents a combination of materials relating to the composer's life and works, including the composer's own essay on his *Sacred service* (pp. 11-16), from a lecture given in San Francisco in 1933.

B22 Bloch, Suzanne. "Ernest Bloch—student of choral music: some personal refections." *American Choral Review*, 10/2 (1968), pp. 51-4.

The author discusses influences on her father's works, especially of Renaissance music on the *Sacred service*.

B23 Boros, James, "The evolution of Robert Moevs's compositional methodology." *American Music*, 8/4 (Winter, 1990), pp. 384-404.

Divides Moevs's works into four stylistic periods and discusses the characteristics of each. Mentions several choral works (with some musical examples), including *Attis*; *Et nunc, reges*; and *Itaque ut*.

B24 Borroff, Edith. *Three American composers*. New York: University Press of America, 1986.

Chapter three covers the music of Finney, with analysis and commentary of three choral works: *Spherical madrigals*, *Edge of Shadow*, and *Still are new worlds* (pp. 161-88).

B25 Broder, Nathan. *Samuel Barber*. New York: G. Schirmer, 1954.

Stylistic analysis of Barber's music, including the early choral works, as well as a listing of works and discography, and a good (though incomplete) bibliography.

B26 Brookhart, Charles E. "The choral works of Aaron Copland, Roy Harris, and Randall Thompson." Ph.D. dissertation, George Peabody College for Teachers, 1960.

Discusses the stylistic characteristics of these three composers, with particular attention given to Harris's *Mass for men's voices* and Thompson's Requiem.

B27 Brown, Cynthia Clark. "Emma Lou Diemer: composer, performer, educator, church musician." D.M.A. dissertation,

Southern Baptist Theological Seminary, 1985.

A comprehensive analysis and evaluation of Diemer's choral music, as well as a biography of the composer and both a catalog of her works and a discography.

B28 Browne, Bruce S. "The choral music of Lukas Foss." D.M.A. dissertation, University of Washington, 1976; also a short article in *The Choral Journal*, 16/8 (1976), pp. 12-13.

The dissertation begins with a stylistic study of Foss's choral works and also includes documentation for three D.M.A. recitals, which contained no works by Foss.

B29 Brunelle, Philip. "Dominick Argento and his music for chorus." *American Organist*, 22/5 (May, 1988), pp. 178-80.

An interview with the composer, discussing many of the choral works and the circumstances surrounding their composition. Especially good information on *I hate and I love*.

B30 Brunner, David L. "The choral music of Lou Harrison." D.M.A. dissertation, University of Illinois, 1989.

B31 Brunner, David L. "Cultural diversity in the choral music of Lou Harrison." *Choral Journal*, 32/10 (1992), pp. 17-28.

A complete stylistic and analytical overview of Harrison's choral works, as well as a biography of the composer, a bibliography for further study, and a discography; written for the composer's 75th birthday.

B32 Bumgardner, T.A. *Norman Dello Joio*. Boston: Twayne, 1986.

Chapter Two is devoted to the vocal music (pp. 26-52). Includes a short biography of the composer.

B33 Cage, John. *Virgil Thomson: his life and music*. See Hoover (B103).

B34 Carnine, Albert Jr. "The choral music of Howard Hanson." D.M.A. dissertation, University of Texas at Austin, 1977.

Examines the reasons for Hanson's popularity as a choral composer, as well as musical characteristics of his works in this genre. Among the important works discussed: *Song of democracy*, *Streams in the desert*, *Lament for Beowulf*, and *The cherubic hymn*.

B35 Carroll, Lucy E. "Remembering composer Richard Yardumian." *Choral Journal*, 26/8 (March, 1986), pp. 23-7.

A rare and excellent introduction to this composer's works, with particular attention to the *Mass: Veni sancti spiritu* and the multi-media *Story of Abraham*.

B36 Carroll, Lucy E. "Three centuries of song: choral music of Pennsylvania composers." Ph.D. dissertation, Combs College of Music, 1982.

Information on the careers and choral works of Vincent Persichetti and Richard Yardumian.

B37 [Carter, Elliott] *Elliott Carter: sketches and scores in manuscript*. Exhibit catalog, New York: Americana collection of the Music Division, New York Public Library, 1973.

B38 Christiansen, Larry A. "The choral music of Daniel Pinkham." *Choral Journal*, 9/2 (October, 1968), p. 18.

Briefly discusses Pinkham's musical style in general terms, without reference to specific choral works.

B39 Christiansen, Sigurd O. "The sacred choral music of Richard Felciano: an analytic study." D.M.A. dissertation, University of Illinois, 1977.

A complete survey of the sacred works until 1974. The author divides the music into those works for "traditional" forces and those with electronic forces, such as pre-recorded tape. A conclusion summarizes Felciano's style, and an appendix gives transcripts of telephone conversation between the author and the composer.

B40 Cooper, Paul. "The music of Ross Lee Finney." *Musical Quarterly* 53/1 (1967), pp. 1-21.

An overview of Finney's music, focusing on dualities in his style, such as a strong rhythmic drive tempered by lyricism. The discussion singles out a number of the choral works, including *Still are new worlds*, *The nun's priest's tale*, and *Pilgrim strangers*. Includes a list of works.

B41 Copland, Aaron, and Vivian Perlis. *Copland: 1900 through 1942*. New York: St. Martins, 1984; and *Copland: Since 1943*. New York: St. Martin's Press, 1989.

These two volumes constitute the most thorough biography of the composer, including much information pertinent to the choral works.

B42 Coppola, Carlo. "Rabindranath Tagore and Western composers: a preliminary essay." *Journal of South Asian Literature*, 19/2 (Summer-Fall, 1984), pp. 41-61.

While the article deals almost exclusively with settings of Tagore's poems in art song literature by Carpenter, Shepherd, Creston, and others, the reader may gain useful insight into why these composers were drawn to the poet and what influenced their musical settings of his works.

B43 Cottle, William Andrew. "Social commentary in vocal music in the twentieth century as evidenced by Leonard Bernstein's Mass." D.A. dissertation, University of Northern Colorado, 1978.

Discusses the sociological implications in Bernstein's work, including religious ecumenism and issues raised in this country during the 1960s (protests, birth control, misuse of religion, the brotherhood of man). Also discusses the Mass as a product of "social-realist" theatre.

B44 Cox, Dennis Keith. "Aspects of the compositional styles of three selected twentieth-century composers of choral music: Alan Hovhaness, Ron Nelson, and Daniel Pinkham." D.M.A. dissertation, University of Missouri-Kansas City, 1978.

Discusses the three composers together primarily because they are eclectic in their compositional orientation. Each of the first three chapters surveys the choral works of one of the composers and analyzes a single major work. Chapter Four compares the musical styles of the three men.

B45 [Cowell, Henry] Scrapbook (on microfilm) of newspaper clippings from 1923-31. Americana Collection, Music Division of the New York Public Library.

B46 Creigh, Robert Hugh. "Stylistic characteristics of Randall Thompson's choral music." M.Ed. thesis, Central Washington University, 1970.

B47 Davis, Deborah. "The choral works of Ned Rorem." Ph.D. dissertation, Michigan State University, 1978.

Divides Rorem's choral works into two stylistic periods, before and after 1961. The later period is characterized by disjunct writing, more frequent polyphonic writing, varied rhythms, and a harmonic language based on secundal, quartel, and quintel harmonies.

B48 Davis, Deborah. "An interview about choral music with Ned Rorem." *Musical Quarterly*, 68/3 (1982), pp. 390-97.

Discusses Rorem's conception of his various works, his musical style, his text choices, and the influences on his choral writing.

B49 DeSesa, Gary. "A comparison between a descriptive analysis of Leonard Bernstein's Mass and the musical implications of the critical evaluation thereof." Ph.D. dissertation, New York University, 1985.

A scholarly musical analysis of the Mass and a discussion of the poor critical reception it received at its Kennedy Center premiere. Provides over 150 musical examples. Focuses on motivic unity and thematic relationships, and includes a summary of research and recommendations for further study.

B50 Detweiler, Greg Jeffrey. "The choral music of Elliott Carter." D.M.A. dissertation, University of Illinois, 1985.

The first chapter deals with Carter's life and those experiences that may have influenced his choral writing. The remainder of the dissertation deals in turn with an analysis of each of the seven major choral works.

B51 DeVenney, David P. *American Masses and Requiems: a descriptive guide.* Berkeley, Calif.: Fallen Leaf Press, 1990.

Comments on and describes Sessions's *Lilacs* and Masses by Bernstein, Chihara, Dello Joio, Harrison, Hovhaness, Menotti, Pasatieri, Persichetti, Pinkham, Rorem, Sessions, Thompson, and Thomson.

B52 Devore, Richard O. "Stylistic diversity within the music of five avant-garde American composers, 1929-45." Ph.D. dissertation, University of Iowa, 1985.

Discusses influences on Cowell and three other composers, as well as stylistic characteristics of each man's works.

B53 Downes, Edward. "The music of Norman Dello Joio." *Musical Quarterly*, 48/2 (1962), pp. 142-72.

Talks of influences on the composer, including Gregorian chant, Italian opera, and jazz. Includes a works list through 1961.

B54 Dox, Thurston J. *American oratorios and cantatas: a catalog of works written in the United States from colonial times to 1985.* Metuchen, NJ: Scarecrow Press, 1986. 2 vols.

Details hundreds of works in the genres of oratorio, cantata, "ensemble [solo] cantatas," and "choral theatre." A major work in the bibliography of American choral music. Many works included in the present Catalog are also surveyed by Dox.

B55 Dox, Thurston J. "Henry Cowell's choral bombshell." *Choral Journal*, 29/10 (1989), pp. 5-11.

Notes the premiere performance of Cowell's *...if he pleases* and the shock it gave an audience prepared for the usual *Messiah* performance at Christmas in 1955. Discusses stylistic aspects of the piece and quotes performance reviews of its first and later performances. Many musical examples.

B56 Dreyfus, Kay. *Percy Grainger's Kipling settings: a study of the manuscript sources.* Melbourne, Australia: University of Western Australia Press, 1980.

While much of this book focuses on settings for solo voice, it also contains many documents valuable to the reader concerned with Grainger's many choral settings of Kipling.

B57 Edwards, J. Michele. *Literature for voices in combination with electronic and tape music: an annotated bibliography.* Ann Arbor, Mich.: Music Library Association, 1977.

Lists and comments on works by Erb, Bernstein, and Felciano.

B58 Evett, Robert. "The music of Vincent Persichetti." *Juilliard Review*, 2/2 (Spring, 1955), pp. 15-30.

An excellent article about Persichetti's compositional style. Musical examples are drawn chiefly from the composer's instrumental works, however. Includes both a photo and a works list.

B59 Ewen, David. *The world of twentieth-century music.* Englewood Cliffs, NJ: Prentice-Hall, 1969.

Gives a short analysis (pp. 831-39) of Thomson's choral works, especially the *Missa pro defunctis.*

B60 [Farwell, Arthur] Scrapbook of newspaper clippings regarding Farwell's career; in the Americana Collection, Music Division of the New York Public Library.

B61 Flostrom, Richard. "The choral warmup: a look at avant-garde music." *Choral Journal*, 14/7 (April, 1974), pp. 22-3.

An aid to choral rehearsal techniques with contemporary music, using as an example Erb's "Kyrie."

B62 Forbes, Elliot. "Americana." *American Choral Review*, 16/4 (1974), pp. 40-55.

Discusses Americanisms as influences on Thompson's work, as well as formative episodes in the composer's life. Mentions many of Thompson's choral works.

B63 Forbes, Elliot. "The music of Randall Thompson." *Musical Quarterly.* 35/1 (January, 1949), pp. 1-25.

A thorough look at Thompson's choral music, but predating the composition of several major works, including the Mass and the Requiem. Includes a photo, a manuscript example from the Second Symphony, and a pre-1949 works list. One long section deals with the choral works, particularly *The peaceable kingdom.*

B64 Foreman, Lewis, ed. *The Percy Grainger companion.* London: Thames Publishing, 1981.

Most useful are the chapters on "Grainger and folksong" (pp. 55-70) and "Orchestral works" (pp. 71-102). Also includes a catalog of works, a bibliography, and a discography.

B65 Foss, Lukas. "Inaudible singing." *Choral Journal*, 13/1 (1972), pp. 5-6.

A transcription of a rehearsal of *Geod* that leads into a discussion by the composer of his ideas behind several of his choral works.

B66 Freedland, Michael. *Leonard Bernstein.* London: Harrap, 1987.

A biography with information on Bernstein's works scattered throughout the text, given in the context of his life. Includes a photo of the Mass in rehearsal between pages 184 and 185.

B67 Fulton, Alvin W. "Ernest Bloch's Sacred service." M.M. thesis, University of Rochester, 1953.

B67.5 Fusner, Henry. "Sowerby's *Forsaken of man*: a forgotten masterpiece?" *American Organist*, 16 (May, 1985), p.48.

This overview of the cantata devotes several paragraphs to each movement. The article was written to inform the members of the AGO before a performance of the work at a forthcoming convention.

B68 Gardner, Effie Tyler. "An analysis of the technique and style of selected Black-American composers of contemporary choral music." Ph.D. dissertation, Michigan State University, 1979.

Discusses the music of Kay in a brief biography of the composer, followed by a complete list of works and a stylistic discussion of representative music.

B69 Gardner, Patrick G. "*La Koro Sutra* by Lou Harrison: historical perspective, analysis, and performance considerations." D.M.A. dissertation, University of Texas at Austin, 1981.

Discusses the combination in this work of tonal, melodic, and rhythmic elements from both the West and the East, in addition to a textual analysis and a discussion of performance considerations.

B70 Garland, Patrick., ed. *A Lou Harrison reader*. Santa Fe: Soundings Press, 1987.

B71 Garofalo, Robert J. "The life and works of Frederick Converse." Ph.D. dissertation, Catholic University of America, 1969.

The author aims to ascertain Converse's importance as a composer and to document his life as a teacher and administrator. Part II is a general discussion of the composer's style and the influences upon it. Includes all of the major choral works.

B72 Gerschefski, Edwin. "American composers: Henry Cowell." *Modern Music*, 23/4 (1946), pp. 255-60.

A brief overview of Cowell's life and works, including the notice he received in Europe as a composer. Several choral works are used to illustrate his musical style, including *American muse*.

B73 Goodwin, Joscelyn. "The music of Henry Cowell." Ph.D. dissertation, Cornell University, 1969.

A discussion of his works, divided into five stylistic periods. The choral works are covered throughout the dissertation, primarily in the earlier chapters. Also includes a nearly 300-page bibliography and a short biography.

B74 Gordon, Eric A. *Mark the music: the life and work of Marc Blitzstein.* New York: St. Martin's Press, 1989.

B75 Gorelick, Brian. "Movement and shape in the choral music of Roger Sessions." D.M.A. dissertation, University of Illinois, 1985.

Identifies significant stylistic characteristics of Sessions through an extensive analysis of *Lilacs*. Concentrates on sound, melody, harmony, rhythm, text, and cadential formulas (tone rows), as well as methods of compositional unification.

B76 Gottlieb, Jack. "The choral music of Leonard Bernstein: reflections of theatre and liturgy." *American Choral Review*, 10/4 (1968), pp. 156-77.
Analyses and musical descriptions of the *Kaddish symphony*, the *Chichester psalms*, and the choruses from *The lark*.

B77 Gottlieb, Jack. "Leonard Bernstein: *Kaddish symphony*." *Perspectives of New Music*, 4/1 (1965), pp. 171-5.
A lengthy performance review that goes considerably beyond a critique into an analysis of melodic material found in the symphony.

B78 Gottlieb, Jack. "Symbols of faith in the music of Leonard Bernstein." *Musical Quarterly*, 66/2 (April, 1980), pp. 287-95.
Includes analysis of music from *The lark*, Mass, *Chichester psalms*, and other works.

B79 Gottwald, Clytus. "Leonard Bernsteins Messe, oder die Konstruktion der Blasphemie." *Melos/Neue Zeitschrift für Musik*, 2/4 (1976), pp. 281-84.
Deals with Bernstein's perception of the crisis of faith that predominates late twentieth-century civilization and how that influenced his composition.

B80 Gradenwitz, Peter. *Leonard Bernstein, the infinite variety of a musician*. London: Berg Publishers, 1987.
"Musical synthesis in the later compositions," pp. 207-224, contains a lengthy and thorough analysis of the Mass. Discusses most of the other choral works, but devotes fewer pages to them.

B81 Gray, Arlene E. *Listen to the lambs: a source book of the R. Nathaniel Dett materials in the Niagara Falls Public Library*. Crystal Beach, Ontario: A.E. Gray, 1984.

B82 Griffen, Malcolm J. "Style in the choral works of William Schuman." D.M.A. dissertation, University of Illinois, 1972.
Seeks to remedy the relative paucity of writings about Schuman's choral music. The author concludes that the focal point of the text in Schuman's works is an overriding factor towards which other aspects of his musical style converge. Primarily deals with the following works: *Pioneers!*, *A free song*, and the *Carols of death*.

B83 Griffith, M.J. "William Schuman's *Carols of death*—an analysis." *Choral Journal*, 17/6 (1977), pp. 17-18.

B84 Griffiths, Richard Lyle. "Ned Rorem: music for chorus and orchestra." D.M.A. dissertation, University of Washington, 1979.
Deals with Rorem's "idiosyncratic" treatment of melody as the distinctive feature of his compositional style.

B85 Gruen, John Erick. *Menotti: a biography*. New York: MacMillan, 1978.
A good biography, focusing more on the operas than the choral works, but including substantial material on the choral works, especially *The unicorn, the gorgon and the manticore*, and *The death of the Bishop of Brindisi*.

B86 Guelker-Cone, Leslie. "Kirke Mechem—an interview." *Choral Journal*, 27/9 (1987), pp. 19-24.
Offers keen insight into Mechem's compositional process and technique. The composer makes a number of

interesting observations, such as "Choral music is, I think, the healthiest sector in the classical area because it is in touch not only with professionals but also with enthusiastic, gifted ... amateurs. It's like art song was in the nineteenth century."

B87 Haar, James. "Randall Thompson and the music of the past." *American Choral Review*, 16/4 (October, 1974), pp. 7-15.

Illustrates how Thompson's knowledge of past music has influenced his own composition. Includes examples from the *Mass of the Holy Spirit*.

B88 Haas, Robert B., ed. *William Grant Still and the fusion of cultures in American music*. Los Angeles: Black Sparrow Press, 1972.

A biography of the composer and a discussion and analysis of his works by genre. Includes a complete catalog of his works as well as a discography and suggestions for programming his music. Discusses the vocal works, pp. 57-68.

B89 Hadley, Richard T. "The published choral music of Ulysses Simpson Kay— 1943 to 1968." Ph.D. dissertation, University of Iowa, 1972.

A biography of the composer, analyses of all the published choral works, and a summary of the composer's musical style, including melodic and rhythmic elements, Kay's treatment of dissonance, and the structural aspects of his choral compositions.

B90 Hall, Roger L. "Randall Thompson." *Journal of Church Music*, 27 (December, 1985), pp. 9-10.

A very brief biography and obituary of the composer, with information on persons who influenced Thompson's

life and works. Includes a list of choral works.

B91 Harris, Carl Gordon. "A study of characteristic stylistic trends found in the choral works of a selected group of Afro-American composers and arrangers." D.M.A. dissertation, University of Missouri-Kansas City, 1972.

Traces the writing of choral music by African-American composers from the late nineteenth century until 1972. Among other composers, the author includes Dett and Kay.

B92 Harris, Carl Gordon. "Three schools of Black choral composers and arrangers, 1900-1970." *Choral Journal* 14/8 (April, 1974), p. 11-14.

The author identifies three distinct compositional periods, characterizing the practitioners in each as "Black trailblazers," "Black nationalists," and "Black innovators." Short biographical sketches and a brief discussion of works may be found regarding Dett, Still, and many others.

B93 Hausfield, Susan Elizabeth. "A study of Mass by Leonard Bernstein." M.A. thesis, The Ohio State University, 1977.

Analyzes the work in four chapters: biographical background, the text and music of the Mass, the Mass as social commentary, and the Mass in the evolution of American musical theatre. Excellent bibliography.

B94 Hawthorne, Loyd F. "The choral music of Gordon Binkerd." D.M.A. dissertation, University of Texas at Austin, 1973.

While surveying all of the choral works, Hawthorne focuses on several he considers most important and representative, particularly *The ebb and flow*. Includes both a listing of works and a bibliography of writings.

B95 Hayes, Laurence M. "The music of Ulysses Kay, 1939-63" Ph.D. dissertation, University of Wisconsin, 1971.

Narrowing his study to the indicated years, Hayes divides Kay's works into two stylistic periods, each roughly a decade long, with a third period emerging toward the 1960s. For purposes of discussion the choral music is divided into those works with instruments (including two operas), and those with unaccompanied choral forces.

B96 Heinz, William, Jr. "New light on Samuel Barber's *Reincarnations.*" *Choral Journal*, 25/3 (1985), pp. 25-7.

Primarily a textual analysis of the three works in this set. Heinz connects ideas and form and structure in the texts with Barber's musical settings, and gives performance suggestions based on his conclusions.

B97 Hendl, Walter. "The music of Peter Mennin." *Juilliard Review*, 1/2 (Spring, 1954), pp. 18-25.

A general introduction to the composer's works. The choral works are given only a paragraph, with the exception of *The cycle*, which is treated in more detail (with two musical examples).

B98 Herrema, Robert D. "The choral music of Ulysses Kay." *Choral Journal*, 11/4 (1970), pp. 5-10.

A biography of the composer is followed by a section discussing style and techniques in his choral works. Includes two musical examples from the *Choral triptych*.

B99 Hinds, Wayne B. "Leo Sowerby: a biography and descriptive listing of the anthems." Ed.D. dissertation, George Peabody College for Teachers, 1972.

Includes an annotated listing of works. A stylistic analysis concludes that Sowerby was a "traditionalist" composer whose writing remained "basically unchanged" throughout his life.

B100 Hinshaw, Don G. "Contemporary composers: Emma Lou Diemer." *Journal of Church Music*, 18 (September, 1976), pp. 13-15.

Discusses Diemer's contributions to church music, as well as aspects of her musical style.

B101 Hobbs, Odell. "A study of selected outstanding Negro college choirs in the United States of America." M.M. thesis, Catholic University of America, 1966.

B102 Holmes, James. "A guide to the sacred choral music of Ned Rorem." *American Organist*, 23/5 (May, 1989), pp. 66-8.

A brief biography and description of style precede a listing of sacred works by Rorem, each with one paragraph of commentary.

B103 Hoover, Kathleen, and John Cage. *Virgil Thomson: his life and music.* New York: Yoseloff, 1959.

Cage discusses various versions of the *Mass in G minor* and the two *Missa brevis* settings (on pp. 130-31), and the *Mass for 2-part chorus* (on pp. 173-4), giving his preferences for various movements in the different works and his reasons for liking them.

B104 Hopkins, John. "Menotti's medieval menagerie: producing *The unicorn, the gorgon and the manticore.*" *Choral Journal*, 26/5 (1985), pp. 21-6.

In a rather practical-minded article, Hopkins gives a brief overview of the work and its genesis. He then explains how (and why) one might mount a performance of the work, and the many production aspects outside the "normal" work of a choral conductor that need attention when performing this piece.

B105 Horowitz, Linda. "Literature forum." *Choral Journal*, 21/4 (1980), pp. 26-9.

A work-by-work description of the choral music of Barber. Devotes several paragraphs to some works, only a few sentences to others.

B106 Hughes, Charles W. "The choral music." *Studies in Music*, 16 (1982), pp. 53-61.

A thorough examination of style and technique in the choral works of Grainger. Readers may also find useful information on different topics concerning this composer in other articles in this periodical, devoted entirely to Grainger.

B107 Hume, Paul. "Liturgy on stage: Bernstein's Mass," in *Sennets & tuckets: a Bernstein celebration*, ed. Stephen Ledbetter. Boston: Boston Symphony Orchestra and David R. Godine, 1988, pp. 57-62.

This short essay on the philosophical underpinnings of the Mass traces the origins of Bernstein's work in relation to his three symphonies.

B108 Jablonski, Edward. *The encyclopedia of American music*. New York: Doubleday, 1981.

An exception to my rule excluding dictionaries and encyclopedias, this relatively unknown book contains a number of very good essays on nearly every composer in this survey, and a particularly fine essay on Foss's *The prairie*.

B109 Jacobs, Arthur, ed. *Choral music*. New York: Penguin Books, 1973.

The chapter on "Twentieth-century Americans" by Robert Sabin is a fine introduction to this subject. Beyond a general discussion of important trends and styles, it includes examples from Hanson's *Lament for Beowulf* and Copland's *In the beginning*.

B110 Jenkins, Gwendolyn N. "The choral style of Randall Thompson." M.M. thesis, University of Rochester, 1955.

B111 Johnson, Axie Allen. "Choral settings of the Magnificat by selected twentieth-century American composers." D.M.A. dissertation, University of Southern California, 1968.

Compares in detail the Magnificats of Stevens and Hovhaness, as well as a setting by Jean Berger, in an attempt to summarize aspects of musical style that might be considered representative of other contemporary settings of this text.

B112 Johnson, Bret. "Still sings the voice: a portrait of Ned Rorem." *Tempo*, 153 (June, 1985), pp. 7-12.

Discusses Rorem's recent orchestral and choral music, especially *An American oratorio*, which the author says beautifully reflects a variety of well-chosen poetry.

B113 Johnson, Craig R. "An examination of Dominick Argento's *Te Deum*." D.M.A. dissertation, University of Cincinnati, 1989.

A musical and textual analysis of this important Argento work. It also includes a short biography of the composer, an annotated listing of the choral works, and a brief summary of other important American settings of this text.

B114 Johnson, Marlowe W. "The choral music of Daniel Pinkham." Ph.D. dissertation, University of Iowa, 1968.

An analysis and discussion of Pinkham's scale materials, vertical sonorities, harmonic connections, counterpoint, form, texts, and use of instruments.

B115 Johnson, Marlowe W. "The choral writing of Daniel Pinkham." *American Choral Review*, 8/4 (June, 1966), pp. 1, 12-16.

Discusses various aspects of Pinkham's compositional style, with particular attention to melodic elements. Gives several musical examples, especially from the Requiem.

B116 Johnston, William R. "Choral settings of Walt Whitman by Norman Dello Joio." Master's thesis, Louisiana State University, 1970.

B117 Jones, Raymond D. "Leo Sowerby: his life and his choral music." Ph.D. dissertation, University of Iowa, 1973.

Biography of the composer and description of his works, in several chapters. Sowerby's church music is covered in Chapter Seven. Particularly good discussion of stylistic elements related to or derived from textual considerations. Includes a thematic catalog.

B118 Jones, Robert E. "*Skyscrapers*: an experiment in design." *Modern Music*, 3 (Jan.-Feb., 1926), pp. 21-6.

Jones discusses the composition of *Skyscrapers* prior to its Metropolitan Opera debut. He explains that Carpenter's jazz-like score preceded any production planning, including a plot line for the ballet.

B119 Kelley, Kenneth B. "The choral music of Leslie Bassett." D.M.A. dissertation, University of Illinois, 1976; also an article in *The Choral Journal*, 19/4 (1978), pp. 16-17.

Divides the choral music into three periods, discussing stylistic and musical characteristics important to each period.

B120 Kimberling, Victoria J. *David Diamond: a bio-bibliography*. Metuchen, N.J.: Scarecrow Press, 1987.

A biography of the composer by stylistic period, especially helpful for material on the genesis of several works, including *To music*. The core of the volume is an annotated catalog of works.

B121 Knapp, Alexander V. "The Jewishness of Bloch: subconscious or conscious." *Royal Musical Association Proceedings*, 97 (1970-71), pp. 99-112.

Traces the influences of Jewish life, thought, and music in the compositions of Bloch, concluding that these changed the most fundamental aspects of Bloch's style.

B122 Kozinn, Alan. "Samuel Barber: the legacy." *Hi-Fidelity/Musical America*, 31 (July, 1981), pp. 45ff.

A survey of Barber's works by genre, with recommended recordings. The choral works are covered on p. 46.

B123 Kummer, Randolph F. "An analysis of the compositional techniques employed in the Requiem by Randall Thompson." M.M. thesis, University of Wisconsin, 1966.

B124 Kushner, David Z. "The 'Jewish' works of Ernest Bloch." *Journal of Musicological Research*, 3/3-4 (Fall, 1981), pp. 259-73.

Discusses those aspects in Bloch's style that might have been influenced by Jewish ideas or philosophies. Among the works given detailed discussion is *Avodath hakodesh*.

B125 Laird, Paul Robert. "The influence of Aaron Copland on Leonard Bernstein." M.A. thesis, Ohio State University, 1982.

Describes Copland's musical influence in chapters devoted to rhythm, melody, harmony, form, Jewish elements, and "Simplicity in Copland and Bernstein." Among choral works discussed are the Mass and *Chichester psalms*.

B126 Larson, Robert M. "Stylistic characteristics in a cappella composition in the United States, 1940-53: as indicated by the works of Jean Berger, David Diamond, Darius Milhaud, and Miklos Rozsa." Ph.D. dissertation, Northwestern University, 1953.

A general discussion of musical techniques and text selections in twentieth-century choral music, drawing upon selections from the works of these four composers.

B127 Latta, John Arthur. "Alice Parker: choral composer, arranger, and teacher." Ed.D. dissertation, University of Illinois, 1986.

Discusses Parker's choral works, as well as her professional associations with both Robert Shaw and Vincent Persichetti. Includes a complete catalog of her works, listing both original works and arrangements.

B128 LePage, Jane W. *Women composers, conductors, and musicians of the twentieth century: selected biographies*. Metuchen, N.J.: Scarecrow Press, 1980-88; 3 vols (2nd volume unavailable to me).

Biographical sketches and stylistic analyses of each subject are followed by a skeletal listing of works. Includes chapters on Diemer and Musgrave in Vol. 1 and Vivian Fine in Vol. 3.

B129 Litton, James. "Electronic music in church." *English Church Music* (1972), pp. 23-8.

Discusses recent American choral music utilizing pre-recorded tapes or other electronic forces. Among the works discussed are Felciano's *Double Alleluia* and *Sic transit*, Bassett's *Collect*, and Pinkham's *In the beginning of creation*.

B130 Lock, William. "Interpretive notes for singers: *Psalm XXIII* by Paul Creston." *Journal of Church Music*, 22 (March, 1980), pp. 6-7.

A brief analysis of the work, with rehearsal and performance suggestions.

B131 Loesch, Robert K. "Alice Parker: composer, teacher, publisher." *Music* (AGO), 9 (February, 1975), pp. 26-7.

Includes commentary on *Seven carols*, *Gaudete*, and *The sermon from the mountian*. Loesch also discusses the composer's ideas on hymn singing.

B132 Loessi, John. "The choral works of Randall Thompson." M.M. thesis, University of Cincinnati, 1955.

B133 Loucks, Richard N. "Arthur Shepherd." Ph.D. dissertation, University of Rochester, 1960.

B134 Loucks, Richard N. *Arthur Shepherd, American composer*. Orem, Utah: Brigham Young University Press, 1980.

One of the few reference volumes on Shepherd, with good general information on the composer, although little specifically on the choral works.

B135 MacNeill, Roger M. "Secular choral chamber music in America since 1950, as represented by the music for this genre by Samuel Adler, Jean Berger,

B134 Loucks, Richard N. *Arthur Shepherd, American composer.* Orem, Utah: Brigham Young University Press, 1980.

One of the few reference volumes on Shepherd, with good general information on the composer, although little specifically on the choral works.

B135 MacNeill, Roger M. "Secular choral chamber music in America since 1950, as represented by the music for this genre by Samuel Adler, Jean Berger, Eugene Butler, and Kirke Mechem." D.A. dissertation, University of Northern Colorado, 1986.

A history of chamber choirs in America, and a history of secular chamber music since the development of the Renaissance madrigal. A useful study for tracing possible influences on contemporary works in this style.

B136 Maggs, J.A. "Literature forum: original settings of the Ordinary for choir and organ." *Choral Journal*, 23/9 (May, 1983), pp. 11-16.

Discusses shorter Masses by predominantly European composers, but includes Sessions's Mass, with several paragraphs about its style and the difficulties its performance presents.

B137 Manion, Martha L. *Writings about Henry Cowell: an annotated bibliography.*

Brooklyn: Institute for Studies in American Music, 1982.

A useful volume, with many entries cited for the choral compositions. Most notices are rather short, usually buried in a longer concert review or article covering several works. Manion's monograph would be useful to anyone pursuing further study of Cowell's works.

B138 Mann, Alfred, ed. *Randall Thompson: a choral legacy.* Boston: E.C. Schirmer, 1974.

Reprinted from an issue of the *American Choral Review* that was devoted to the composer's choral music. See Thompson (B215).

B139 Mark, Michael L. "The life and works of Vittorio Giannini (1903-66)" D.M.A. dissertation, Catholic University of America, 1970.

Describes Giannini as a reactionary composer whose works are rooted in a nineteenth-century Romantic idiom. The dissertation focuses on Giannini's work as a music educator and administrator; in regards to his music, the discussion centers primarily around the composer's band scores.

B140 McBrier, Vivian Flagg. "The life and works of Robert Nathaniel Dett." Ph.D. dissertation, Catholic University of America, 1967.

A critical study of the composer's life and works, drawn not only from interviews with Dett's friends and acquaintances as well as primary sources, but also from observations by the author, who was a pupil of Dett's. The choral works that receive the most attention include *Listen to the lambs*; *The ordering of Moses*; *Don't be weary, traveler*; and *Juba*.

B141 McCray, James. "American choral music with organ: Emma Lou Diemer." *American Organist*, 21 (November, 1987), pp. 64–71.

The most thorough article in this series, with detailed commentary and many musical examples.

B142 McCray, James. "American choral music with organ: Kirke Mechem." *American Organist*, 20 (February, 1986), pp. 66-9.

The following works are each given several paragraphs of description and analysis: *The Lord is in his holy temple, The children of David, I will sing alleluia, Why art thou cast down,* and *It is good to give thanks.*

B143 McCray, James. "American choral music with organ: the music of Richard Felciano." *American Organist*, 17 (March, 1983), pp. 66-7.

A brief but valuable overview of each of Felciano's published choral works with organ.

B144 McCray, James, "Daniel Pinkham's published music for chorus and electronic tape." *Choral Journal*, 19/7 (1979), pp. 10-16.

McCray discusses style in the choral/electronic music of Pinkham, with information on sixteen works in this genre.

B145 McCray, James. "Lukas Foss' *A parable of death*: comments on structure and performance." *American Choral Review*, 18/3 (1976), pp. 12-13.

A very short structural overview of this work.

B146 McCray, James. "Ned Rorem's music for chorus and organ." *Diapason*, 71 (February, 1980), pp. 16-18.

B147 McCray, James. "Norman Dello Joio's Mass settings: a comparative introduction." *Diapason*, 80 (September, 1989), pp. 14-16.

B148 McCray, James. "Vincent Persichetti's music for women's chorus." *Choral Journal*, 21/7 (1981), pp. 9-15.

An extensive article that provides a stylistic analysis of each choral work for women's voices, in addition to giving the difficulty level of the composition, the source of the text, and other information.

B149 McGilvray, Bryan Wendol. "The choral music of Randall Thompson, an American eclectic." D.M.A. dissertation, University of Missouri-Kansas City, 1979.

A study of the musical and extra-musical forces influencing Thompson's choral output, including the composer's philosophies of music and composition. Includes analysis of text, modal and tonal counterpoint, and a descriptive analysis of the major choral works. The author conducted extensive interviews with Thompson and some of his colleagues and students.

B150 Mechem, Kirke. "Alienation and entertainment, continued: choral music and its effect on audiences and students." *Choral Journal*, 13/7 (1973), pp. 9-10.

A response by Mechem to an earlier article; here, he discusses distinctions between learned music and entertainment music, and concludes by admonishing the reader to forget about shaping public opinion and instead to develop "our singers' respect and love for integrity and beauty."

B151 Mechem, Kirke. "The choral cycle." *Choral Journal*, 10/7 (1970), pp. 8-11.
A valuable discussion by a composer who has written several works in this genre. Includes a listing of choral cycles.

B152 Meier, Ann. "An interview with Norman Dello Joio." *Music Educators Journal*, 74 (October, 1987), pp. 53-6.
Discusses possible influences on the composer, his compositional style, and a number of other topics. Includes two photos.

B153 Merritt, Susan. "Text and tune: back to basics with Alice Parker." *Choral Journal*, 25/1 (1985), pp. 5-9.
Following a few paragraphs of biography, the author undertakes a discussion of Parker's compositional techniques and gives rehearsal suggestions for performing her choral music. Several musical examples.

B154 Miller, Donald Bruce. "The choral music of Kirke Mechem: a study and performance of representative works." D.M.A. dissertation, University of Southern California, 1981.
Chapter Three analyzes *Songs of wisdom*, *The children of David*, *Psalm 23*, and *It is good to give thanks*. Dissertation includes a biography of the composer.

B155 Miller, Donald Bruce. "The choral music of Kirke Mechem." *American Choral Review*, 12/4 (1970), pp. 163-71.
Probably the best short introduction to Mechem's music, including an analysis of his style and influences on his work.

B156 Mincar, Paul S. *Death set to music: masterworks by Bach, Brahms, Penderecki, Bernstein*. Atlanta: John Knox Press, 1987.

Surveys four works, including Bernstein's Mass, concentrating on the text and its musical setting. Minear also discusses implications for performance based on his ideas.

B157 Mize, Lou Stem. "A study of selected choral settings of Walt Whitman poems." Ph.D. dissertation, Florida State University, 1967.
Includes an investigation of the mutual influences of poetry and music in Whitman settings by Dello Joio, Hanson, Harris, and Schuman.

B158 Moe, Orin. "The music of Elliott Carter." *College Music Symposium*, 22/1 (Spring, 1982), pp.1-31.
Delineates Carter's stylistic periods, devoting a brief discussion to the choral works. Many musical examples, mostly from the instrumental works, illustrate Carter's stylistic development.

B159 Moore, James W. "A study of tonality in selected works of Leonard Bernstein." Ph.D. dissertation, Florida State University, 1984.
Investigates Bernstein's tonal practice by examining six works, including *Chichester psalms* and the Mass.

B160 Mosher, Lucinda. "Children's choral corner: Alice Parker on composing for children's voices." *Choral Journal*, 24/6 (1984), p. 23.
A short article that relates part of the author's correspondence with Parker regarding her underlying philosophy and the musical techniques she uses when writing for children's voices.

B161 Mottola, Gail Louise H. "A survey of the choral works by Thea Musgrave with a conductor's analysis of the *Five ages of* *man* and *Rorate coeli."* D.M.A. dissertation, University of Texas at Austin, 1986.

The author discusses the primacy of dramatic elements in Musgrave's choral music and demonstrates her thesis through examination of two specific works.

B162 Muilenburg, Harley W. "A study of selected unpublished choral compositions of Leo Sowerby." M.S. thesis, University Wisconsin-Eau Claire, 1976.

B163 Murphy, James L. "The choral music of Halsey Stevens." Ph.D. dissertation, Texas Tech University, 1980.

Discusses his text choices, harmonic practice, formal structures, and use of rhythm, meter, and tempo. Surveys all of the choral music and includes a number of quotes from Stevens based upon interviews with the author. Includes a biography.

B164 Newman, William S. "Arthur Shepherd." *Musical Quarterly,* 36/2 (April, 1950), pp. 159-79.

In this article, written to commemorate the Shepherd's seventieth birthday, Newman surveys the composer's works and stylistic development, using many musical examples (including one from *Psalm 42*).

B165 Olmstead, Andrea. *Conversations with Roger Sessions.* Boston: Northeastern University Press, 1987.

Discusses the vocal works (on pp. 103-45), and the *Mass for unison voices* (on pp. 33, 122-27). Sessions comments on, among other things, the genesis of the Mass and its melodic elements. *Lilacs* is treated even more fully in its own chapter. The book includes a good discography and bibliography.

B166 Olmstead, Andrea. *Roger Sessions and his music.* Ann Arbor: UMI Research Press, 1985.

More generally biographical than the author's later book (above). The text briefly mentions the Mass (on p. 109) and *Lilacs* (on pp. 157-162), as well as *Psalm 140, Turn O Libertad,* and *Three choruses on biblical texts.* Excellent although limited material, with a good discography and bibliography.

B167 Orton, Fred. "Morton Feldman: interview." *Studio Int.,* 192 (November-December, 1976), pp. 244-48.

A wide-ranging interview, useful to the reader for its questions regarding Feldman's association with Mark Rothko and other artists, and the importance of those friendships to *Rothko chapel* and other works.

B168 Page, Robert. "In quest of answers." *Choral Journal,* 14/3 (1973), pp. 5-8.

An interview with Persichetti, in which the composer discusses his life and influences on his choral music.

B169 Parks, O.G. "A critical study of the works of Leo Sowerby." M.M. thesis, North Texas State University, 1941.

B170 Parmentier, Richard. "Richard Felciano's *Sic transit." Diapason* 62/5 (April, 1971), p. 14.

A brief analysis and discussion. The author concludes that "the composer creates a new metaphor for passionate subjectivity."

B171 Perlis, Vivian. See Copland, *Copland: 1900-1942* and *Copland: Since 1943* (B41).

B172 Perrison, Harry D. "Charles Wakefield Cadman: his life and works." Ph.D. dissertation, University of Rochester, 1978.
Concludes that Cadman's style is a fusion of European Romanticism and American nationalism. Although the dissertation discusses many of the choral works, it centers around an investigation of Cadman's song literature.

B173 Peyser, Joan. *Bernstein: a biography*. New York: Beech Tree Books/William Morrow, 1987.
Discusses the Mass on pp. 411-17 and 420-22, with a few other passing references. Useful for examining Bernstein's personal reasons for composing the work, and the place it occupies generally in his life and music.

B174 [Pinkham, Daniel] Papers, 1949-1972. Houghton Library, Harvard University. Contains manuscripts and printed scores of Pinkham's compositions, concert programs, and miscellaneous items.

B175 Plum, Nancy. "A conversation with composer Ned Rorem." *Voice*, (Nov.-Dec., 1985), pp. 1ff.
An interview, in which Rorem discusses various works, including the *Missa brevis* and *The poet's Requiem*.

B176 Pollack, Howard J. "Walter Piston and his music." Ph.D. dissertation, Cornell University, 1981.
Discusses both published and unpublished works. Among the choral works included, *Carnival song* is given substantial and detailed analysis. Includes a biography of the composer, with interviews.

B177 Pooler, Frank, et al. "In quest of answers." *Choral Journal*, 13/6 (1973), pp. 5-15.
A lengthy interview with Schuman that covers a wide variety of topics, with many insights into his life and works.

B178 Powers, Harold S. "Current Chronicle." *Musical Quarterly*, 58 (1972), pp. 297-307.
Discusses the genesis of Sessions's *Lilacs*, as well as its musical language and compositional procedures. Many musical examples.

B179 Restagno, Enzo. *Elliott Carter in conversation*. Brooklyn: Institute for Studies in American Music, Monograph No. 32, 1989.
A wide-ranging series of interviews. Includes information on several choral works, as well as Carter's own experiences as a chorister.

B180 Restine, James H. "The choral idiom of Randall Thompson." M.A. thesis, West Texas State University, 1959.

B181 Revicki, Robert K. "A study of recent settings of the Mass by American composers." Master's thesis, Brown University, 1960.

B182 Riegger, Wallingford. "The music of Vivian Fine." *American Composers Alliance Bulletin*, 8/1 (1958), pp. 2-6.
A brief introduction to Fine's musical style, followed by an annotated listing of her works.

B183 Robinson, Ray. "Gian Carlo Menotti's new Mass." *Choral Journal*, 20/5 (January, 1980), pp. 5-7, 21.
An analytical discussion of *Missa O pulchritudo*.

B184 Roma, Catherine. "The choral music of Thea Musgrave." *American Choral Review*, 21/1 (Winter, 1989), pp. 5-13.

A relatively short stylistic analysis of the composer's works in chronological order. Several musical examples illustrate the text.

B185 Rosenfeld, Paul. *Discoveries of a music critic*. New York: 1936.

On pp. 164-170, a discussion and critical analysis of Bloch's *Sacred service*.

B186 Rosner, Arnold. "An analytical survey of the music of Alan Hovhaness." Ph.D. dissertation, State University of New York at Buffalo, 1972.

The author states that his study is the first, and to that date only, serious study of the composer's compositional style. A short biography of Hovhaness is followed by chapters dealing with his rhythmic, melodic, and harmonic style, orchestration, and stylistic periods. Most musical examples are drawn from the instrumental works.

B187 Ryder, Georgia A. "Another look at some American cantatas." *Black Perspective in Music*, 3/2 (May, 1975), pp. 135-140.

Discusses Still's *And they lynched him on a tree* and Dett's *The ordering of Moses* by placing these works in perspective with other dramatic works (especially opera) by other African-American composers.

B188 Ryder, Georgia A. "Melodic and rhythmic elements of American Negro folk songs as employed in cantatas by selected American composers between 1932 and 1967." Ph.D. dissertation, New York University, 1970.

Identifies and investigates folksong elements in the works of Dett and Still, among other composers.

B189 Saladino, David A. "Influence of poetry on compositional practices in selected choral music of Gordon Binkerd." Ph.D. dissertation, Florida State University, 1984.

Three areas of exploration: influences on the composer, his use of borrowed music, and his choices of text. The author surveys not only the choral works as a whole, but also a number of specific compositions in greater detail.

B190 Schiff, David. *The music of Elliott Carter*. New York: Da Capo Press, 1983.

Commentary on and stylistic analysis of all of Carter's major works, including *The defense of Corinth*, *Harmony of morning*, *Musicians wrestle everywhere*, and *To music*.

B191 Seigle, Cecilia Segawa. "The choral music of Vincent Persichetti." *American Choral Review*, 7/3 (March, 1965), pp. 4-5.

A very short article that serves as a quick overview to the composer's choral oeuvre.

B192 Shackelford, Rudy. "Conversation with Vincent Persichetti." *Perspectives of New Music*, 20/1-2 (1981-82), pp. 104-34.

A wide-ranging interview with the composer, in which he talks at some length about *The creation*, among other works.

B193 Shackelford, Rudy. "The music of Gordon Binkerd." *Tempo*, 114 (September, 1975), pp. 2-13.

Gives an overview of Binkerd's music. In the choral music, the author examines Binkerd's settings of Herrick and

Hardy to support his theses regarding the composer's preoccupation with "the metaphysical imagination."

B194 Simpson, Ralph R. "William Grant Still—the man and his music." Ph.D. dissertation, Michigan State University, 1964.

A somewhat partial and admiring look at this composer and his music. Simpson deals with Still's compositional style and musical development by examining a large number of works, including much choral music.

B195 Skulsky, Abraham. "The music of William Bergsma." *Juilliard Review*, 3/2 (Spring, 1956), pp. 12-26.

A discussion of style in Bergsma's works, especially the instrumental works. Briefly describes the choral music, on p. 20.

B196 Slaterry, Thomas. "The life and work of Percy Grainger." *The Instrumentalist*, 22 (November, 1967), pp. 42-3; (December, 1967), pp. 47-9; and (January, 1968), pp. 36-8.

These three articles, concerned primarily with Grainger's band scores, also give good information on the choral works with band, including *The lads of Wamphray*, *Immovable Do*, and *Lost lady found*.

B197 Smedley, Bruce Robert. "Contemporary sacred chamber opera: a medieval form in the twentieth century." Ph.D. dissertation, George Peabody College for Teachers, 1977.

Examines twentieth-century operas suitable for church performance, by a number of composers, including Thompson's *The nativity according to St. Luke*. Discusses influences on this body

of music, as well as common compositional procedures used by the composers studied.

B198 Smith, James A. "Charles Sanford Skilton (1868-1941): Kansas composer." M.A. thesis, University of Kansas, 1979.

B199 Smith, Julia. *Aaron Copland: his life and contribution to American music.* New York: E.P. Dutton, 1955.

An early biography, but with helpful information on the earlier choral works, especially *Canticles of freedom*, *In the beginning*, the choruses from *The North Star*, *Old American songs*, *The tender land*, and several smaller works.

B200 Somerville, Thomas. "Some aspects of the choral music of Halsey Stevens." *Choral Journal*, 14/5 (1974), pp. 9-13.

A survey of style and musical characteristics in thirty-three published choral works by Stevens, with eleven musical examples. Also includes a list of works.

B201 Southern, Eileen. "Conversation with William Grant Still." *Black Perspective in Music*, 3/2 (May, 1975), pp. 165-75.

The composer discusses his life and works, including the cantata *And they lynched him on a tree* and several other dramatic works.

B202 [Sowerby, Leo] Sketchbook of holograph scores for various choral works, at the Music Division, the Library of Congress, Washington, D.C.

B203 Sparger, A. Dennis. "A study of selected choral works of Randall Thompson." M.A. thesis, Eastern Illinois University, 1965.

B204 Spencer, Jon Michael. "The writings of Robert Nathaniel Dett and William

Grant Still on Black music." Ph.D. dissertation, Washington University, 1982.

Includes a survey of the writings by these two men, many of which are valuable aids to the interpretation of their choral music, particularly those writings dealing with traditional African-American folk songs and spirituals.

B205 Stallings, M. E. "Representative works for mixed chorus by Daniel Pinkham, 1968-83." D.M.A. dissertation, University of Miami, 1984.

A biography of the composer with a general analysis of his works. There follows a more in-depth look at the "representative works": *Ascension cantata, Daniel in the lion's den,* and *Fanfares.* Includes quotes from Pinkham taken from interviews and correspondence.

B206 Stallings, Valdemar L. "A study of *Forsaken of man,* a sacred cantata by Leo Sowerby." M.S.M. thesis, Southern Baptist Theological Seminary, 1956.

B207 Stambler, Bernard. "Robert Ward." *American Composers Alliance Bulletin,* 4/4 (1955), pp. 3-11.

A brief overview of Ward's stylistic characteristics, followed by an annotated listing of his works.

B208 Stehman, Dan. *Roy Harris: a bio-bibliography.* Westport, Conn.: Greenwood Press, 1991.

Discusses the choral works in the section on "Life, Works, Style" (pp. 15ff). An annotated catalog of works follows, as well as a discography and a bibliography, which together form the major portion of the book.

B209 Stehman, Dan. *Roy Harris: an American musical pioneer.* Boston: Twayne Publishers, 1984.

Discusses the works for chorus (pp. 227-39); gives especially good information on Harris's settings of Whitman and his use of folksong.

B210 Strimple, Nick. "An introduction to the choral works of Roy Harris." *Choral Journal,* 22/9 (1982), pp. 16-19.

An excellent overview of the composer's works, beginning with a stylistic analysis that covers the important pieces, followed by a listing of all the works giving title and performing forces. Includes a lengthy quotation from a speech Harris delivered in a UCLA lecture, ca. 1960, which characterizes the "vast choral audience" as an untapped source for composers in the twentieth century.

B211 Studebaker, Donald. "The choral cantatas of Daniel Pinkham: an overview." *Choral Journal,* 29/5 (1988), p. 15-20.

The author gives a brief biography of the composer and a quick, general overview of his style, followed by an interview with Pinkham discussing his compositional process. Also lists the larger choral works with performing forces, publisher, and duration.

B212 Studebaker, Donald. "The sacred choral music of Norman Dello Joio." *Journal of Church Music,* 28 (October, 1986), pp. 10-12.

An interview with Dello Joio discussing influences on his work. Deals with all three Mass settings and a number of the composer's shorter anthems.

B213 Thompson, Randall. "On choral composition: essays and reflections," David Francis Urrows, compiler. *American Choral Review*, 22/2 (1980), entire issue.

Useful essays by Thompson about "Writing for the amateur chorus," "On contrapuntal technique," "The story of an 'Alleluia,'" and "Five love songs."

B214 [Thompson, Randall] Papers, 1917-1978. Houghton Library, Harvard University.

Contains manuscript scores, some with annotations; printed scores; photocopies of scores; and preliminary drafts of Thompson's choral and non-choral works. Also, miscellaneous printed and photocopied scores by other composers from his library, as well as his own pencil sketches and other fragments of compositions.

B215 Thompson, Randall. "Requiem: notes by the composer." *American Choral Review*, 16/4 (October, 1974), pp. 16-32.

Thompson provides an invaluable movement-by-movement guide to compositional procedures used and performance practices desired in the Requiem. He also gives a history of the commissioning of the work.

B216 Thomson, Virgil. *Virgil Thomson*. New York: Knopf, 1966.

This rather chatty volume includes information on the Mass settings, *Capital capitals*, and other choral works.

B217 Tircuit, Heuwell. "Alan Hovhaness: an American composer." *American Choral Review*, 9/1 (1966), pp. 8, 10-11, 17.

Deals with the compositional style of Hovhaness's choral works, with attention to his New England upbringing and similarities between his style and that of William Billings, and the influences of the *Bay Psalm Book* and the Boston Symphony Orchestra on his music.

B218 Tortolano, William. "The Mass and the twentieth-century composer: a study of musical techniques and style, together with the interpretive problems of the performer." D.S.M. dissertation, University of Montreal, 1964.

A thorough study, dealing with important settings of the Mass by major European and American composers of this century, as well as works by lesser composers. Discusses texts and their formal structures, rhythm, melody, harmony, and polyphony. Details the Masses of Creston, Harrison, Persichetti, Sessions, Thompson, and Thomson, some with musical examples.

B219 Tortolano, William. "Melody in the twentieth-century Mass." *Diapason*, 60/5 (April, 1969), pp. 18-19.

A chapter drawn from the author's dissertation. Mentions Persichetti's Mass several times, and traces Persichetti's use of a Gregorian theme throughout the Mass. Also mentions the Mass compositions of Sessions and Harrison.

B220 Tuthill, Burnet C. "Leo Sowerby." *Musical Quarterly*, 24/3 (1938), pp. 249-64.

A short analysis of Sowerby's style, with particular attention to instrumental works. Among other things, the author compares Sowerby to Brahms and traces compositional practices common to both. Includes a brief biography.

B221 Ulrich, Homer. *A survey of choral music*. New York: Harcourt Brace Jovanovich, 1973.

Chapter Eleven discusses twentieth-century American choral composers and their works, including Thompson, Thomson, Bernstein, and Pinkham.

B222 Urrows, David Francis. "The 'lost' choral work of Randall Thompson." *American Choral Review*, 23/1-2 (Winter/Spring, 1990), pp. 8-16.

Deals with the circumstances surrounding the composition of *Poscimur*, originally intended to be the first of the *Odes of Horace*. Discusses the work in the context of several other Thompson compositions, and argues for its inclusion in this composer's canon.

B223 Van Allen, Janice Kay. "Stylistic and interpretive analysis and performance of selected choral compositions by three American composers: Vincent Persichetti, Virgil Thomson, and Daniel Pinkham." Ed.D. dissertation, Columbia University, 1973.

The works in question: Persichetti's *Spring cantata* and *Winter cantata*; Pinkham's *Emily Dickinson mosaic*, *Magnificat*, and *Three Lenten poems of Richard Crashaw*; and Thomson's Mass and *Seven choruses from Medea*.

B224 Vanderkoy, Paul Arthur. "A survey of the choral music of Halsey Stevens." D.A. dissertation, Ball State University, 1981.

Examines the choral music of this composer and summarizes its stylistic characteristics, including performance considerations. Includes a number of music examples and a chronological list of works.

B225 Voorhees, Larry D. "A study of selected vocal-choral works of Samuel Barber." M.A. thesis, Eastern Illinois University, 1965.

B226 Willoughby, Dale E. "Performance preparation of various choral works representing selected periods of music history." D.M.A. dissertation, University of Miami, 1971.

Pinkham's *Stabat mater* was chosen as representative of the modern period. Willoughby discusses the various aspects of historical period, composer, text, musical analysis, and "technical considerations," drawing conclusions relevant to the rehearsal preparation of the work for performance.

B227 Wilson, J.H. "A study and performance of *The ordering of Moses* by Robert Nathaniel Dett." D.M.A. dissertation, University of Southern California, 1970.

A thorough examination of this work, as undertaken by the author prior to his performance of it. The dissertation includes a short biography of the composer and a performance history of the piece.

B228 Wolf, Robert Erich. "France." *Musical Quarterly*, 47/3 (1961), pp. 400-07.

A lengthy review/critical analysis of Thomson's *Missa pro defunctis*, following its European premiere. The author compares the Mass to similar works by Berlioz and Poulenc. Many musical examples.

B229 Yancy, Henrietta Miller. "The contribution of the American Negro to the music culture of the country." *School Musician*, 41 (March, 1970), pp. 60-1.

Discusses the contriubtions of Dett, Still, and others to American music; cites many choral works, but with only brief discussion.

Index to Titles

A

A solus ortu, 1963
A Venus, regina Cnidi, Paphique, 1899
Abigail Adams, 1096
Above the Pate Valley, 824
An absent friend, 1537
Ad bibinem cum me rogaret ad cenam, 60
Ad lyram, 884
Ad te, Domine, 712
Ad te levavi animam meam, 1646
Adam in the garden pinnin' leaves, 1097
Adeste fideles, 1286
Adieu, farewell earth's bliss, 1545
Adieu, Mignonne, when you are gone, 380
Adon olom, 698
Adonai, Elohim, 200
Adoration, 885
Adoro te devote, 378
Advent, 1156
After, 1455
After the battle, 581
Las agachadas, 302
Against jealousy, 665
Agnus Dei, 61, 93, 1647, 1914, 1915
Agnus Dei—I once loved a boy, 286
Aguinaldo, 1848
Ah, sinful nations, 1609
Ah! sunflower, 822
Ahavas Olom, 976
Air Force, Ballad of hurry up, 194
Air held her breath, 317
The airborne, 194
The akond of swat, 1918
Alas! alack!, 713
Alice in Wonderland, 1153
All circling point, 693
All creatures are the voice, 51
All for love, 1582

All glorious God, 1523
All hail, adored Trinity, 1648
All in green my love went riding, 440
All my heart this night rejoices, 1649
All over joy!, 1582
All Saint's Day, 1567
All the ends of the earth, 1808
All the world's a dream, 461
All they from Saba shall come, 1650
All things are thine, 1651
All this night shrill chanticleer, 1819
Alleluia, 462, 870, 886, 1070, 1201, 1368,
    1403, 1652-56, 1874
Alleluia, Christ is risen!, 463
Alleluia for Michaelmas, 1233
Alleluia, proclamation and carol, 1369
Alleluia, tell the tidings, 1393
An alleluia super round, 1
Alleluia to the heart of the matter, 609
Along about cockcrow, 1122
Ambivalence, 1272
Amen and hallelujah, 441
Amen! praise and glory, 1393
Amens, 1370
America, 867
America, an epic rhapsody, 201
America, we love your people, 827
American cantata, 699
American muse, 318
An American oratorio, 1524
American love songs, 1525
American madrigals, 1159
Americana, 1875
Las Americas unidas, 1160
America's vow, 605
The amphisbæna, 1813
Ample make this bed, 1074
Anabasis, 887
Anchor song, 741

B

D

E

O

Index to Authors and Sources of Texts

C

Index to Performing Forces

Children's Voices

Bacon, 19
Bernstein, 120, 125, 128
Binkerd, 167, 180
Cadman, 214, 231
Carpenter, 271
Cowell, 325, 330, 333
Diamond, 452, 454
Diemer, 482
Erb, 574, 580
Felciano, 625, 647
Foss, 711
Gaburo, 713
Grainger, 788, 801
Hanson, 810
Hovhaness, 907
Mechem, 1177
Mennin, 1203, 1209
Menotti, 1213, 1218, 1224
Musgrave, 1266
Parker, 1276, 1278, 1281, 1319
Persichetti, 1347, 1360
Pinkham, 1466
Rorem, 1554
Skilton, 1638
Sowerby, 1662, 1743
Thompson, 1905
Thomson, 1917, 1946, 1950
Ward, 1953

Unison Voices

Albright, 1
Barber, 66
Binkerd, 150, 183
Carpenter, 268, 272
Copland, 309
Cowell, 348

Creston, 368
Diemer, 500, 565
Farwell, 581, 596, 604
Felciano, 610-611, 621, 649-650
Grainger, 753, 784, 801
Harris, 836, 857, 861
Harrison, 872, 876, 880-881
Hovhaness, 948, 963
James, 1033, 1066
Kay, 1080
Larsen, 1144
Mechem, 1177
Moevs, 1233
Parker, 1272, 1278, 1281, 1302, 1308
Pinkham, 1393, 1402, 1428, 1447-1448, 1505, 1507, 1513
Rorem, 1565-1566, 1574
Sessions, 1608
Skilton, 1642
Sowerby, 1673, 1710, 1716, 1721, 1737, 1740, 1746, 1764, 1795
Thomson, 1932
Ward, 1958
Wuorinen, 1968

Women's Chorus

Albright, 1
Argento, 18
Bacon, 19, 22-24, 26-27, 34-36, 47-48, 50-51, 56, 59
Barber, 62, 66, 79
Bassett, 83, 85, 97
Bauer, 101, 106, 109-110
Bergsma, 114
Binkerd, 134, 137, 148, 151, 153-154, 160, 177, 182, 184, 189-190
Blitzstein, 195, 197
Bloch, 201

Men's Chorus

Mixed Chorus, 2–4vv

(Works with fewer than four parts are marked with an asterisk.)

Mixed Chorus, 5vv or More

Works with Instrumental Accompaniment (Solo or small ensemble)

(Works with accompaniment for solo instrument other than keyboard are marked with an asterisk. List does not include works accompanied by solo keyboard.)

Works with Orchestra or Band Accompaniment

Index to Durations

Indeterminate Length

Albright, 1
Feldman, 659, 661
Harrison, 874

Under 5 Minutes

Argento, 7-8, 11, 17
Bacon, 21-24, 26-28, 30-31, 36-41, 44, 47, 49-50, 52, 54-56, 58-60, 63, 65
Barber, 69, 71, 76-79
Bassett, 82, 84, 86-87, 92, 94, 96-97
Bauer, 98, 100-101, 103-104, 106, 110
Bergsma, 113-114, 116, 117, 121
Bernstein, 124, 129
Binkerd, 133, 135-137, 139, 141, 143, 145-146, 148, 153-156, 160, 161, 163, 165-168, 171, 176, 180, 183, 185-186, 192
Blitzstein, 198
Cadman, 203-204, 207, 209-215, 218-219, 221, 224, 226-230, 232, 234, 236, 238-239, 244-245, 247-259, 262-264, 266-267
Carpenter, 268
Carter, 278
Chihara, 285
Converse, 291, 293, 296, 300
Copland, 311, 313, 315-316
Cowell, 317, 322, 326-329, 334-349, 351, 353-355
Creston, 360-361, 364, 372, 374-375, 379
Dello Joio, 380, 383-384, 387, 389, 393, 400, 402-403, 410, 413, 415
Dett, 421-423, 425-426, 428, 430-431, 433, 435-436, 438-439
Diamond, 440, 444-446, 450, 455, 457-458
Diemer, 461-463, 465-467, 469-470, 472-474, 481, 486, 488, 498-502, 504, 506-507, 509-510, 514, 517, 520-521, 523-524, 526-528, 531, 533, 535, 540, 543, 546, 549, 557, 560-562, 564-565
Erb, 574, 578
Farwell, 581-582, 587, 590-594, 596, 601, 608
Felciano, 609-611, 613-614, 616-621, 623-625, 630, 632, 634-637, 639-640, 645, 648-649, 651, 653-654
Fine, Irving, 667, 669-671, 673
Finney, 689, 695
Foss, 698
Gaburo, 712-713, 716-717, 719-720, 723-724
Giannini, 730, 738-740
Grainger, 741, 743, 745, 747, 750, 752, 754, 757-758, 760, 764, 767, 769-775, 777-779, 781, 783-784, 786-787, 789, 791-792, 794, 799, 801
Hanson, 805-806, 812, 814
Harbison, 820
Harris, 830, 835, 839-841, 843, 846, 851, 855, 862-863, 868-869
Hovhaness, 886, 888, 891, 896-897, 903-904, 909, 912, 916, 919, 923, 926-932, 934, 938, 940-941, 944-945, 949, 957-958, 964
Jacobi, 976, 979-983
James, 990-994, 997-1000, 1002-1003, 1005-1006, 1008-1009, 1012-1015, 1017-1018, 1020, 1022-1025, 1027, 1029-1030, 1032, 1034-1035, 1038-1039, 1042-1048, 1054, 1056, 1059, 1061, 1064-1067
Kay, 1071-1072
Kubik, 1096, 1098, 1104, 1108-1110, 1113-1114, 1116, 1118, 1120-1121, 1124, 1129, 1131
Larsen, 1140, 1147-1148, 1150, 1152

5' to 10' Duration

11' to 30' Duration

Over 30' Duration

Index to the Bibliography of Selected Writings

Reference numbers used in this index refer to the "B" numbers used in the Bibliography of Selected Writings. For information on a specific choral work, refer to that piece in the Catalog of Works under the annotation "Bib."